STEP-BY-ST
PASTA COOK
(and more...)

P

OOK

CHARTWELL
BOOKS, INC.

**CHARTWELL
BOOKS, INC.**

General Editor:
Stephen Schmidt

Consultant:
Nicoletta Grill
Kerry Milis

Production Services:
SBC Enterprises, Inc.

Adapted from CUCINARE OGGI by Simonetta Lupi Vada

Summary

HOMEMADE   PASTA

How to Make Pasta

The kneading together of flour and water was perhaps one of man's first actions if you look back through his history. The first bread was simply dough made from flour and water without yeast: even today, among some primitive populations, the use of yeast is completely unknown. However, all cultures have known the art of kneading even if they have not all used the same ingredients, which are usually chosen according to what is available locally: the flour of various cereals either mixed with water alone or enriched with eggs and perhaps oil, and so on.

Pasta casalinga (homemade pasta), or so-called fresh pasta, now generally means egg pasta; it contains one egg for every 2½ ounces of American all-purpose white flour and is extremely nutritious. Why not prepare it every now and then in order to rediscover forgotten aromas and flavors especially since modern equipment has greatly reduced the time and effort once involved in the preparation of pasta? Some have objected that homemade pasta is a food that is hardly suitable for the sedentary life of modern man because it contains too many calories: in fact, a normal plate of *pastasciutta* contains about 360 calories, most of which are derived from carbohydrates, with only a few calories coming from protein. The most up-to-date nutritional science has now ascertained that pasta is not fattening if it is properly seasoned and included within a correct and well-balanced diet. Indeed, it is advisable to introduce pasta into the daily diet because wheat flour, especially "natural" wheat flour that has not been treated chemically during refining and that has been cultivated using natural fertilizers, contains mineral salts and many important vitamins including some from the B and E groups. Moreover, pasta made with one egg for every 2½ ounces of flour has considerable nutritional value. If soft-grain wheat flour is less rich in proteins than the hard-grain durum wheat flour used in making industrial pastas, this deficiency is largely compensated by the nutritious substances contained in the eggs: albumin, other proteins of animal origin, and fatty substances.

After the above considerations, it is easy to realize how important this food is in our diet. If one also considers that fresh pasta is mainly seasoned with foods that are also very nourishing—cheeses and other such ingredients—or that it may be stuffed with succulent meat, fish, and vegetable fillings, one can definitely conclude that it has great chances of becoming a dish with an unmatchable flavor, within everyone's means and ready to satisfy even the fussiest and most refined palates.

How to make pasta by hand

The utensils — The pasta rolling pin is still the instrument most used nowadays for making homemade pasta. Another indispensable tool for those who use the rolling pin is the pastry board. Also handy are a small serrated or smooth cutting wheel and a scraper for removing the dough from the pastry board (1).

The ingredients and the proportions — For egg pasta made at home, one large egg for about 9 tablespoons of flour is usually necessary (2). The quantity of flour varies according to what you intend to use the pasta for: 3½ cups for *pastasciutta,* 2⅔ cups if you intend to dress the pasta with a rich sauce, and 1¾ cups for pasta in broth. The proportions are intended for four persons. The flour you use must be fresh.

Pasta dough — Place the flour on the pastry board and break the eggs into the center (3). If you like, you can break the eggs into a plate, beat them in the same way you do for an omelette, and pour them into the center. You may replace one egg with shellful of water in order to make a less rich pasta or you may add a tablespoon of oil to render the dough more elastic. In some cases you may even add a little white wine. Remember, though, that authentic recipes do not allow for these variations.

Add a pinch of salt and begin to incorporate flour and eggs (4) slowly with your fingertips. Now use your hands to knead the dough for at least 10 to 15 minutes, flouring the pastry board every now and then and removing the dough that has stuck to it with a scraper (5). Knead the dough until it is soft, smooth, and elastic (6). Every so often, stretch out the dough and fold it back on itself (7). When air bubbles start to form in the dough, gather it into a ball, wrap it tightly in plastic wrap and leave it to stand for about 15 minutes, covered with a bowl or with a cloth.

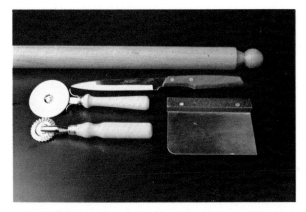

1 Utensils necessary for making pasta: rolling pin, pasta cutting wheels and wide metal scraper.

2 The basic ingredients for homemade pasta with eggs: all-purpose white flour and very fresh eggs.

3 Place the flour on the pastry board, make a well in the middle, and break an egg into it.

4 Begin blending the flour and eggs together, using your fingertips, and work the dough...

5 ...with your hands for 10 to 15 minutes, removing the dough that has stuck to the pastry board.

6 Knead the dough with the heels of your hands, until it is soft, smooth, and elastic.

The dough — If you are experienced, leave the dough in one piece. If you are a beginner, it is advisable to divide it into two or three parts and work with one piece at a time.

In order to roll out the dough, first flatten it a little with your hand and then press down on it with the pasta rolling pin (8). Starting from the center, roll out the dough in all directions, rotating it as you proceed so that it becomes round and of uniform thickness (9). When the piece of dough reaches a certain size, wrap it around the rolling pin (in order to turn it without breaking it) and turn it onto its other side. Towards the end, wrap the dough partially around the rolling pin, rolling it out slightly towards the left and pulling it at the same time (10); repeat this operation until the desired thickness is achieved.

A thickness of a little less than 1/16 of an inch is the most suitable for general uses. However, in the case of certain types of pasta, it could be thicker or thinner.

For those who own a special pasta-making machine, electric or manual, time and effort can be saved.

The working procedure is very simple: pass a piece of dough, slightly flattened by hand and folded back on itself, 4 or 5 times through the rollers set at the maximum width. When the characteristic bubbles form, turn the special small wheel and begin tightening the rollers gradually, passing the piece of dough through them each time until the desired thickness is achieved. As the piece gets longer, join the two ends together to make a kind of ring; continue passing this ring through the rollers, holding it up with the back of your left hand.

7 While working the dough, stretch it out every now and then and fold it back on itself.

8 After having flattened the dough by hand, begin rolling it out by pressing down on the rolling pin.

9 Starting from the center, roll out the dough in all directions, rotating it to make it round.

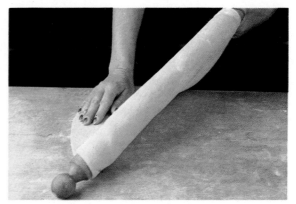

10 Wrap part of the dough around the rolling pin, turn it slightly and stretch it.

Colored pasta

Once you have understood that making pasta at home is fairly easy, you can amuse yourself by making it with a particular color or flavor, modifying the basic recipe and introducing new ingredients.

Green pasta — The proportions for this pasta are 3½ cups of all-purpose white flour, ½ lb. of raw spinach, 5 large eggs and a pinch of salt. This is for approximately 4 persons.

Wash the spinach well, place it in a saucepan with only the water that clings to the leaves after washing, add a pinch of salt, and cook for 5 to 10 minutes. Allow to cool, then squeeze well by hand and pass through a vegetable mill or purée in a blender or food proccessor.

Place the flour on the board. Break the eggs into the middle, add the spinach and a pinch of salt, and mix. Bear in mind that the proportion of flour may be slightly increased if the dough is too soft. Knead the ingredients together and proceed as you would in the case of ordinary pasta. The only difference between green pasta and other pasta is that green pasta dough is less elastic and thus the dough is rather difficult to roll out and it will not be as thin as ordinary egg pasta dough. We would advise beginners to divide it into two or three pieces and roll them out one at a time. The spinach can be replaced by the green leafy part of Swiss chard. Tender nettle leaves make an unusual change, and they will yield an unexpectedly velvety and tasty pasta. Remember that green pasta takes longer to dry than the normal egg pasta.

Green pasta can be used together with ordinary pasta for preparing *paglia e fieno* (straw and hay) dishes, as well as exquisite baked pasta dishes.

Red pasta — The proportions are more or less the same as those required for green pasta: about 3½ cups of all-purpose white flour, ½ lb. of carrots, 5 large eggs, salt and 1 tbsp. of tomato paste.

Clean and scrape the carrots well. Cut them into small pieces, then boil them until tender in a little salted water. Pass them through a vegetable mill and dry the purée in a small saucepan over a low flame, sitrring with a wooden spoon; add the tablespoon of tomato paste to the purée. Proceed as for normal pasta, placing the flour on the board and adding the eggs and mashed carrots. The quantity of flour necessary will vary slightly according to how dry the mashed carrots are. Also, in this case it will be rather difficult to roll the dough very thin. In order to have an even redder pasta, some people use an entire small can of tomato paste in place of the carrots: we would recommend this only to those who particularly like the slightly acid flavor of tomatoes, which is very noticeable even after cooking the pasta.

Violet pasta — The quantities are the usual 3½ cups of all-purpose white flour, ½ lb. beets, 4 "large" eggs and a pinch of salt. Buy canned beets, cut them up, and pass them through a vegetable mill. Squeeze the beets well between your hands so as to extract all the juice possible, then add the juices and the eggs plus a pinch of salt to the flour. (The quantity of flour necessary will vary slightly according to the quantity of juice obtained.) Proceed as for the other pastas. This pasta cannot be rolled very thin. Since this pasta dries out very quickly, sprinkle it with corn meal or semolina when you roll it out.

Orange pasta — The proportions are 3½ cups all-purpose white flour, 1 lb. of pumpkin, 4 "large" eggs, and a pinch of salt. Cut the pumpkin into slices and bake it for about an hour, or boil it in salty water for half an hour. Remove the peel and seeds and pass through a vegetable mill. If the pulp is too liquid, dry in a saucepan over a flame, mixing rapidly with a wooden spoon. Knead the pumpkin together with the flour, eggs, and salt as in the the case of the other pastas.

Cocoa pasta — One of the latest novelties in the way of colored pasta is cocoa pasta, which is obtained by adding about ⅓ cup of bitter cocoa to the usual ingredients (3½ cups of flour and 6 "large" eggs). If you prefer a pasta with a lighter color, decrease the amount of cocoa. Cocoa pasta is excellent with duck, pigeon, or game sauce.

Cheese pasta — Use 1¾ cups of all-purpose white flour, 6 ounces of Parmesan cheese, 4 "large" eggs, and a pinch of salt (not too much salt because the cheese is salty). Remember that this pasta cannot be stored but should be used immediately due to the cheese content. Finely grate the cheese (you will end up with about 1½ cups) and mix with the flour; then proceed as for ordinary egg pasta.

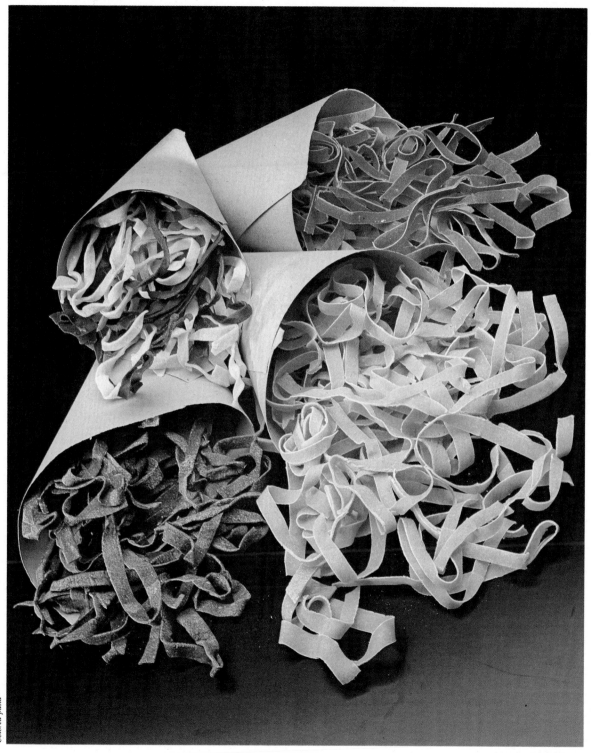

Colored pasta

Pasta-making machines

Very few things are necessary for making pasta: a marble slab or wooden pastry board, a pasta rolling pin—and two strong arms. In order to roll the dough very thin, as the clever Emilian housewives once did, and still do, you really need a lot of strength and patience! The pasta rolling pin has been replaced by the pasta machine for some years now in many homes. The first machines were manually operated; some are now electric.

The manual machine with a handle is still the most widely used of all because it is reasonably priced and very easy to use. This machine has smooth rollers for making *tagliatelle* and *tagliolini*. The space between the two rollers is narrowed by turning the wheel on the side of the machine to obtain thinner dough at every click.

The electric machine works in the same way except for the fact that it is run by electricity; the machine usually comes with several accessories. Then there are the electric kneading machines where all you have to do is pour the recipe ingredients into the special bowl, put the lid on, and turn on the machine; small blades then start turning slowly, mixing everything until a smooth and compact dough is formed, ready for whatever use is intended. Even more automatized machines exist which are supplied with small discs for obtaining the various pasta shapes. You put the flour in the special basin, dropping in the eggs one at a time while the machine is working; once a compact dough has been formed, a type of shutter comes down and the finished pasta comes out. There are, in short, many types of pasta-making machines on the market today. Each of them has its own particular characteristics and needs precise quantities in order to perform really well. Follow the instructions attached to the machine very carefully the first time; once you have gained experience you can make personal variations.

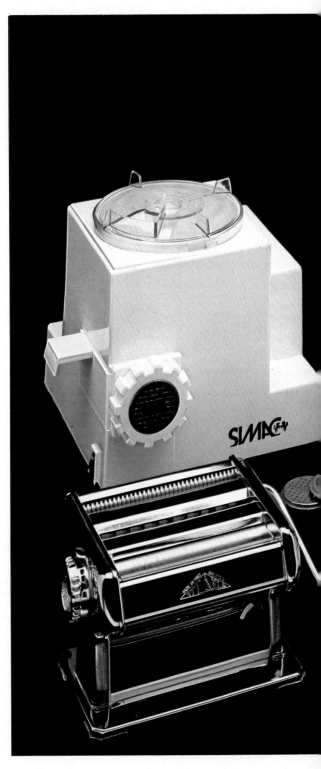

How to make shaped pasta

When using an electric machine, you can prepare the dough and proceed at once to form the desired pasta shape. On the other hand, if you follow the traditional system, i.e. "rolling pin and elbow grease," after having obtained a thin sheet of dough, you must let the dough stand for a few minutes. When cutting pasta dough by hand, bear in mind that you need a heavy knife with a wide and very sharp blade—this is very important—or you risk squashing the pasta instead of cutting it cleanly. Proceed as follows to obtain the most common pasta shapes.

Tagliatelle or fettucce — These are pasta strips about ⅜-inch wide. To obtain these, roll the sheet of pasta dough up quite tightly and cut it with a wide-bladed knife (as mentioned above) into ⅜-inch strips (1). Open the small rolls of pasta by hand or by inserting the blunt edge of a knife and lifting them up; alternatively, you may pick up the rolls a small handful at a time and drop them onto the board, allowing the coils to open on their own.

Tagliatelle are usually served *asciutte* ("dry"; i.e., on a plate rather than in broth) and are excellent even when they are simply dressed with butter and Parmesan cheese or with fresh tomato sauce.

Fettuccine or linguine — These are strips of pasta, like *tagliatelle,* but a little less than ¼-inch wide. They are mainly served "dry," dressed with oil or butter, with or without cheese, or with cream, peas and ham, or white sauce.

Tagliatelline or tagliolini or taglierini — These are even narrower strips of pasta (about ³⁄₁₆ths of an inch wide). Though usually served in meat broth, they are also good eaten "dry" and are especially well liked by children.

Quadrettini or quadrucci — These are small pasta squares measuring ½-inch square. To obtain these shapes, roll up the pasta as usual and cut it

1 *Tagliatelle* or *fettucce:* roll up the dough and then cut into ⅜-inch strips.

2 *Quadrettini* or *quadrucci:* roll up the dough and cut it first into strips and then horizontally.

3 *Maltagliati:* roll up the dough and then cut so as to obtain small irregular diamond shapes.

4 *Farfalle* or *nodini:* make rectangular shapes with a cutting wheel and squeeze the middle.

5 *Pappardelle:* use a serrated cutting wheel to cut long strips ¾-inch to 1-inch wide.

6 *Lasagne:* use a smooth cutting wheel to make squares or rectangles from the rolled-out dough.

into strips ½-inch wide; now turn the small rolls of pasta and cut them crosswise, thus obtaining ½-inch squares (2). In order to make these squares with a machine, you simply reduce *tagliatelle* noodles to the same length as the rollers of your machine and then feed the noodles sidewise to the machine a small group at a time. Pasta squares are mainly served in meat, chicken, or vegetable broth.

Maltagliati — These are small pieces of pasta cut irregularly, usually in a diamond shape. After rolling up the dough as described above for *tagliatelle,* cut it into random strips ⅜-inch wide along one side (3). In this way, you will obtain small pasta shapes mainly served in broth with such vegetables as chick-peas or beans.

Farfalle or nodini or galani — These are small pieces of pasta squeezed in the middle to make a characteristic butterfly form. Without letting the dough dry too much, cut horizontal strips ⅜-inch to ¾-inch wide with the cutting wheel. The width depends on whether you want to serve the pasta in broth, in which case the pieces should be narrow. Without moving the strips, cut them into 1½-inch rectangles. Form the butterflies by squeezing the rectangles in the middle (4). Butterflies can be dressed with tomato sauce, peas and ham, meat sauce, the juices from stews or roast joints, or with cream sauces.

Pappardelle — These are long strips of pasta ¾-inch to 1-inch wide that are cut with a serrated cutting wheel (5) from a flat sheet of pasta dough. They are almost always served with rich meat, giblet, game, or mushroom sauces, but they may also be served in broth.

Lasagne — These are strips of pasta at least 2½ inches wide that are cut with a knife or with a smooth cutting wheel into squares or rectangles of the desired size (6). They are then spread out on a floured board for drying. They are used for baked pies or for *cannelloni ripieni* (large stuffed pasta rolls).

Pasta trita — To conclude the subject of homemade pasta shapes, we must not forget *pasta trita,* or grated pasta, a Mantua specialty that is also eaten in many cities in the Lombardy and Venetian regions. The basic dough is ordinary egg pasta dough but it must be a little harder than usual and very well prepared. Grate the dough on the shredding side of a grater so that it falls onto the floured board; let it dry. This pasta is especially suitable for cooking in broth, but for small children and convalescents, it can also be prepared "dry," dressed with olive oil and cheese.

Storing and cooking

Fresh homemade pasta can be stored for several days if it has been set out on a floured cloth or covered with semolina and dried in the open. It should then be sealed in a plastic bag and put in a dry environment. It can also be stored for several months in a freezer. After being cut into one of the various shapes, the pasta should be left to dry. It is then divided up into portions sufficient for one meal, placed on a tray, and put into the freezer. When the pasta has hardened, it should be put into plastic bags, sealed, and put back in the freezer.

For cooking pasta, the pot must be sufficiently large to contain a quart of water for every quarter pound of pasta. The water must reach up to three-quarters of the height of the pot. When the water is very hot, salt is added in the proportion of 2 teaspoons for every quart of water. As soon as the water boils, throw in the pasta and stir constantly either with a wooden spoon, (if the pasta is short), or with a large fork, (if the pasta is long). Cover the pot and bring everything to the boil, then remove the lid and lower the flame slightly (the water must, however, remain at a lively boil).

Stir every now and then until the pasta has reached the right degree of doneness, bearing in mind that the cooking time depends above all on the thickness of the dough, which should be thin and uniform. The only way to discover whether the pasta is ready for eating is to taste it: it should not be soft or gluey but rather quite chewy or *al dente*.

As soon as the pasta is cooked, stop the boiling by pouring a ladle or a glass of cold water into the pot. Drain the pasta at once, keeping a few tablespoons of cooking water to add when dressing the pasta. *Note:* According to recent studies the best way to preserve all the mineral salts, enzymes, and vitamins in pasta is to throw the pasta into boiling water, cook the pasta one minute from the time the water starts boiling again, turn off the flame, cover the saucepan with a kitchen towel and lid, and then let the pasta stand for the normal cooking time.

Farfalle with salmon

Regional pasta and equipment

Regional pastas, like egg pasta, are made by kneading flour and liquid together and require patient and skillful work with the hands. In the past, food meant a direct relationship with nature and a communion with the vital forces contained therein. Where is this relationship best expressed? In the countryside, where the farm worker sows, looks after, gathers, and grinds the wheat, using both the outside (bran) of the grain and the inside (flour). In the countryside, cooking methods transmitted from mother to daughter for generations have joined with a love of good food to preserve culinary traditions. Regional equipment expresses the local culture: from the presses of the more industrialized areas to the rudimentary tools of poorer areas, where imagination and the ability of the hands have had to compensate for the lack of means.

A quick trip through Italy — In the Venetian region we find *bigoli*, a rudimentary spaghetti made entirely from bran, and *bigoli bianchi*, made from a mixture of half bran and half white flour. This pasta is also prepared with whole-wheat flour and called *bigoli mori*. It is eaten on Good Friday and Ash Wednesday just as in Medieval times.

This pasta is made with a press or *trafila* which is called a *bigolaro* in the Venetian region. Every family had one in their house in the past, but today it is almost a museum piece. This press is soldered onto a wooden trestle seat on which the person who makes the pasta sits; the dough is inserted in small pieces into the press and pushed through the strainer by turning the screw. The threads of pasta obtained (or *bigoli*), drop into a wide tray or basket which is floured so that the pasta does not stick together. There was a time when *bigoli* were hung out to dry on ropes over sheets of newspaper which caught strands that dropped. This was common practice in country houses where there was no lack of space. Poorer families prepared this pasta with only flour and water but those who could added eggs and butter to obtain a tastier and softer dough. *Bigoli* are dressed today with various sauces (one of which is the famous duck sauce) or, more simply, with an onion and anchovy sauce.

Now let us move on to Valtellina in northern Italy, one of the few regions where buckwheat is still cultivated and used. The ancient Romans called buckwheat *pulmentum*. As in those times, buckwheat is ground and toasted and then combined with other flours for making the typical dishes that demonstrate the loyalty of the people of Valtellina to their past—the *pizzoccheri,* a type of dark *tagliatelle* that are cooked with the most typical mountain vegetables, potatoes and savoy cabbage, and seasoned with *bitto,* a tasty local cheese similar to *fontina*. The result is a nutritious dish which is a complete meal which can be served on its own. Excellent industrially prepared *pizzoccheri* can be found on the market as is the case with

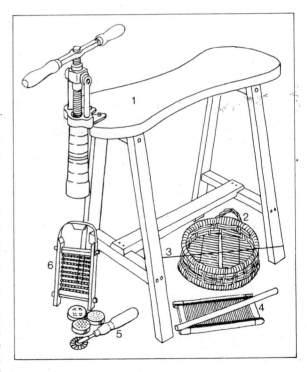

1-*bigolaro* or press for *bigoli;* 2-*ciuliri*, a sieve made of rushes for *malloreddus;* 3-rod for tubular macaroni; 4-comb for *garganelli;* 5-pasta cutting wheel; 6-wooden grater.

most kinds of pasta, but their flavor, according to gourmets, is quite different from that of homemade *pizzoccheri*, perhaps because the love and mountain spirit are lacking.

We travel from the mountains to the Ligurian coast in order to taste some genuine Ligurian cooking specialities that have remained in the shadows due to the character of the population itself, which is rather reserved. The temperate climate and sunshine of the Riviera cause the vegetables and herbs to grow healthily, impregnated with taste and aroma. These vegetables and herbs are the basic ingredients for all the preparations, from basil for *pesto* sauce, to garlic and borage for pasta fillings. We should not forget the genuine olive oil and the pine nuts, a precious gift from the maritime pines which the people of Liguria often use in their sauces. Among the homemade pastas, there are the *trofie*. These are small twisted dumplings *(gnocchi)* thinned at the ends and prepared with white flour to which a little bran is added. Sometimes a small quantity of chestnut flour is also added, which sweetens the gnocchi and blends well with the flavor of *pesto* sauce with which this dish is almost always seasoned. In some localities, the *trofie* are mixed with a small quantity of boiled fresh white beans; it is in fact a typical local custom to mix the pasta with vegetables.

Another Ligurian speciality are the *corzetti* (stamped pasta pieces). They get their name from their resemblance to the ancient silver coin of this one-time seafaring Republic, the *crosazzo*. They are made with a special chiselled stamp or hand-made in the form of an eight. They are seasoned with melted butter, scented with sweet marjoram and pine nuts.

On the Tuscany and Liguria border, we find *testaroli*, so-called because they are cooked in wide earthenware pans, *testi*, which are filled with charcoal and ash to keep the temperature constant. The pasta has a flour and water base and is served cut into wide strips, seasoned with a Genoese *pesto* sauce.

At the border between Lombardy and Emilia in the Piacenza area, we find *pisarei*. These are prepared with white flour, water and bread crumbs and are served "dry," dressed with a bean sauce. Their name seems to derive from *biscia*, which means snake, because of the snakelike form of the pasta.

Garganelli are typical of Romagna. In order to prepare these you need a special utensil, the "comb." *Garganelli* can be served in broth or "dry" with tomato and chicken liver sauce.

In Umbria they still make *stringozzi* or *ceriole*, very long thin hollow macaroni typical of the Terni area made with a special square knitting needle or an ordinary round one. They are dressed either with spicy sauce made with tomato, garlic, and oil or simply with lightly sautéed garlic and oil.

The Apulia region derives its principal gastronomic ingredients from the countryside and the sea. In fact, agriculture prospers along the whole length of the "Tavoliere di Puglia" and there is still abundant fishing off the coasts. The most famous pasta is *orecchiette* (little ears). This pasta is prepared with white flour and hard-wheat flour (semolina). These pasta shapes look like hats, which is why they are also called "priests' hats". These may be served with turnip greens, potatoes and tomatoes, or rolled veal or pork. A variation on *orecchiette* are *strascinari*. These small pasta *gnocchi* are made with a dough similar to that of the *orecchiette* and are *strascinati*, that is, dragged across a special grooved paddle with the tips of three fingers.

In Calabria, a rough and picturesque land, cooking is the most immediate expression of a way of life. The characteristics of this cuisine are those of all southern Italian cooking: vegetables, good oil, and pasta of all types. The *maccheroni inferrettati* (hollow macaroni), called *fusilli* in some areas, are patiently made at home using the special square-sided knitting needle or even a willow branch. The use of a needle is not isolated to Calabria alone but is common to all of southern Italy, from Apulia to Sicily and as far as Sardinia. The typical Sicilian pasta is *maccaruni*, small hollow macaroni which are prepared with a needle and generally seasoned with a sauce made of pork and pecorino. Elsewhere, hollow macaroni are seasoned with sauces made of local products including tomato, olives, and capers; garlic, oil, and small red peppers; or tomato and eggplant.

We can hardly ignore another important Italian region: Sardinia. Scholars assure us that this land was once joined to the African continent, and we are inclined to believe this because the food, as well as the flora and fauna, has Arab tendencies. Semolina pasta predominates in Sardinian cooking and in fact the small Sardinian *gnocchi* called *malloreddus* are made with this. *Malloreddus* means "small bulls" in Sardinian dialect. Saffron is used freely in both pasta sauces and pasta doughs and adds fragrance and color to the regional ingredients. The sauces are based on tomatoes, young goats' meat, lamb, game, and venison.

Regional Pasta

Garganelli

■ **Yield: 4 servings**
■ **Time needed: 1½ hours**
■ **Difficulty: ****

Pasta ingredients: 3½ cups all-purpose white flour, 6 large eggs, 4 tbsp. grated Parmesan cheese, pinch nutmeg and salt.
Sauce ingredients: 1 thick slice of smoked bacon weighing 5 to 6 oz. 1 cup homemade tomato sauce, olive oil.

This is a typical Romagnese dish.

Prepare the pasta: Knead together the flour, eggs, grated cheese, nutmeg, and salt. Prepare the pasta until it is smooth, then roll it out until it is fairly thin, flouring the board every now and then. Using a knife, cut the dough into squares measuring about 1¼ inches (1). Pile the squares on top of each other and cover with a cloth so the pasta does not dry out. Starting at the corners fold two squares around the little stick, placing the squares at a distance from one another (a smooth pencil could be used) (2) and roll them, passing them over the "comb" made of close-set canes inserted into two cross bars (3). In this way, you will obtain macaroni like *penne rigate* (grooved quills) commonly found on the market. When carrying out this operation, press down at the point where the pasta is joined so the edges stick

together to prevent the rolled-up pasta from opening during cooking. Delicately remove the *garganelli* from the stick (4), place them on the floured board, spread apart and continue until you have used all the pasta.

Dice the bacon and brown in a few tablespoons of oil, place the macaroni, previously cooked to *al dente* in boiling water, in the frying pan, (5) and finish by adding the boiling tomato sauce. Stir briefly and then remove the pan from the flame. If you like, you can sprinke the dish with grated Romano cheese.

Garganelli can also be prepared with green pasta, adding boiled and mashed spinach to the basic dough (see recipe on page 14).

1 After having rolled out the dough with a rolling pin, cut it into squares of approximately 1¼ inches.

2 Space two squares of dough on the special round stick and fold from the corners.

3 Roll the pasta over the special utensil called a "comb," made of close-set canes.

4 Carefully remove the *garganelli* from the stick, spreading them out on the floured board.

5 Lightly fry the boiled macaroni and mix well with a wooden fork.

Guitar macaroni

- ■ **Yield: 4 servings**
- ■ **Time needed: 1½ hours**
- ■ **Difficulty: ***

Ingredients: About 3½ cups all-purpose white flour, 6 "large" eggs, and salt.

These macaroni are typical of Abruzzi cooking.

The pasta is made by using a utensil called a "guitar", a wooden frame over which are stretched steel threads to make an implement that reminds one of the musical instrument of the same name. This utensil cuts the homemade pasta into many thin strips with square edges.

In order to prepare this pasta, place the flour on a board and make a well in the center, and break in the eggs. Once this has been done, add a pinch of salt and start kneading the dough energetically for about 15 minutes. With a floured pasta rolling pin, roll out the dough quite thickly and cut it into pieces that are as long and as wide as the "guitar" strings. Wrap a piece round the rolling pin and stretch it over the guitar (1). Then, with the special small rolling pin, press down firmly so as to cut the dough in one go (2). The macaroni will drop, as shown, into the lower part of the "guitar" (3).

Pick up the strands of pasta and spread them out on the floured board. Let them dry a little before cooking.

For dressing the pasta, you can either prepare a sauce of tomatoes, olives, anchovy fillets and capers or a sauce of tomatoes, fresh red peppers, eggplant, and small hot peppers. For a quick sauce, use cut-up raw tomatoes mixed with excellent olive oil and pinches of oregano; sprinkle the dish with grated Parmesan or, even better, Romano cheese.

Abruzzi lamb sauce is a characteristic seasoning for the macaroni. To prepare this sauce, brown ¾ lb. of ground lamb in oil and pork fat, season with salt and pepper, and add a few fresh mushrooms, previously sautéed with a little onion. Flavor the sauce with a little concentrated tomato sauce and finally with a little chopped parsley. This dish is served sprinkled with grated Romano cheese.

1 Unroll the dough from the rolling pin onto the "guitar," stretching the dough out.

2 Cut the pasta into thin strips by pressing down firmly with the special small rolling pin...

3 ...in this way the macaroni will drop into the lower part of the "guitar."

Guitar macaroni

Lasagna pie

- Yield: 4 servings
- Time needed: 2½ hours
- Difficulty: **

Ingredients: homemade egg lasagna prepared with 3½ cups flour and 6 eggs, ½ lb. canned tomatoes thoroughly drained, ½ lb. lean minced beef, 2 oz. prosciutto, ¾ oz. dried boletus mushrooms, 2½ tbsp. flour, ½ medium onion, 1 small carrot, 1 small celery, ¼ tsp. each dried basil and chopped fresh parsley, 3½ tbsp. butter, ½ cup red wine, 4 oz. (1 cup) grated Parmesan, 2 cups milk, olive oil, nutmeg, pepper, salt.

In order to make the sauce, sauté the minced prosciutto in a little olive oil, add all the chopped vegetables (but not the herbs), brown slightly, add the beef, and then add the mushrooms, which should be softened for 30 minutes in a little tepid water, then squeezed and chopped roughly. Cook everything for a few minutes, then add the red wine, chopped parsley and basil, salt, pepper, and a pinch of nutmeg. When the wine has evaporated, add half a tablespoon of flour mixed with a little

1 Grease a pyrex dish with butter, spread a layer of sauce, top with pieces of boiled pasta...

2 ...add another layer of sauce, spreading it over the entire surface of the pie...

3 ...cover with a layer of white sauce prepared with butter, flour, and milk...

4 ...sprinkle with Parmesan cheese. Alternate layers until all the ingredients are used up.

water, allow the sauce to boil for a few more seconds, and then add the tomato pulp. Simmer the sauce over a moderate flame until it thickens.

Now prepare the white sauce. Melt the butter (except ½ tablespoon), add the flour, and mix well. Off heat, slowly add the boiling milk, then add salt. Return pan to heat and, stirring with a wooden spoon, simmer the sauce for a few minutes.

Grease a pyrex dish with the remaining ½ tablespoon butter, then make layers in the following order: meat sauce, the previously boiled and drained pasta (1), meat sauce again (2), white sauce (3), a sprinkling of Parmesan cheese (4), pasta again, and so on, until all the ingredients have been used up. Place the lasagna in the oven and bake at 375° until the pie is brown and bubbling.

Lasagna is eaten all over Italy and infinite recipe variations exist. Lasagna with mushrooms is an excellent variation.

In order to prepare the mushroom sauce, grate a scraped carrot, and chop an onion, a celery stalk, and a handful of parsley. Sauté the vegetables until tender in 3½ tablespoons butter. Add 5 ounces ground veal and 1 pound sliced fresh mushrooms and sauté briefly. Add 1 cup well-drained canned tomatoes, season with salt and pepper, cook slowly for about half an hour, eventually adding a little broth if the mixture seems dry.

Grease a pyrex dish with ½ tablespoon butter, and make alternating layers of sauce, boiled and drained pasta, and 7 ounces prosciutto cut into very thin strips. Cover the top of the lasagna with grated Parmesan cheese and dots of butter. Bake the lasagna at 375° until the pie is brown and bubbling.

Sicilian tagliatelle

■ Yield: 4 servings
■ Time needed: 1½ hours
■ Difficulty: *

Ingredients: Homemade *tagliatelle* prepared with 3½ cups flour and 6 eggs, ½ lb. spicy sausage, ¼ lb. pork fat or bacon, 3 oz. grated Romano cheese, 1 eggplant, olive oil, salt.

Remove the tips of the eggplant, wash it, and cut it into dice without removing the skin; brown in a frying pan in a few tablespoons of oil.

Mince the pork fat or bacon and fry it briefly in a casserole dish. Add the spicy sausage, cut into small pieces, and let it brown well. Boil the *tagliatelle* in abundant salted water until *al dente,* drain, and place on a heated china plate. Cover with the sausage and the pan drippings, diluted with a tablespoon of cooking water from the pasta. Toss with the eggplant and cheese and serve immediately.

Tagliatelle with ham and peas

■ Yield: 4 servings
■ Time needed: 1½ hours
■ Difficulty: *

Ingredients: Homemade *tagliatelle* prepared with 2⅓ cups flour and 4 eggs, 3 oz. ham, ½ lb. fresh shelled peas, 1 small onion, 1 tbsp. chopped fresh parsley, 4 tbsp. butter, pinch sugar, Parmesan cheese, heavy cream, oil, salt, pepper.

Sauté the onion, finely chopped, in 2 tablespoons butter and a few tablespoons of oil. Add the diced ham and when everything is well browned, add the peas. Stir, add half a glass of water and a pinch of sugar, cover, and cook over moderate heat until the peas are tender. Add salt and pepper, chopped parsley, a little cream. Boil the *tagliatelle* and toss with the remaining 2 tablespoons butter. Stir in the ham and pea sauce and finally sprinkle with a little Parmesan cheese.

"Straw and hay" with *mascarpone*

■ Yield: 4 servings
■ Time needed: 1 hour
■ Difficulty: *

Ingredients: Homemade small *tagliatelline* prepared with 1¾ cups flour and 3 eggs, green *tagliatelline* prepared with 1½ cups flour, ¼ lb. spinach, and 2 eggs, 5 oz. *mascarpone* (an Italian cream cheese) or ordinary American cream cheese, 2 oz. (½ cup) grated Parmesan cheese, 2 tbsp. butter, 2 egg yolks, white pepper, salt.

Boil the yellow and green *tagliatelle* in salted water, drain when *al dente,* and toss with a mixture of melted butter and *mascarpone* cheese beaten together with 2 egg yolks. Finish by tossing with Parmesan cheese and pinches of white pepper and salt.

"Straw and hay" with uncooked tomatoes

■ Yield: 4 servings
■ Time needed: 1 hour
■ Difficulty: *

Ingredients: Homemade small *tagliatelline* prepared with 1¾ cups flour and 3 eggs, green *tagliatelline* prepared with 1½ cups flour, ¼ lb. spinach, and 2 eggs, 1¼ lbs. very ripe fresh tomatoes, a handful of fresh basil, 4-5 tbsp. strong fruity olive oil, salt, and pepper.

Peel the tomatoes by dipping them first into boiling water for a few seconds, then slipping off the skins. Remove seeds and cut the pulp into small strips. Add 1 teaspoon salt and allow to drain for 15 minutes in a colander or sieve.

Boil the pasta in abundant salted water. Chop the basil. Drain the pasta when it is *al dente,* add the strips of tomato, the basil, 4 to 5 tablespoons of oil, and a fair quantity of freshly ground pepper. Serve at once.

Fettuccine with zucchini

■ Yield: 4 servings
■ Time needed: 1 hour
■ Difficulty: *

Ingredients: Homemade *fettuccine* prepared with 3½ cups flour and 6 eggs, 10-12 ounces fresh, young zucchini, a large handful flat-leaf parsley, 1 garlic clove, 2 oz. (½ cup) grated Parmesan cheese, large pinch of oregano, 4 tbsp. olive oil, salt, and pepper.

Mash the garlic and sauté in the oil, add the diced zucchini, and brown. Season with salt and pepper, and when the squash is almost ready, add the chopped parsley and the oregano. Boil the pasta until *al dente,* drain, and pour it into the pan with the zucchini. Stir quickly, add the cheese, stir again, and serve.

Pappardelle delight

■ **Yield: 4 servings**
■ **Time needed: 1½ hours**
■ **Difficulty: ***

Ingredients: Homemade *pappardelle* prepared with 3½ cups flour and 6 eggs, ¼ lb. smoked bacon, ¼ lb. shelled peas, 4 tbsp. butter, 1 small handful flat-leaf parsley, 2 eggs, ¾ oz. dried boletus mushrooms, 1 small onion, 1 garlic clove, 1 small piece of hot red pepper, a little heavy cream, 2 tbsp. grated Romano cheese, olive oil, salt, and pepper.

Melt half the butter, add the peas and a pinch salt, and cook slowly until the peas are tender, adding a little water every now and then. In a separate skillet sauté the bacon, cut into small pieces, in two tablespoons of oil; add the hot pepper and sauté for a few more seconds. Finely chop the onion, garlic, and parsley and sauté in the remaining butter. Add the mushrooms, which should be softened for 30 minutes in warm water and cut into small pieces. Season with salt and pepper and cook slowly for several minutes. Beat the eggs with the cream and Romano cheese in a large serving bowl. Boil the pasta, drain and pour into the bowl, stirring energetically. Add the bacon and mushrooms mixture, then the peas, and stir again. Serve at once.

Pappardelle with chicken livers

■ **Yield: 4 servings**
■ **Time needed: 1½ hours**
■ **Difficulty: ****

Ingredients: Homemade *pappardelle* prepared with 3½ cups flour and 6 eggs, ½ lb. chicken livers, 1 thick slice of smoked bacon, 1 lb. canned tomatoes thoroughly drained, 4 tbsp butter, 2½ oz. (about ⅔ cup) grated Parmesan cheese, 1 chopped small onion, 1 chopped celery stalk, 1 chopped carrot, ½ cup dry white wine, oil, salt, and pepper.

Cut the livers in half. Place half the butter and a few tablespoons of oil in a skillet over a flame. Add the onion and the other vegetables and sauté until they wilt. Add the diced bacon and the livers and sauté slowly for 5 minutes. Add the wine, letting it evaporate over moderate heat, then add the tomato pulp, salt, and pepper and cook for half an hour. Boil the pasta and toss with the remaining butter. Stir in the sauce and sprinkle with Parmesan cheese.

Spaghetti with tomato and anchovies

■ **Yield: 4 servings**
■ **Time needed: 1 hour**
■ **Difficulty: ****

Ingredients: Homemade spaghetti prepared with 3½ cups flour and 6 eggs, 1 lb. canned tomatoes, thoroughly drained, 5 flat anchovy fillets, drained, 1 chopped onion, 1 chopped carrot, 1 chopped stalk celery, 1 whole garlic clove, 2 tbsp. chopped fresh parsley and/or basil, 2 tbsp. capers, well drained, olive oil, salt, and pepper.

Sauté the chopped vegetables and whole garlic clove in 2 to 3 tablespoons of oil. Add the anchovies, capers, tomatoes, and a little salt and pepper. Cook the sauce until it is rather thick; when nearly ready, remove the garlic and add the chopped herbs.

Boil the pasta in salted water, drain, and toss with the sauce.

Farfalle with salmon

■ **Yield: 4 servings**
■ **Time needed: 45 minutes**
■ **Difficulty: ****

Ingredients: Homemade *farfalle* prepared with 3½ cups flour and 6 eggs, 5 oz. smoked salmon, 1 cup heavy cream, 2-3 tbsp. red caviar, freshly ground pepper, salt.

Reserve two or three slices of salmon and dice; purée the rest in a blender. Boil the *farfalle* in salted water and drain. Put the puréed salmon into a serving bowl and mix with the cream, heated separately. Turn the pasta into the serving bowl, stir and garnish with the salmon and caviar. Season with salt and pepper and serve. A photo is on page 21.

Trofie with pesto

- **Yield: 4 servings**
- **Time needed: 1½ hours**
- **Difficulty: ****

Pasta ingredients: 2½ cups all-purpose white flour, ½ cup bran, salt.
Pesto **ingredients:** 2 large handfuls (about 2 packed cups) fresh basil leaves, 1 tablespoon grated Romano cheese, 1 tablespoon grated Parmesan cheese, 1 garlic clove, ⅓ cup pine nuts, ½-⅔ cup olive oil, salt.

This is a typical Ligurian dish and comes from the Riviera in particular.

In order to make the pasta, combine the flour, bran (if you are unable to obtain bran, use dry bread crumbs), and a pinch of salt on a board, make a well in the center, and gradually pour in as much water as is necessary to obtain a rather stiff dough (1). Knead well and then cut the dough into pieces. Roll each piece on the floured board into the shape of a stick and cut the sticks into small pieces the size of a thimble (2).

If you want to follow the traditional method, first roll the pieces of pasta on the board with the thumb of your right hand so as to obtain small *gnocchi* (dumplings); then twist the pieces while pulling on them at the ends, to make pasta shapes about 1 inch in length which look vaguely like *fusilli*.

In order to quickly prepare *trofie* it is sufficient to roll the pieces of dough along the prongs of a fork, in practically the same way as you do in the case of potato *gnocchi* (3). If you want a nice decorative spiral effect, you can roll the dough pieces at a slant along the prongs.

In order to prepare the *pesto* sauce, wash the basil leaves and lay them out on a cloth to dry. Put basil leaves into the container of a blender or food processor, along with the garlic clove, pine nuts and a pinch of salt. Purée, add the oil gradually. Finally stir in the Romano and Parmesan cheeses, previously grated and mixed together.

When you have finished preparing all the *trofie*, boil them in abundant salted water, drain, and toss generously with *pesto* sauce.

1 Lay out the flour and bran, make a well in the center, add salt, and pour in the water.

2 Roll up a piece of dough by hand and cut it into pieces the size of a thimble.

3 Roll the small *gnocchi* along the prongs of a fork, pressing lightly with a finger.

Trofie with pesto

Corzetti Ligurian style

- **Yield: 4 servings**
- **Time needed: 1 hour**
- **Difficulty: ****

Pasta ingredients: 2⅔ cups all-purpose white flour, 3 "large" eggs, salt.
Sauce ingredients: 5 tbsp. butter, 3 tbsp. pine nuts, pinch marjoram, 2½ oz. (⅔ cup) grated Parmesan cheese, salt, and pepper.

The *corzetti* are a typical Ligurian dish. The origin of the name *corzetti* seems to derive from the fact that, in size and shape, these pasta shapes resemble the *crosazzo,* a silver coin used by the ancient Genoa Republic.

Besides being yellow, the pasta can also be green if a certain amount of finely chopped well-squeezed spinach is added to the flour and eggs.

When preparing the homemade *corzetti,* proceed as follows: Place the flour on the board, make a well in the middle, and break in the eggs, adding some pinches of salt. Beat well with a fork and then add 4 to 6 tablespoons of tepid water (1), kneading until a firm, smooth dough is obtained.

Pinch off small pieces of dough about the size of chickpeas (2) and stretch the pieces while pressing at both ends with the fingertips so that they have the form of the number '8' (3). When all the *corzetti* are ready, spread them out on a cloth and leave them to dry. The *corzetti* are usually left to dry for a few days before being cooked.

In Liguria, the *corzetti* are sometimes made as follows. You roll out a rather thick sheet of dough and form it into small circles using a special stamp (*crosetti* iron) that engraves one side of the circle with arabesques.

Place abundant salted water over a flame and bring to a boil. After boiling the *corzetti* (4), remove them with a slotted skimmer to an earthenware pot or other serving dish, dressing them in layers (5) with 5 tablespoons butter melted with a pinch of marjoram, plus the pine nuts, the grated Parmesan cheese, and a goodly pinch of freshly ground pepper. *Corzetti* can also be seasoned with meat or mushroom sauce.

1 Knead the eggs, flour, and salt together with sufficient water to obtain a cohesive dough.

2 When the dough is nice and smooth, pinch off small pieces about the size of chickpeas.

3 Stretch the pieces while pressing at both ends so that they have the form of the number '8'.

4 After having left the *corzetti* to dry well, cook them in abundant boiling salted water.

5 Remove to a serving dish, seasoning layers with melted butter, marjoram, pine nuts, and cheese.

Pizzoccheri

■ **Yield: 4 servings**
■ **Time needed: about 2 hours**
■ **Difficulty: ***

Pasta ingredients: 1½ cups buckwheat flour, ½ cup all-purpose white flour, 2 "large" eggs, 2-4 tbsp. milk, salt.
Other ingredients: 6 oz. *fontina* cheese, 7 tbsp. butter, 3 or 4 medium-size potatoes, 1 small savoy cabbage, ¼ tsp sage, 1 garlic clove, salt, and pepper.

This is a typical dish from Valtellina.

Mix the buckwheat flour and the white flour together on the board, (make a well in the middle, and break in the whole eggs). Knead, adding just enough milk and water to obtain a cohesive and rather stiff dough, continue to knead energetically for a few minutes until the dough is nice and smooth (2). Roll out the dough into a fairly thick sheet (3), cut the dough into strips approximately ⅜-inch wide (4), and then divide these strips into pieces approximately 2 inches long (5).

Separate the savoy cabbage into leaves choosing the nicest ones and wash, drain and cut the cabbage leaves into strips. Peel the potatoes, wash, and cut into cubes. Bring abundant salted water to a boil. Add first the potatoes (6), then the savoy cabbage (7), and, when the vegetables are half cooked, add

the pasta (8). Mix gently every now and then, preferably using a wooden spoon or fork (9).

While the pasta and vegetables are cooking, place the butter, the whole garlic clove and the sage over a low flame and sauté briefly without allowing the butter to brown. Cut the cheese into very thin slices so that it can melt when heated.

Drain the pasta together with the vegetables when the pasta is still *al dente,* and arrange the mixture in layers in the traditional wooden plate (10) or in some other serving dish, seasoning each layer with slices of cheese, pepper, butter, and, if you like some grated Parmesan cheese (11). Stir just before serving.

Pizzoccheri are traditionally served with a separate dish of horseradish roots, which are dipped into salt that has been spread out on the tablecloth.

1 Mix the two flours together, making a well in the middle, add the eggs, salt, a little milk.

2 Knead the ingredients together energetically in order to obtain a smooth, cohesive dough.

3 Roll out the dough on the board with a pasta rolling pin until you have a not-too-thin sheet.

4 With a knife, cut the dough into strips approximately ⅜-inch wide...

5 ...then divide these strips into smaller pieces about 2 inches long forming numerous rectangles.

6 Peel the potatoes, wash and cut them into cubes, and put them into boiling water.

7 Choose the nicest leaves from the cabbage, wash and cut into strips, and drop into boiling water.

8 When the vegetables are half cooked, add the freshly-made pasta.

9 Stir every now and then with a wooden spoon to prevent the pasta from sticking.

10 Drain the pasta and the vegetables and arrange in layers in the traditional wooden plate...

11 ...seasoning each layer of pasta with thin slices of *fontina* cheese, pepper, and melted butter.

Bigoli with sardines

■ **Yield: 4 servings**
■ **Time needed: 1½ hours**
■ **Difficulty: ****

Pasta ingredients: 2⅔ cups wholewheat flour, 2 tbsp butter, 4 "large" eggs, milk, and salt.
Sauce ingredients: 10 oz. fresh sardines (or smelts, if fresh sardines are unavailable), 1 garlic clove, 3 tbsp. olive oil, freshly ground pepper, salt.

This is a typical dish from the Venice and Mantua regions.

To prepare the *bigoli*, pour the flour onto a board and break the eggs into the center. Add the melted butter and a pinch of salt, and knead the ingredients together, adding as much milk as necessary to obtain a rather stiff dough (1). Pass the pasta through a *bigolaro,* an old-fashioned press used in the Venice and Mantua regions where this dish originated (2) to obtain long solid strings of pasta with a rather granular consistency, rather like large spaghetti. If you do not have a press, use the ordinary pasta-making machine. Using a floured knife cut the *bigoli* into approximately 12-inch lengths as they gradually come out of the *bigolaro* or press (3).

Spread the *bigoli* far apart on the board or in a basket (4) and allow them to rest without letting them dry too much.

In order to make the sauce, clean, bone, wash, and dry the sardines. Sauté the garlic clove, crushed, in the oil, then remove the garlic and add the sardines. Mash the sardines well with a fork and cook slowly over a moderate flame (the sardines must not fry in the oil).

Boil the *bigoli* in abundant salted water, drain when they are *al dente,* and pour the sardine sauce on, stirring quickly to blend everything well. Serve very hot.

If you like, you can vary the *bigoli* sauce by replacing the fresh sardines with 2 tins of anchovy fillets which have been drained, minced, and sautéed in a little oil. Crush the anchovies with a fork, add a cup of homemade tomato sauce, and cook. Add a handful of finely chopped parsley. Before serving season with freshly ground pepper.

1 Break the eggs into the flour, add butter and a pinch of salt, and knead together adding milk as necessary.

2 Pass the dough through the *bigolaro,* to make thick strands.

3 Cut the *bigoli*, with a floured knife into lengths of about 12 inches.

4 Spread the *bigoli* on the board or in a large floured basket and leave them to dry.

Bigoli with chicken giblets

■ Yield: 4 servings
■ Time needed: 1½ hours
■ Difficulty: **

Ingredients: 1 recipe homemade *bigoli* (page 41), ½ lb. chicken giblets, cut into small pieces, 7 tbsp. butter, ½ tsp. sage, salt, grated Parmesan cheese.

Warm the butter with the sage leaves, add the giblets, except for the livers, season with salt, and cook for about twenty minutes over a moderate flame (add a bit of chicken broth if the mixture looks too dry.) A few seconds before removing from the flame, add the livers and sauté just until the livers stiffen.

Boil the *bigoli* in abundant salted water, drain when *al dente*, and toss with the sauce and cheese.

Bigoli with anchovy sauce

■ Yield: 4 servings
■ Time needed: 1½ hour
■ Difficulty: **

Ingredients: 1 recipe homemade bigoli (page 41), ½ lb. yellow onions, 1 tin flat anchovy fillets, drained, 4 tbsp. olive oil, salt and pepper.

Sauté the onions thinly sliced, in 3 tablespoons of oil. When they start browning, add a little water, cover the dish (preferably of terra cotta), and cook until they have completely lost their shape. At this point, add the anchovy fillets and smash well with a fork until they become a pulp. Continue to cook for another couple of minutes, then add a tablespoon of oil, stir, and turn off the flame.

Boil the *bigoli* in abundant salted water, drain, and toss with sauce and some freshly ground black pepper.

Serve the pasta immediately.

Bigoli with duck

■ Yield: 4 servings
■ Time needed: 2½ hours
■ Difficulty: **

Ingredients: 1 recipe homemade *bigoli* (page 41), 1 5-lb. duck, 4 tbsp. butter, 1 small onion, 1 small carrot, 1 celery stalk, ½ tsp. sage, 1 bay leaf, 3 tbsp. grated Parmesan cheese, oil, freshly ground pepper, and salt.

Wash the duck and set aside the giblets. Boil the duck in salted water with the onion, carrot, and celery all cut into small pieces, until the meat is tender. Warm the butter and a tablespoon of oil in a pan with the sage and bay leaf, add the duck giblets, cut into very small pieces, and sauté slowly for 10 minutes. Add a little broth, (the classic recipe requires two tablespoons of pomegranate juice) and cook over a low flame for about ten minutes.

Boil the *bigoli* in the duck broth, drain, and toss them with the giblet sauce and with Parmesan cheese.

Serve the *bigoli* as a first course and follow with the boiled duck as a main dish. Accompany the duck with a *peverada* sauce, a very highly peppered sauce made of game giblets sautéed in oil, and a little broth, and finished with chopped parsley and the juice of half a lemon.

Bigoli and olives

■ Yield: 4 servings
■ Time needed: 1½ hours
■ Difficulty: **

Pasta ingredients: 3 cups wholewheat flour and salt
Sauce ingredients: 12 oz. canned tomatoes, well drained, 4 oz. green olives, ½ yellow or green pepper, 1 small onion, 1 garlic clove, 1 tbsp. chopped parsley, 4 tbsp. oil, 2 tbsp. grated Parmesan cheese, freshly ground pepper, and salt.

Sift the flour onto a board, make a well in the center, add a few pinches of salt, and add as much water as is necessary to obtain a rather stiff dough. Pass the pasta through the *bigolaro* press. You will obtain long strings of solid pasta, similar to large spaghetti. You can also make the pasta with an ordinary pasta-making machine.

Sauté the chopped onion and garlic in the oil, add the chopped pepper. Sauté for a few minutes and then add the tomatoes, puréed in a blender, a pinch of salt, some freshly ground pepper, and the olives, pitted and halved. (Reserve a few whole olives for the garnish.) Simmer the sauce for 10 minutes to blend the flavors.

Just before removing the sauce from the flame, add the parsley. Boil the *bigoli*, drain, and toss with olive sauce and the cheese. Garnish with the whole olives and serve immediately.

Pisarei with beans

■ **Yield: 4 servings**
■ **Time needed: 2 hours**
■ **Difficulty: ****

Pasta ingredients: 3½ cups all-purpose white flour, ¾ cup dry bread crumbs, a few pinches of salt.
Sauce ingredients: ½ lb. dried pinto beans, 4 tbsp. butter, 2 oz. pork fat, 1 small onion, 1 small bunch parsley, 1 garlic clove, 10 oz. ripe tomatoes (or 1 can of peeled tomatoes weighing 8 to 9 oz.), 1 small bunch basil, olive oil, freshly ground pepper, and salt.

This is a typical dish from the Piacenza area.

Soak the beans overnight in cold water. The next morning, drain the beans, put them into a saucepan, cover with cold water, add half an onion and a tablespoon of oil, and cook slowly with the lid off. Remove the beans from the flame when they are about half cooked and keep them in their water.

In the meantime, prepare the pasta. Place the flour on the board, make a well in the center, and add the bread crumbs, previously soaked in enough boiling water to make a mixture with the consistency of very thick oatmeal (1). Knead ingredients together with a little hot water (2), just enough to obtain a rather stiff dough. Continue to knead until the dough becomes smooth (3). After about ten minutes, take a piece of dough and roll it under the palms of your hands so as to obtain a long roll about as thick as your little finger (4). Pinch off a piece about as big as a bean (5), and then press with your thumb to form the classic shape of a *gnocchetto* (small dumpling) (6).

Prepare the sauce for the *pisarei*. Melt the butter, and add finely chopped pork fat, garlic, and parsley (7). Sauté for a few minutes and then add the remaining half of the onion chopped (8), stirring with a wooden spoon until the mixture is slightly browned. Pour the fresh tomatoes, peeled and seeded or the can of tomatoes into the dish (9), and add the drained beans (10), the whole basil leaves, a little freshly ground pepper (11), and a little of the bean cooking water. Mix all ingredients together and cover the dish. Cook over a low flame until the beans are tender, stirring every now and then. Add the salt only towards the end of cooking to prevent the skin of the beans from hardening. When done, the sauce should be thick but abundant.

Cook the *pisarei* for about a quarter of an hour in boiling salted water, drain and toss with sauce.

Bean sauce is traditionally used with *pisarei* because the beans are similar in size to the *gnocchetti*. You could also prepare this sauce with chickpeas or fava.

The following is a suitable recipe. Boil ½ pound of fresh fava beans, shelled and washed, in lightly salted water. In the meantime, grate a carrot, a small piece of celery and a small onion and sauté in a skillet with 2 tablespoons butter and 2½ ounces diced bacon. Add 1 pound canned tomatoes and a bit of salt, and reduce the sauce a little over moderate flame. Mix in the broad beans, add half a cup of broth (or water and half a bouillon cube), and cook for approximately ten minutes over a moderate flame. Flavor the sauce with some chopped garlic and basil. Toss with the sauce.

1 Place the flour on the board, make a well in the center, and add the bread crumbs.

2 Knead ingredients together, adding just enough hot water to obtain a rather stiff dough.

3 Knead the dough energetically until it is smooth and elastic.

4 Roll a piece of the dough under the palms of your hands until you obtain a long stick.

5 Pinch off a small piece about the size of a bean from the stick.

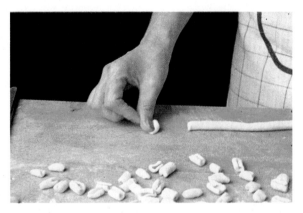

6 Using your thumb, give each small piece the form of a *gnocchetto* by pressing it against the board.

7 In order to make the sauce, sauté a mixture of pork fat, garlic, and parsley in a casserole dish.

8 When the mixture has begun to brown, add finely chopped onion and mix well.

9 Add the peeled and seeded tomatoes or the canned peeled tomatoes together with the canning liquid.

10 After a few minutes, add the partially cooked beans, drained.

11 Finish the sauce with a few whole fresh basil leaves and freshly ground pepper.

Testaroli with pesto

- ■ **Yield: 4 servings**
- ■ **Time needed: 1½ hour**
- ■ **Difficulty: ****

Pasta ingredients: 2⅓ cups all-purpose flour, lard, or vegetable shortening and salt.
Pesto **sauce ingredients: 2 large handfuls (about 2 packed cups) fresh basil leaves, 1 tbsp. of grated Romano cheese, 2 garlic cloves, ⅓ cup pine nuts, a small handful walnuts (1-2 tbsp.) about ½-⅔ cup olive oil, and salt.**

This dish is from the Lunigiana area.

Mix the flour and a pinch of salt with enough water to make a viscous batter like glue. Grease a pan with a little lard or vegetable shortening, pour in two tablespoons of batter, and swirl the pan in order to cover the bottom with the batter. When the pancake has cooked on one side, turn it over. Cook on the other side and remove. Proceed in this way until you have finished all the batter.

Prepare the *pesto* by puréeing the basil, garlic, pine nuts, walnuts, and a pinch of salt in a blender or food processor, adding the oil gradually. Stir in the cheese.

Immerse the *testaroli* in salted boiling water, then turn off the flame. Drain after 4 to 5 minutes, cut into strips, and toss with the *pesto* sauce.

Ciriole

- ■ **Yield: 4 servings**
- ■ **Time needed: 1½ hours**
- ■ **Difficulty: ****

Pasta ingredients: 3 cups semolina flour.
Sauce ingredients: 1 lb. canned tomatoes, well drained, 2 garlic cloves, 1 hot red pepper, 3 tablespoons olive oil, salt, and pepper.

This is a typical Umbrian dish.

Mix the flour with a pinch of salt and knead together with enough water to obtain a rather stiff dough. Knead the dough hard for at least 15 minutes, slapping it down repeatedly onto the board. Roll out a rather thick sheet of dough and cut it into wide but rather short noodles. With flour-covered hands, twist the pieces of pasta round a large knitting needle, allow to dry briefly, then boil.

Sauté the garlic, cut into strips, in the oil, add the crushed hot pepper, the minced tomatoes and a pinch of salt, and reduce the sauce over moderate flame until it is quite thick. Toss the pasta with the sauce immediately after draining.

Cavatieddi

■ **Yield: 4 servings**
■ **Time needed: 2½ hours**
■ **Difficulty: ****

Ingredients: 1 cup hard-wheat flour ("semolina"), 1½ cups all-purpose flour, salt.

This is a traditional Apulian dish.

Place the two types of flour on a board (1), make a well in the center, and mix with enough tepid salty water to obtain a dough as similar to bread dough as possible (2). Knead the dough very well, then roll a small piece of the dough into a cylinder ⅜-inch thick (about as thick as your little finger) and approximately 16 inches long.

Once you have finished the first cylinder, make a second one, but do not roll all of the dough into cylinders at once because the cylinders will dry out too quickly; remember, in fact, to keep unrolled dough covered with a cloth.

Cut each cylinder into lots of small pieces (3). As you are cutting the pasta, press each piece with the point of a floured knife against the board (4) to obtain the *cavatieddi* (or very small shells). Once you have made all the *cavatieddi,* allow them to dry in the open. After boiling the pasta, season with a good meat sauce, or with fresh tomatoes, basil, and oil, or with garlic, oil, and hot pepper.

Cavatieddi with arugula

■ **Yield: 4 servings**
■ **Time needed: 1½ hours**
■ **Difficulty: ****

Ingredients: 1 recipe homemade cavatieddi (page 48), 1 can peeled tomatoes weighing 8-9 oz., drained, 1 lb. arugula, 1 onion, 1 garlic clove, 2½ oz. (about ⅔ cup) grated Romano cheese, oil, salt, and pepper.

This is a typical Apulian dish that uses the local variety of arugula, a leafy plant with a very strong odor and rather sour flavor. In the kitchen arugula is mainly used as an ingredient in salads; sometimes its juice and even its seeds are used in addition to the leaves. The seeds were used in the past to prepare a very tasty sauce to go with meat.

In southern Italy, especially in the Apulian region, arugula is cooked and eaten with *cavatieddi*.

Choose the best leaves of the arugula and wash under running water. Discard the stems. Chop the onion and sauté in a few tablespoons of oil until it wilts. Add the whole garlic clove and the skinned tomatoes, season with salt and pepper, and cook the sauce over a very low flame until the juice of the tomatoes has evaporated and the sauce is nice and thick. Remove the garlic.

Place abundant salted water over a flame and, as soon as it starts boiling, immerse the arugula. When the arugula is cooked, add the pasta and cook until *al dente*.

Drain the pasta and arugula together, pour them into an earthenware bowl or other serving dish, toss with the tomato sauce.

Finish the dish with grated Romano cheese.

1 Place the white flour and the semolina on a board, mix, and make a well in the center.

2 After kneading the flour with tepid water, work the pasta until it is smooth and elastic.

3 After rolling the dough into small cylinders the thickness of a little finger, cut into small pieces.

4 Press each small piece of dough with the tip of a floured knife against the board.

Orecchiette with potatoes

■ **Yield: 4 servings**
■ **Time needed: 1½ hrs. approx.**
■ **Difficulty: ****

Pasta ingredients: 2½ cups all-purpose white flour, ¾ cup hard-wheat flour (semolina), and salt.
Other ingredients: 4 medium-size potatoes, a few sprigs of fresh rue or 1 tbsp. fresh basil, ¾-1½ cups fresh tomato sauce, ½-1 cup grated Romano cheese, salt.

This is another traditional Apulian dish.

Mix the two types of flour and a pinch of salt together, make a well in the middle, and add as much tepid water as is necessary to make a firm dough. Knead the dough for about ten minutes, or until small blisters form. The dough should be a little stiffer than bread dough (like *cavatieddi* dough). Remove a piece of dough and roll it on the board, obtaining a cylinder as thick as a pencil. Cut it into ⅜-inch pieces (1) and, with the rounded point of a knife, press each piece against the board (2) to form a small shell. With the tip of your thumb (and with the help of a knife blade if necessary) poke the shell from behind, thus turning it inside-out (3). Continue in the same way until you have used all the dough. Leave the *orecchiette* to dry until the following day (but no longer, or the pasta will break up when cooked). Bring abundant salted water to the boil, add first the potatoes, previously peeled and cut into small pieces (4), then the sprigs of rue or basil (5), and finally the *orecchiette* (6). When cooked, drain everything (7), remove the rue or basil and turn the *orecchiette* and potatoes into a serving dish, adding warmed tomato sauce and sprinkling Romano cheese. Serve at once.

You can serve homemade *orecchiette* with various ingredients. A typical Apulian dish consists of *orecchiette* combined with turnip greens or brussel sprouts. You can boil the brussel sprouts in abundant salted water and cook the *orecchiette* in the same water. Drain the pasta and toss with very hot tomato sauce flavored with a garlic clove. Top the *orecchiette* with the brussel sprouts, cut into small pieces and serve with lots of Romano cheese.

1 Roll the pasta into cylinders, then cut into pieces measuring ⅜-inch.

2 Press the small pieces of pasta against the board using a knife with a round tip...

3 ...forming a shell, which you turn inside-out by poking with your thumb and the blade of the knife.

4 Cut the potatoes into medium-size pieces and put them into the boiling salted water.

5 Add a bunch of fresh basil, just picked if possible, to the water...

6 ...finally throw the *orecchiette*, prepared the previous day, into the water.

7 When cooked, drain all the ingredients together: *orecchiette*, potatoes, and basil.

Orecchiette with meat rolls

- Yield: 4 servings
- Time needed: 2 hours
- Difficulty: **

Ingredients: 1 recipe homemade *orecchiette* (page 51), 7 oz. sliced veal cutlets and, 7 oz. pork cutlets cut into 4 in. squares, 3½ oz. sliced smoked bacon in strips, 2 oz. (about ½ cup) grated Parmesan cheese, 1½ oz. (about ⅓ cup) grated Romano cheese, 1 lb. canned tomatoes, 1 small onion, a small handful of chopped parsley, ½ cup red wine, oil, salt, and pepper.

Lay the strips of bacon on the slices of veal and pork and sprinkle with chopped parsley and a bit of Parmesan cheese. Roll the meat slices up into roulades and tie with kitchen string. Sauté the chopped onion in 2 to 3 tablespoons of oil, add the roulades, and pour in the red wine, allowing the wine to evaporate over moderate heat. Season with salt and pepper and add the tomatoes, breaking them up with a spoon. Cover and cook slowly until the rolls are completely tender, about 45 minutes.

Boil the *orecchiette* in abundant salted water. Drain, toss the pasta with the meat-roll sauce, sprinkle with Parmesan and Romano cheese. Place the meat rolls on top and serve immediately.

This substantial dish needs only a salad or vegetable to become a complete meal.

Note: The meat rolls can also be prepared with beef that has been cut into very thin and rather wide slices; obviously, the cooking will take longer.

Hollow macaroni

- ■ **Yield: 4 servings**
- ■ **Time needed: 1½ hours**
- ■ **Difficulty: ****

Pasta ingredients: ⅔ cups all-purpose white flour, 1 cup hard-wheat flour (semolina), salt.
Sauce ingredients: 2 cups homemade tomato sauce, 2-3 tbsp. olive oil, oregano.

These macaroni, widespread throughout southern Italy, are also called *fusilli*. You need a square rod about a foot long for preparing them. Place the flour on a board with a well in the middle, add a few pinches of salt, and knead in just enough tepid water to obtain a rather stiff dough. Some people also add a whole egg to the dough.

Knead the dough energetically until it is elastic and smooth. Cut the dough into pieces. Keep the pieces of dough that you are not working with wrapped in a cloth to prevent them from drying out. Roll a piece of dough with the floured palms of your hands into a cylinder the width of a pencil (1). Cut the cylinder into small pieces approximately 1 inch long. Line up three or four small pieces of dough on the board, place the rod over the center of the pieces of dough (2), and press down on the rod with your hands, moving it back and forth thus rolling the dough round it (3). Press the rod firmly to seal the macaroni (4). The dough will lengthen during this operation and will take on the appearance of long hollow macaroni. Slide the dough off the rod (5). Spread the pasta out on the floured board and allow to dry well. Boil the macaroni in salted water, drain when *al dente,* and toss gently with boiling tomato sauce, a few tablespoons of olive oil, and oregano to taste. You can add some freshly ground pepper if you like.

The pasta produced here is rather short but you can also cut 2½-inch pieces and make much longer macaroni. In this case you can toss the pasta with a tasty sauce made with pork and sprinkle with lots of chopped fresh basil leaves and a good handful of grated Romano cheese.

1 Roll a small piece of dough under your hands to obtain a cylinder the width of a pencil.

2 Line up three or four small pieces of dough on the board and place the rod over them.

3 Roll the dough around the utensil by pressing down, lifting your hands every now and then.

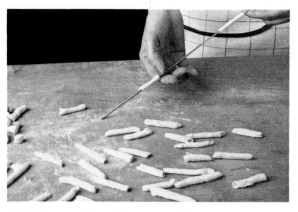

4 After having pressed down repeatedly on the dough, give one firm push to seal the macaroni.

5 Remove the small macaroni from the rod and spread them out on the board.

Malloreddus

1 Mix the flour with a little tepid water in which you have dissolved the saffron.

2 Roll a small piece of dough with your hand until you have a stick about ³⁄₁₆ inch in diameter.

3 Press the *gnocchetti* against the *ciuliri* pressing the center with your thumb.

Malloreddus

- Yield: 4 servings
- Time needed: 1½ hours
- Difficulty: **

Pasta ingredients: 3 cups semolina flour, a pinch of saffron, a little white flour, salt.
Sauce ingredients: 1¾ lbs. fresh tomatoes, 2 oz. bacon, 1 small onion, 3 basil leaves, 1 garlic clove, ½ bouillon cube, grated Romano cheese, olive oil, salt, and pepper.

Place the flour on a board and mix with tepid water containing the salt and saffron (1). Knead until you obtain a smooth but fairly soft dough. Remove a small piece of dough and roll it until you obtain a stick with a circumference of about ³⁄₁₆-inch (2). Sprinkle the dough with flour and pinch off very small pieces about as long as a bean with your thumb. As you pinch off the pieces, press down on them in the center with your thumb. To get a better shape, press the pieces against the bottom of an ordinary basket. (3). Let the pasta dry in the open for a couple of days.

To make the sauce, sauté the bacon and chopped onions in a casserole dish with 2 tablespoons of oil. Stir in the smashed garlic and basil, then add the tomatoes, the crumbled bouillon cube, and a pinch of salt and pepper. Cook until a thick sauce is obtained. Boil the *malloreddus* and toss with the sauce and Romano cheese.

Malloreddus with lamb ragout

- Yield: 4 servings
- Time needed: 2 hours
- Difficulty: **

Ingredients: 1 recipe of homemade *malloreddus* (above), a piece of leg of lamb weighing approximately 2¼ lbs., 10 oz. canned tomatoes, ½ tsp. rosemary, 1 small onion, 3 garlic cloves, about ⅓ cup grated Romano cheese, oil, white wine, salt, and pepper.

Cut slits in the leg of lamb and insert rosemary and pieces of garlic. Sprinkle lamb with pepper, place in an oval casserole dish, and brown in oil. Pour a glassful of white wine over the lamb and allow it to evaporate, then add the chopped onion and tomatoes and bake, covered, for about two hours in a 350° oven. If the cooking juices dry up, add a little boiling water.

Boil the *malloreddus* in salted water, drain when *al dente,* and toss with the sauce from the braised lamb, which should be quite thick.

Finally sprinkle the pasta with the Romano cheese. Serve the pasta first and follow with the leg of lamb as the main course.

Gnocchi

When you talk about *gnocchi*, everyone thinks of those made with potatoes, which are undoubtedly the most famous. But potato *gnocchi* are not the original kind. Potatoes were unknown in Europe until 1500, when the Spanish imported them from Peru, their land of origin. In other words, in the beginning *gnocchi* were made with various doughs based on cereal flours, vegetables, cheeses, or bread. The tastiest and most popular *gnocchi* recipes today are those based on vegetables (in addition to potatoes, you can use spinach, the green leafy part of swiss chard, pumpkin, carrots, etc.), boiled or baked, chopped fine or puréed, and mixed with flour, bread, eggs, cheese, and other ingredients until a dough of the correct consistency is achieved.

The semolina *gnocchi* are the most refined. They should be gratineed in a very hot oven until they are a slightly golden color, a finishing touch which renders even the simplest dishes inviting. Almost all *gnocchi* are cooked in abundant boiling salted water, from which they are removed with a slotted skimmer as soon as they start to float. They are then dressed in various ways. Melted butter plus Parmesan cheese and cream sauces are delicious with *gnocchi*. *Gnocchetti*, small, delicately flavored gnocchi, made with *ricotta* cheese, should be seasoned with tomato sauce whereas potato *gnocchi* require a meat sauce.

In order to prepare ordinary *gnocchi* all you need is a wooden board or a good-sized table top on which to prepare the dough. In the case of semolina *gnocchi*, however, you need a marble slab of some other nonabsorbent surface on which to cool the dough. You need a potato ricer to make potato *gnocchi*, a vegetable mill for pumpkin *gnocchi*, and a "rocker" chopping knife for spinach *gnocchi*. A blender or food processor may also be handy, but you should never use a vegetable mill or an electric appliance to mash potatoes, for they will be gluey. For chopping fresh or frozen spinach, the best utensil is still the old-fashioned "rocker" chopping knife because it reduces spinach to just the right consistency.

Roll floured *gnocchi* over the prongs of a fork or along the back of a grater. The first method will produce rather deep grooves, while the second results in small knobs. One way or the other, the *gnocco* will have roughed, irregular surface which will hold the sauce well.

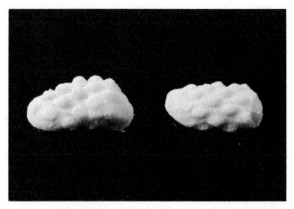

1 *Gnocchi* pressed against the back of a grater have small uniform knobs.

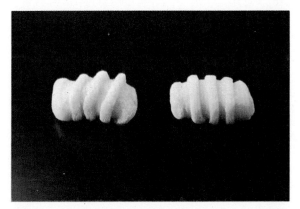

2 *Gnocchi* pressed against the prongs of a fork have very deep grooves.

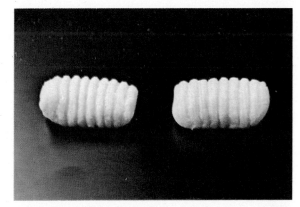

3 *Gnocchi*, pressed against a small grooved wooden board are ideal for holding sauces.

Potato gnocchi

- **Yield: 4 servings**
- **Time needed: 1½ hours**
- **Difficulty: ***

Gnocchi ingredients: 2¼ lbs. baking potatoes, about 2¾ cups all-purpose white flour, 1 "large" egg, nutmeg, salt.
Sauce ingredients: Tomato sauce flavored with basil, a few tablespoons grated Parmesan cheese, salt.

Boil the potatoes in their skins, peel them and pass through a potato ricer, letting the riced potatoes fall onto the board. Mix in a goodly pinch each of salt and nutmeg, make a well in the center, add the egg and a little flour, and begin kneading, gradually adding as much of the remaining flour as necessary (1). At the end, you should have obtained a soft dough which does not stick to your fingers. Remove a piece of dough and roll it over the floured board until you obtain a long stick (2). Cut the stick into lots of small pieces measuring about ¾-inch in length (3). Proceed in the same way until you have used up all the dough, flouring your hands and the work surface every now and then.

Press the *gnocchi* against the back of a grater with your thumb, one at a time (4), over the prongs of a fork (5) or over the special little wooden paddle (6). If you have to make many *gnocchi,* the little hand-cranked machine may be of help.

Cook the *gnocchi* in boiling salted water, skimming them from the water as they gradually float to the top. Serve with tomato sauce and Parmesan cheese.

Potato gnocchi with cheese

- **Yield: 4 servings**
- **Time needed: 1½ hours**
- **Difficulty: ***

Ingredients: 1 recipe potato *gnocchi* (above), ½ lb. *fontina* cheese, 7 tbsp. butter, salt.

Boil the *gnocchi* in salted water and drain well. In a pyrex dish greased with butter, make alternating layers of *gnocchi* and thin slices of *fontina* cheese. Finally cover with the butter, cut in pats, and place in 450-degree oven for 15 to 20 minutes, or until lightly browned.

Potato gnocchi with anchovies

- **Yield: 4 servings**
- **Time needed: 1½ hours**
- **Difficulty: ***

Ingredients: 1 recipe potato *gnocchi,* 4 frankfurters, 4-5 flat anchovy fillets, drained, 3 tbsp. oil, 1 crushed garlic clove, salt.

Sauté the crushed garlic clove in the oil, remove the garlic, and add the anchovies, mash them with a fork. Add the sliced frankfurters and cook slowly for about ten minutes. Boil the *gnocchi,* drain, and dress with the sauce.

Ricotta and spinach gnocchetti

- **Yield: 4 servings**
- **Time needed: 1 hour**
- **Difficulty: ***

Gnocchetti ingredients: 1½ pounds spinach, ½ lb. *ricotta,* 1 cup all-purpose white flour, 4-5 tbsp. Parmesan, 2 eggs, nutmeg, pepper, salt.
Sauce ingredients: 7 tbsp. butter, pinch of sage, 4 tbsp. grated Parmesan, salt.

Cook the spinach and drain thoroughly, squeezing out excess water. Press the spinach through a sieve or food mill. Add to it the *ricotta,* Parmesan, eggs, nutmeg, salt and pepper. Blend well, then stir in the flour little by little until you have a medium firm dough. Grease your hands and form small *gnocchetti* with the dough, spreading them on a floured plate as you make them.

Gently drop them into boiling salted water for about 3 minutes. When they are cooked, drain them and dress them in layers with melted butter flavored with sage and Parmesan.

Ricotta gnocchetti

- **Yield: 4 servings**
- **Time needed: 1½ hours**
- **Difficulty: ***

Ingredients: 10 oz. *ricotta* cheese, about ¾ cup all-purpose white flour, 7 tbsp. butter, 5 oz. (about 1¼ cups) Parmesan cheese, 1 whole egg and 2 egg yolks, salt, pinch nutmeg.

Mix the *ricotta* cheese with a little less than a cup of the grated Parmesan cheese, the flour, whole egg, egg yolks, salt, and, if you like, nutmeg. If necessary add a little more flour. Make the *gnocchi* from the dough, immerse in boiling water for 3 minutes, and dress with the remaining grated Parmesan cheese and the butter melted.

1 Mix the riced potato, egg, and flour and knead together well.

2 Roll the dough, piece by piece, over the board until you obtain long sticks.

3 Cut the sticks into pieces approximately ¾-inch long flouring the board every now and then.

4 Press the *gnocchetti* one by one against the back of a grater, pushing them down a little with your thumb.

5 If you do not have a concave grater, you can press the *gnocchi* against the prongs of a fork...

6 ...or against a special wooden paddle in order to make *gnocchi* with close-set grooves.

Parisian gnocchi

- **Yield: 4 servings**
- **Time needed: 1¼ hours**
- **Difficulty: ****

Pasta ingredients: 2½ cups milk, 1 cup all-purpose white flour, 6 tbsp. butter, 4 "large" eggs, 4 tbsp. grated Parmesan cheese, nutmeg, pepper and salt.

Sauce ingredients: 5 oz sweet *gorgonzola* cheese, 3 oz. *mascarpone* cream cheese (or ordinary American cream cheese), 5 tbsp. butter, salt, and pepper.

Place the milk, a pinch of salt, and 6 tbsp. softened butter in a small saucepan. When the mixture starts boiling, remove the pan from the flame and add the flour all at once (1), beating hard to prevent lumps from forming. Return to the flame and continue mixing until the paste makes a slight hissing noise and comes away from the bottom of the pan (2). At this point, remove the pan from the flame and add the eggs to the paste one at a time (3), adding one egg only after the previous one has been absorbed. Add the Parmesan and a pinch of nutmeg, mixing again.

For the sauce, melt 5 tbsp. butter in a small casserole dish, add the pieces of *gorgonzola* cheese and the *mascarpone* (or regular) cream cheese and

melt over a low flame. A little freshly ground pepper helps if you like it.

Place a large pot with abundant salted water over a flame. Place the *gnocchi* paste in a cloth pastry bag fitted with a round tip (4). To form the *gnocchi*, squeeze the pastry bag directly over simmering water cutting off pieces of the paste with a small knife (5). Immerse the blade of the knife every so often in the boiling water to prevent the dough from sticking to it and to permit the *gnocchetto* to drop easily into the pot.

Cook the *gnocchetti* for 3 to 4 minutes, then remove them with a skimmer and cover with the prepared sauce. This very delicate dish should be served steaming hot.

1 Bring the milk to the boil and pour in the flour all at once, beating hard.

2 Continue mixing the paste until it begins to come away from the bottom and sides of the saucepan.

3 Remove the saucepan from the flame and beat the whole eggs into the dough one at a time.

4 When the dough is nice and smooth, turn it in a cloth pastry bag fitted with a round tip.

5 Squeeze the pastry bag, letting the paste drop into the boiling water in small pieces.

Semolina gnocchi

- ■ **Yield: 4 servings**
- ■ **Time needed: 1½ hours**
- ■ **Difficulty: ***

Pasta ingredients: 3½ cups hard-wheat flour, 3 tbsp. butter, ⅓ cup grated Parmesan cheese, 3 egg yolks, pinch nutmeg, 1 quart milk, salt.
Sauce ingredients: 5 tbsp. butter, about ⅔ cup grated Parmesan cheese.

This is a typical Roman dish.

To prepare the *gnocchi* paste bring the milk, butter, and a few pinches of salt to the boiling point while gradually adding the semolina in a steady stream and stirring constantly (1). Boil, stirring with a wooden spoon or a spatula, until the paste has become as thick as oatmeal or *polenta* and starts coming away from the bottom and sides of the saucepan. Now remove the pan from the flame and add the egg yolks one at a time (2). Beat in the nutmeg, the Parmesan cheese, and, if you like, a few pinches of pepper. Mix well so that all the ingredients are thoroughly blended.

Pour the paste onto a marble slab or some other smooth surface that has been greased with butter and spread with a metal spatula to a thickness of about ⅜-inch (3). Dip the spatula into boiling water every now and then to prevent the paste from sticking to it. Allow the paste to cool completely and then, with a 1½-inch cookie cutter or drinking glass, cut the dough into circles (4), dipping the cutter or glass every now and then into boiling water. Finally place the semolina *gnocchi* in a baking dish greased with butter, overlapping them slightly (5). With the remaining dough, roll small balls for decorating the edge of the baking dish. Drizzle with melted butter and sprinkle with Parmesan cheese. Place dish in a 350-degree oven and bake until the *gnocchi* are well browned on top.

If you like, you can cover the *gnocchi* before baking, with a thin white sauce to which you may add an egg yolk and four or five tablespoons of heavy cream.

The *gnocchi* can be prepared a few days before and kept in the freezer, covered with cellophane.

1 Bring the milk, butter, and salt to the boil, while adding the semolina in a slow, steady stream.

2 When the paste has become as thick as oatmeal or *polenta*, add the egg yolks one at a time.

3 Spread the paste ⅜-inch thick on a marble slab, using a spatula.

4 Cut the paste into circles using a round cutter with a diameter of about 1½ inches.

5 Lay the *gnocchi* in an oven-safe dish greased with butter, overlapping them slightly.

Pumpkin gnocchi

■ Yield: 4 servings
■ Time needed: 2 hours
■ Difficulty: *

Paste ingredients: 2 cups mashed pumpkin (a 1-lb. can), 1½ cups all-purpose white flour, 1 large egg, a few pinches of nutmeg, salt.

Sauce ingredients: Tomato sauce flavored with basil, a few tbsp. grated Parmesan cheese, salt.

Place the pumpkin and flour in a bowl (1), then mix in the egg, a pinch of salt and the nutmeg (2). Add a bit of flour if the paste is too thin, an extra egg if it seems too thick or dry.

Form the *gnocchi* by dropping them with a tablespoon into abundant boiling salted water (3). Drain the *gnocchetti* as soon as they float (4). Dress with tomato sauce and Parmesan cheese and serve steaming hot.

For a more substantial dish, replace the tomato sauce with a tasty sausage ragout. Sauté some excellent spicy pork sausage, cut into small pieces, with chopped onion and then add a mashed garlic clove and some fresh tomatoes, peeled and seeded. Cook long enough to blend the flavors.

1 Sift flour over the mashed pumpkin in a bowl.

2 Add an egg, a pinch of salt, and nutmeg, beating everything together well.

3 Cook the pumpkin *gnocchi* in abundant boiling salted water, dropping the paste by spoonfuls.

4 When the *gnocchi* start to float, drain with a slotted skimmer and arrange in a serving dish.

Pumpkin gnocchi with mushroom cream sauce

■ **Yield: 4 servings**
■ **Time needed: 2 hours**
■ **Difficulty: ***

Ingredients: 1 recipe pumpkin *gnocchi* (page 66), 1½-2 oz. dried boletus mushrooms, 4 tbsp. butter, 1 garlic clove, 1 cup dry white wine, 1 cup heavy cream, 1 beef bouillon cube, salt, and pepper.

First prepare the mushroom cream sauce for the *gnocchi*. Soften the mushrooms in tepid water for about an hour, then wash them well, drain, and chop roughly with a "rocker" chopping knife.

Place the butter over a flame, add the finely chopped garlic clove, and sauté slightly. Add the mushrooms, salt, and pepper and cook very slowly for 10 minutes. Add the bouillon cube, dissolved n 3 tablespoons tepid water. When the mushrooms have wilted and the sauce is rather thick, pour in the white wine, then boil off the wine over a high flame.

When the mushrooms are tender, add the heavy cream and reduce the sauce over moderate heat until it has thickened lightly. Remove sauce from the flame, purée in a blender or food processor, and keep hot until serving. Prepare the *gnocchi* following the recipe on page 66, and, after draining them, place them in a large, fairly deep dish which you have warmed slightly. Pour the boiling mushroom cream sauce on top and stir gently. If you like, you can accompany this dish with grated Parmesan cheese.

STUFFED PASTA

The Ravioli Family

When the Italian housewife of a hundred years ago bought meat, she almost always bought a large piece. More often than not she had a large family to feed, and butchers of the time rarely cut and dressed the meat of the animals they slaughtered. Therefore, she saw to it that the piece of meat she had bought yielded the cuts she needed, and from this delicate task she inevitably obtained some scraps that she put aside and ground up. The same situation arose when she cooked a chicken, a goose, or a rabbit. The giblets, heart, and liver were added to sauces; or they were stewed, grilled, or ground and combined with other ingredients to make meatballs, meat loaves, or, more likely, fillings to put inside homemade pasta. Raw and cooked meat was soon mixed with other ingredients, such as cheeses, salami, vegetables, fish, and eggs. These combinations, which were originally based on what one had on hand, gave rise to the stuffed pastas that are the pride of Italian cooking today. Egg pasta is a delicious dish in itself, even if simply dressed; but it becomes sublime when it encloses a fine filling.

Although the fillings that have won Italy's first courses world-wide fame vary from region to region, many kinds of stuffed pasta have well-known origins. *Agnolini, tortellini,* and *cappelletti,* for instance, were certainly invented in Emilia-Romagna; and Piedmont is the undisputed home of *agnolotti.* Stuffed pasta has existed in one form or another since the fourteenth century, or so it seems. But if one goes looking for early recipes, one finds that history and legend are hopelessly intertwined.

Even today every city, every village, and almost every family has its own original and delicious recipes. In the following pages you will learn all about preparing pasta the traditional way, with a pasta rolling pin, or with a pasta-making machine. We will also talk about fillings, which, as we have seen, can be made up of different ingredients—including meat, salami, and sausage for a rich filling; or fish, spinach, ricotta, and other cheeses for a light one. Later on, in the recipe section, we will suggest how to dress each dish to the best advantage, in order to create a perfect harmony of flavors. In addition to describing the basic technique for preparing these dishes, we will show you the more famous stuffed-pasta recipes. We will also suggest a number of variations. In the end, though, it will be up to you to put your ability and imagination to work to turn the recipe of your choice into a truly personal creation. Before going further, a word of advice: because these preparations take time, it will be worthwhile to get a "head start" on the work by beginning to prepare the filling the day before. That way you will be able to divide the work into two parts, making everything much easier.

How to make stuffed pasta

The dough — To make egg dough you need one egg for every 8 to 10 tablespoons of flour, and ideally no other liquid. If the dough is to be stuffed, however, it will have to be fairly soft, in order to be rolled thinly. You will want to use fewer eggs, and you may add water and in some cases a little olive oil or white wine.

The recipes that follow will tell you just how much of each ingredient to use. Here we will show you how to obtain a perfect dough. First of all it is very important to allow yourself enough time, and to work in a cool room where the dough can dry well but not too quickly. Place flour (nearly 1 cup per serving for pasta to be served with a sauce; about ½ cup for pasta to be served in broth) in a mound on a flat working surface, and make a hollow in the middle. Add eggs and salt, in the hollow. Mix the ingredients with your fingertips, beginning in the center and slowly blending all the flour into the eggs. Bearing down with the heels of your hands, knead the dough until it is smooth and elastic. Let it rest for a while in a cool room (not in the refrigerator), wrapped in cellophane and protected from drafts that might dry it out, then roll it into a sheet with a pasta rolling pin or with a hand-operated or elastic pasta-making machine.

Stuffing the dough — Stuffed pasta must be prepared before the dough has a chance to dry. Therefore it is a good idea to use dough right away, as soon as it has been rolled out. At this point you can begin to place the filling on the sheet of dough, remembering to cover the area you are not using with a clean cloth in order to keep it from drying in the air. Fold and cut the dough as your recipe suggests. If the dough seems a bit dry when you close it over the filling, wet the edges with a little beaten egg or egg white. To keep the dough from opening up while cooking, firmly join the two layers by pressing lightly with your fingers all along the edges: this way the filling won't seep out.

Stuffed pastas

Pasta fillings

Today fillings may be infinite in number and variety if one skillfully combines the ingredients and if the final product pleases a delicate palate. In these pages, however, we will talk about tested fillings and classical preparations—the ones that are best known and most widespread in Italy.

Meat fillings — The classic meat filling is the one used in *tortellini,* made from pork loin or from breast of turkey, browned first, then chopped ground together with bologna, *prosciutto*, eggs, and spices. *Tortellini* filling is one of the quickest and easiest to prepare, but it is also one of the most costly because of the high quality of the ingredients used. A more economical variation of this filling can be made with braised beef flavored with pork fat or bacon and a mixture of herbs that will be ground together with the meat and other flavoring. A generous helping of grated Parmesan cheese and spices will complete the work. Another meat filling is the one used to make *cappelletti;* this, however, varies considerably from town to town. The most frequently used meats are pork, veal, and beef braised with the classic spices and then finely ground. To the meat filling may be added green, leafy vegetables and fresh *ricotta* cheese. Some kinds of filling can be made with beef stewed with fine herbs, cloves, and a pinch of cinnamon. At the end of cooking some shredded bread (without the crust) may be added to the sauce to increase its volume in an extremely flavorful manner. A classic example of this technique are the *"casonsei"* typical of Brescian cookery, made with a mixture of bread soaked in milk and then squeezed dry, sausage, and grated cheese. Other meat fillings are enriched by the addition of vegetables and lots of spices. The famous Piedmont *agnolotti* (or *"agnellotti"),* made with roast pork and veal or braised beef, all ground, call for the addition of green, leafy vegetables; the original recipe calls for cabbage and a tuft of endive. Last but not least are those meat fillings that call for the addition of variety meats such as brain, and sweetbreads which, after trimming and precooking are then browned, chopped, and added to the other ingredients. All meat-based fillings should be mixed with eggs to bind the ingredients together and flavored with grated Parmesan cheese, salt, and spices (nutmeg, pepper, and cloves).

Vegetable fillings — These originally appeared as the poor man's alternative to the rich man's meat fillings. The most classic are those which use green, leafy vegetables such as garden herbs or spinach, which are readily available, and ricotta cheese. These are commonly called *ripieni di magro,* or "meatless fillings," because they were eaten especially in the days on which it was necessary to abstain from meat. One must admit that they offer very little in the way of penance, as they richly satisfy both the palate and the stomach. Nor are they very economical these days, as vegetables and ricotta now cost as much as meat.

Another famous and typical vegetable filling is based on pumpkin. It comes from the area around Mantua, where pumpkin is abundant. The pumpkin is baked or steamed, then chopped together with spicy pickled fruit and mixed with macaroons, honey, or jam (sometimes a drop of cognac or rum is also added), and a copious amount of Parmesan cheese. This recipe is very old, and it probably did not use pumpkin, originally. More likely, it resembled the unusual filling today still in use in and around Cremona, which consists of macaroons, raisins, candied citron, crumbled *"mostaccini"* cookies, mint candies, and lemon peel, mixed together with toasted bread crumbs and Parmesan cheese.

Fish fillings — In towns and country areas along the seashore it was natural to invent fillings using fish. Most of these recipes utilize leftovers of large baked or boiled fish. They make very delicate fillings for ravioli, which, when cooked in a good fish or vegetable broth, are not only delicious but light and easy to digest, too. A richer variation calls for the addition of garden or wild herbs and even very tender nettles. A typical example of such ravioli are the *ravioli di magro* that are made in Liguria.

If one looks closely at the various types of filling, one notices that here, as elsewhere, environment and standard of living are of fundamental importance. The preparations of northern Italy—where pork, beef, and all kinds of fowl are plentiful—are richer in every sense. In central Italy, in contrast, meat has been almost completely eliminated and replaced by vegetables and cheese; in the South stuffed pasta is almost unknown.

How to make shaped pasta

1 Cut dough with a cutting wheel into 1½ inch squares.

No writer has yet succeeded in classifying all the various types of stuffed pasta, because this eminently Italian dish gives the imagination free rein in the choice of fillings and in the invention of shapes, so that every region of the country has several "original" recipes with hundreds of variations and hundreds of different names. We will briefly touch on the more well-known stuffed pastas: *agnolini, tortellini, cappelletti, agnolotti,* and *ravioli*—all little envelopes of dough stuffed with different kinds of fillings.

These pastas are served in a sauce or in broth depending on the type, and different shapes have different names. Except for *raviolini,* which are square, they are all round in shape with a hole in the center made by turning the stuffed pasta (sealed in a half-moon shape or a triangle, depending on whether it has been cut into circles or squares) around one's index finger to seal the two ends together.

Agnolini — A specialty of Mantuan cookery, *agnolini* have spread from Mantua throughout lower Lombardy and Emilia, where, depending on the area, their filling, and even their name, may vary.

They are usually served either *in bianco*—that is, with butter and cheese, or with butter, cheese, and cream—or boiled in broth, which in this case must be excellent. An example of the latter are the typically Emilian *agnolini* cooked in capon and beef broth.

To make *agnolini,* use a pasta cutting wheel to cut dough into 1½-inch squares (1); form the filling into little balls, and place one ball at the center of each square. Fold the dough over the filling to form a triangle (2). Firmly seal the package of dough, so that the filling doesn't seep out during cooking. Wrap the triangle around your index finger, pressing together the two opposite corners, while at the same time pushing the third corner toward the outside (3).

2 Place a bit of filling in the middle of each square and fold dough over to make a triangle...

3 ...press and roll the dough around your index finger, pinching the corners together.

Tortellini — A specialty of Emilia, and particularly of Bologna, *tortellini* are traditionally served in broth, but they are also very good with a meat or tomato sauce.

To make *tortellini*, form the filling into little balls and place them about 1 to 1½ inches apart and about 1½ inches from the edge of the dough (1). Lift the edge of the dough and fold it over the little mounds of filling (2). With a cutting wheel, cut the pasta close (but not too close) to the filling to obtain a strip of stuffed pasta (3). Press down with your fingertips around the filling to seal it perfectly. Run the cutting wheel between the mounds of filling to cut the strip of pasta into small rectangles (4). Finally, draw one of the corners at the base of the rectangle over the other, shaping the pasta at the same time into a little hat (5).

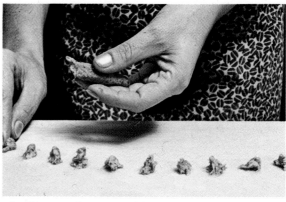

1 Place small mounds of filling on the dough, about 1 to 1½ inches apart.

2 Lift edge of dough and fold it over the mounds of filling...

3 ...then with a cutting wheel cut stuffed dough to make a long strip.

4 Press down on dough around filling to seal, then cut dough into rectangles.

5 Fold together the two corners at the base of the rectangle turning out the opposite side.

Ravioli — Ravioli, the most famous of stuffed pastas, receive their name from the old Italian term *raviolo,* which was used generally to describe any pasta wrapped around a filling. *Ravioli* are almost always square or rectangular in shape. To make them, place small mounds of filling (but not too small because the best *ravioli* are those with the most filling) in a single row about 1½ inches apart and 1½ inches from the edge of the dough. Lift the dough and fold it over the mounds of filling (1). Then, with a pasta cutting wheel, cut the dough close (but not too close) to the filling to make a strip of stuffed pasta (2). Press down around the filling with your fingertips to seal it tightly (3). Then use the pasta cutting wheel to cut the strip into fairly big rectangles (4).

Ravioli may be stuffed in any number of ways, then served with a sauce that complements their filling. Typical are *ravioli alla genovese,* which are made with paper-thin dough (using very few eggs and a lot of water) so that they cook in five minutes. They are round, and they are stuffed with meat and vegetables, or with fish. Fish *ravioli* may also be served in strained fish stock. Another kind of *ravioli* typical of Liguria are *pansotti* or "pot bellies." They are meatless *ravioli* in the shape of even-sided triangle filled with cheese, eggs, and wild and garden herbs; they are served in a walnut sauce.

Another well-known variety of *ravioli* are the half-moon *casonsei* of Brescia, whose name derives perhaps from the cheese they are dressed with. They are fairly large, round or square packages of dough which are sometimes formed to resemble large *tortellini.*

1 Lift outer edge of dough and fold it over evenly distributed mounds of filling.

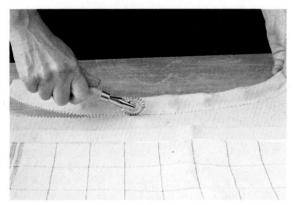

2 Cut along edge of folded dough, not too close to the filling, with a pasta cutting wheel.

3 Seal dough around filling with your fingertips...

4 ...then cut the strip into rectangles, and your ravioli are ready.

Cappelletti — When finished these look like little hats *(cappelletti* in Italian), but the procedure for making them is practically the same as that for making *tortelli*. They should be served in beef or chicken broth. In their homeland, Romagna, it is customary to serve them in capon broth for Christmas dinner.

Agnolotti — A specialty of Piedmont, *agnolotti* are generally square and stuffed with meat. They are usually served in a sauce based on the roasts or braised meats used in making the filling. They have many variants because families almost always made them on Mondays, using Sunday leftovers.

Agnolini, tortellini, ravioli . . .

Some useful suggestions

At this point you are ready to make some of the stuffed pastas we've been talking about. For best results, bear in mind the following basic rules:

—Make your dough as thin as possible, and don't let it dry out.

—To dry your finished *ravioli,* etc., spread them out over a flour-dusted work surface, and cover with a clean cloth, keeping them in a cool room but not in the refrigerator. Turn them at least once, but avoid unnecessary handling.

—To store them for brief periods, spread them on a tray covered with a cloth dusted with flour. Place the tray in a plastic food bag, and seal the bag, letting the excess air out first, then set in the refrigerator.

—To store for longer periods, spread *ravioli,* etc., on a flour-dusted tray and place them for about an hour in the coldest part of the freezer. When they are hard, drop them into a plastic food bag and seal it. This way they may be stored for two or three months.

—Cook fresh *ravioli,* etc., in lots of boiling water if you want to serve them in a sauce, or in boiling broth if you want to serve them in broth. Put in a few at a time when the water comes to a boil, and let them cook in an uncovered pot, stirring with a wooden spoon. It is preferable not to cook *ravioli* that will be served with a sauce in broth, because the fat content of the broth will keep the pasta from blending perfectly with its dressing. Bear in mind that a few particular dishes are prepared in just this way, and that the recipe in these cases will say so explicitly. In preparing these dishes the fat will have to be carefully skimmed from the broth.

—Some stuffed pastas, especially *tortellini* and *cappelletti,* are traditionally served in broth. Consequently, it is important that the broth does the pasta honor. Your butcher will know the cuts of beef (soup cuts) that are best for this purpose. Meat should be placed in a large pot and covered with cold water (one quart per pound), then slowly brought to a boil. When the water boils, add vegetables—celery, carrots, onions, parsley, and, if you like, a clove of garlic (potatoes are optional but are good to add if the broth seems too salty or too fatty). If you want a highly aromatic broth, add a bay leaf or a teaspoon of thyme, or stick an onion with one or two whole cloves. The heat should be turned down and the broth skimmed several times before being salted and perhaps flavored with a piece of bouillon cube. The pot should always be covered, with the lid slightly ajar so the broth doesn't boil over. When the broth is ready it is best to filter it through a fine strainer or, better yet, through a piece of cheesecloth or gauze placed in the bottom of a strainer, to eliminate the vegetables and all other residues. The broth should then be placed in the refrigerator and the layer of fat that forms on the surface should be scraped off. To tone down the flavor of beef broth, which is sometimes a bit too strong, you can substitute chicken bones and even half a hen for some of the beef, remembering, though, to add them later because they cook more quickly. The beef broth must boil, or better, simmer, for at least three hours. To save time, a pressure cooker may be used.

—Cook frozen *ravioli* in boiling water or broth, either thawed first at room temperature or straight from the freezer.

—Test the pasta for doneness by biting into it, especially where two layers of dough have been joined together, before draining it. The cooking time of fresh pasta varies 12 to 20 minutes, according to the thickness of the dough and the volume of filling it contains. If you cook it straight from the freezer, you'll have to allow a little additional time.

—Remove *ravioli,* etc., from their cooking liquid a few at a time with a slotted skimmer or a loosely woven straw palette and let them stand for a few seconds in a colander.

—If you serve the *ravioli,* etc. with a sauce, dress them in a preheated serving bowl, making layers of *ravioli,* sauce, and cheese. Remember that sauces must complement fillings and not overwhelm them.

—If you serve the *ravioli,* etc. in broth, place them in the bottom of separate serving bowls and then pour the broth over the top. For a special dinner the broth must be clear; therefore it is better not to use the broth the pasta was cooked in. The cooking broth, however, is usually fine on informal occasions. Cheese is served separately.

—To warm *ravioli,* etc., place them in the oven with a little butter, cream, or plain white sauce. You can also warm them in a pan or, to make a lighter dish, steam them or warm them in a double boiler.

—Leftover *ravioli* with sauce may be frozen in a covered, sealed, and labeled aluminum dish, and reheated in a moderate oven.

Necessary equipment

First of all, to roll the dough you need a flat surface, preferably of wood, sprinkled with flour and a 32-inch pasta rolling pin with fixed handles. If you want to save a little labor, you can use a pasta-making machine. Both the hand-operated and the electric kind will roll dough evenly and as thin as you like. Once the dough has been prepared, you have to place the filling on it and cut the dough into the desired form. You will usually use one of the specially made round or square molds for this task. Naturally, you can also use the traditional serrated pasta cutting wheel, or even a simple knife if all you want to do is cut the dough without giving it a serrated edge.

Special metal trays with *raviolo*-shaped depressions can be found in some stores. They are a great help for making *ravioli*. You roll a sheet of dough

over the tray (1), press down lightly with your fingers to make it stick to the sides of the mold (2), fill the molds with the filling of your choice, prepared beforehand (3), cover with another sheet of dough (4), and seal the *ravioli* with the small rolling pin that comes in the package, pressing firmly to bind the two sheets of dough together forming a *raviolo* in every mold (5).

Also for *ravioli,* there is a special attachment that can be fitted to hand-operated pasta-making machines. This accessory comes with a container to put the filling into and a molded roller so that the dough is automatically filled and formed into a *ravioli* as it passes through the machine.

1 Lay a rectangular sheet of homemade dough over the special tray for making *ravioli.*

2 Dip your fingers in flour and press down on dough until it sticks to the tray.

3 Place mounds of filling in the molds of the tray.

4 Cover filling with a rectangle of dough the same size as the first one.

5 Seal with the little rolling pin that comes in the package, pressing the two sheets together firmly.

Cappelletti pie

■ **Yield: 6 servings**
■ **Time needed: 3 hours**
■ **Difficulty: ****

Pasta ingredients: 1 lb. *cappelletti* **(also see Agnolotti piedmont style p. 92), 3 cups all-purpose white flour, 10 tbsp. butter, ¼ cup sugar, 3 egg yolks, a little dry white wine, 1 egg for glazing pastry, butter and bread crumbs sufficient for lining pie, salt.**
Sauce ingredients: 5 oz. pork loin, ½ lb. beef, ¼ lb. bacon, 7 tbsp. butter, 2½ oz. (about ⅔ cup) grated Parmesan cheese, a few chicken livers, 1 cup heavy cream, 1 carrot, 1 onion, 1 stalk celery, 10 oz. drained canned tomatoes, 1 clove, 1 bay leaf, 2 tbsp. flour, 2 cups milk, nutmeg, pepper, salt.

To make a meat sauce, sauté chopped vegetables and bacon in 3½ tablespoons of butter, add the meat, finely chopped, and brown together, stirring constantly, for a few minutes. Add the drained canned tomatoes, spices, and a pinch of salt and pepper. Continue cooking over moderate heat, adding a little cream from time to time. Five minutes before removing from heat, add cleaned, diced chicken livers.

While the sauce cooks, prepare the pastry. Sift together flour, sugar, and a pinch of salt. Add 10 tablespoons butter (cut up in small pieces) and egg yolks (1) and blend rapidly with flour (2), adding one or two tablespoons of wine, if necessary. When the dough is smooth and even, wrap it in plastic and refrigerate for about one hour.

With the remaining 3½ tablespoons butter, flour, and milk, prepare a fairly thin white sauce and flavor with salt, pepper, and nutmeg. Boil the *cappelletti* in lots of salted water, drain while still very *al dente,* and flavor with part of the sauce (or the juice of a roast or pot roast). Divide the pastry dough into two parts, one almost twice as large as the other. Roll out the larger piece in a circle about ⅛-inch thick and line the bottom and sides of a 10-inch spring-form pan that has been buttered and sprinkled with bread crumbs (3). Cut away excess dough and pierce the bottom with a fork (4). Pour a layer of *cappelletti* into the pie shell (5), and cover with a bit of meat sauce (6), white sauce (7), and Parmesan cheese. Proceed until the last layer made of Parmesan cheese. Cover the filled shell with the second piece of dough, which should be rolled out to the size of the pie pan (8). Cut away excess dough (9) and join the two layers along the edges by pressing lightly with a fork (10). Leftover dough may be cut out, moistened, and used to decorate the pastry. With a piece of aluminum foil, make a "chimney" and place it in the center of the pie crust (11) so that steam may escape during baking. Brush the surface with a beaten egg (12), then bake at 350° F for about an hour. Before serving, let the pie rest outside the oven for a few minutes, then open the hinge on the pan (13) and carefully lift out the pastry crust with a spatula (14).

1 Sift together flour, sugar, and salt, add softened butter in pieces, and finally egg yolks.

2 Blend by hand, gradually kneading together flour and other ingredients.

3 Using a rolling pin, place pastry over pie pan and press into place.

4 Trim off excess dough and pierce bottom of pastry shell with a fork.

5 Pour a thin layer of *cappelletti* into shell and spread evenly.

6 Pour in meat sauce slowly and evenly.

7 Pour in white sauce and spread evenly over *cappelletti*.

8 Cover with a sheet of pastry the same diameter as the pie pan.

9 Use a cutting wheel to trim off excess dough around edges.

10 Join the two halves of the pastry shell at the edges by pressing lightly with a fork.

11 Decorate the pie with leftover dough and insert a "chimney."

12 Brush dough with beaten egg to glaze.

13 After letting the pastry crust rest in its pan, unhinge pan and remove wall.

14 Lift the crust off bottom of pan with the aid of one or two broad metal spatulas.

Cappelletti pie

Agnolini in cream sauce

■ **Yield: 4 servings**
■ **Time needed: 2 hours 15 minutes**
■ **Difficulty: ****

Pasta and filling ingredients: Pasta dough made with 3½ cups flour and 6 eggs, ½ lb. turkey or chicken, 2½ oz. *prosciutto*, 2 tbsp. butter, 5 oz. *ricotta* cheese, 3 oz. (about ¾ cup) grated Parmesan cheese, 4 thin slices bologna, 2 chicken livers, 2 tbsp. bread crumbs, 1 egg, ¼ tsp. sage, 2 tbsp. Marsala wine, 1 tbsp. olive oil, nutmeg, pepper, salt.
Sauce ingredients: 3 tbsp. butter, 1 cup heavy cream, 2 oz. (about ½ cup) grated Parmesan cheese, ¼ tsp. sage, pepper, salt.

First prepare the filling. Brown sliced poultry, *prosciutto* and bologna in butter and oil, season with salt and pepper, add sage and chicken livers, and sprinkle with Marsala. When wine has evaporated, chop meats. Add *ricotta,* Parmesan cheese, bread crumbs, egg, and a little nutmeg. Mix well and add a little salt, if necessary. With dough and filling prepare *agnolini* as described on p. 75. Boil *agnolini* in lots of salted water. Meanwhile, prepare the sauce. Melt butter with sage, add cream, season with salt and pepper, and heat thoroughly. Drain and dress *agnolini* in layers with cream sauce and Parmesan cheese.

Agnolini in a puff pastry shell

■ **Yield: 6 servings**
■ **Time needed: 2 hours**
■ **Difficulty: ****

Pasta and filling ingredients: 1 lb. homemade or frozen puff pastry dough, pasta dough made with 3½ cups flour and 6 eggs, ½ lb. chicken breast, 2 tbsp. butter, 2½ oz. *prosciutto*, 5 oz. cream cheese, 1 egg and 1 egg yolk, 2 tbsp. grated Parmesan cheese, a little brandy, pepper, salt.
Sauce ingredients: 5 tbsp. butter, 7 oz. boiled peas (fresh, frozen, or canned), 3 oz. diced boiled ham, ¼ cup heavy cream, ½ beef bouillon cube, ½ small onion, 3 tbsp. grated Parmesan cheese, pepper, salt.

First make the puff pastry. If you use frozen pastry dough, let it thaw well before beginning. Roll dough to a thickness of about ¼-inch. Using the lid of a 10-inch pan as a guide, cut out a circle of dough holding the knife at a slight angle. Wrap the pastry around the rolling pin, and place it on a lightly buttered baking sheet top-side-down. Center another lid about 6 inches in diameter over the pastry circle, and make a shallow incision with the knife all the way around, cutting about half way into the dough. Now, use the blunt side of the knife to make shallow vertical dents around the outside edge of the dough. Brush dough with egg yolk and place in the oven at 375° F for about 25 minutes. When the time is up, lift the inner circle of the pastry shell out with a fork and place it upside-down, on a plate (you will use it later to cover the filling). Then scrape out the dough inside the pastry shell which will be very soft, and put the pastry shell back in the oven for 5 more minutes longer before setting it aside to cool.

Meanwhile prepare the filling for the *agnolini.* Chop and sauté the *prosciutto* in 2 tablespoons butter. Add the chicken breast, sauté, and cook over moderate heat, sprinkling from time to time with a little brandy.

Finely chop the cooked chicken, and combine it with its cooking juices, the cream cheese, an egg, the grated Parmesan cheese, and a pinch of salt and pepper. Mix the filling well and place it in small mounds on the sheet of homemade dough. You should make *agnolini* about 1 to 1½ inches square (for instructions see p. 75).

For the sauce, melt 5 tablespoons butter in a large pan and sauté the chopped onion. Add diced *prosciutto*, peas, and the half bouillon cube, dissolved in a little hot water. Mix well and, after cooking about ten minutes, add the cream. Boil the *agnolini* in lots of salted water, drain while still a bit *al dente,* and pour into the pan with the peas. Add Parmesan cheese, a good pinch of salt, and continue to mix well for a few moments. Pour the mixture into the pastry shell (ready and waiting on its plate). Put it back in the oven for about ten minutes, and serve the pastry shell with its cover on.

Tortellini Bolognese

■ **Yield: 4 servings**
■ **Time needed: 2 hours**
■ **Difficulty: ****

Pasta and filling ingredients: Pasta dough made with 3½ cups flour and 6 eggs; 5 oz. pork loin, 5 oz. chicken or turkey breast, 3 oz. bologna, ¼ lb. *prosciutto*, 5 oz. about 1¼ cups grated Parmesan cheese, 2 tbsp. butter, 1 egg, nutmeg, pepper, salt.
Sauce ingredients: A meat sauce or tomato sauce, 3 oz. (about ¾ cup) grated Parmesan cheese.

Melt the butter in a saucepan, add the pork and poultry, cut into small pieces, and brown over moderate heat for about ten minutes. Next, chop the meat very finely (or put it through a meat grinder) together with the *prosciutto* and bologna.

Add the egg, Parmesan cheese, a little salt, pepper, and nutmeg, and mix until smooth.

With dough and filling, make *tortellini* as indicated on p. 76. Boil in lots of salted water, then drain and dress with meat sauce or tomato sauce and Parmesan cheese.

Tortellini in broth

- **Yield: 6 servings**
- **Time needed: 2½ hours**
- **Difficulty: ***

Pasta and filling ingredients: Pasta dough made with 3½ cups flour and 6 eggs; 10 oz. beef, 1 slice *prosciutto* weighing ¼ lb., 1 mild Italian link sausage, 3 oz. about ¾ cup grated Parmesan cheese, 2 tbsp. butter, 2-3 tbsp. bread crumbs, 1 egg, 1 small onion, 1 celery stalk, 1 carrot, 1 bay leaf, ½ tbsp. tomato sauce, 2 juniper berries (optional), ½ cup red wine, nutmeg, olive oil, pepper, salt.
Other ingredients: An excellent broth, preferably one made from 1 small capon, 1 carrot, 1 celery stalk, 1 small onion, 1 bunch parsley, salt.

To make the filling, sauté the onion and chopped *prosciutto* in a few tablespoons of olive oil and butter. Add chopped celery and carrot, bay leaf, juniper berries, and, after a few minutes, the meat. Season with salt and pepper, brown, sprinkle with wine, and let wine evaporate. Add the tomato sauce dissolved in a little water, and, halfway through cooking, the sausage. At end of cooking, chop the meat and sausage and put them back into the sauce, which in the meantime will have thickened (take out the bay leaf and juniper berries). Add Parmesan cheese, a pinch of nutmeg, egg, and bread crumbs, and mix well. Combine dough and filling to make *tortellini,* as described on p. 76. Bring broth to a boil, and cook *tortellini* for about half an hour.

Ravioli with meat sauce

- **Yield: 4 servings**
- **Time needed: 2 hours**
- **Difficulty: ***

Pasta and filling ingredients: Pasta dough made with 3½ cups flour and 6 eggs; 10 oz. ground veal, 2 tbsp. butter, 2 oz. *prosciutto*, 5 oz. sausage, 1 slice bologna weighing ¼ lb. 1 oz. about ¼ cup grated Parmesan cheese, 1 egg, 1 small onion, 1 beef bouillon cube, dry white wine, 2 tbsp. olive oil, nutmeg, pepper, salt.
Sauce ingredients: 7 oz. ground beef, 14 oz. drained canned tomatoes, 1 oz. bacon, ¾ oz. dried boletus mushrooms, 3 oz. (about ¾ cup) grated Parmesan cheese, 1 small onion, 1 celery stalk, 1 garlic clove, 1 bay leaf, 1 clove, red wine, olive oil, pepper, salt.

To make the sauce, chop up bacon, celery, onion, and garlic, and sauté in a few tablespoons of olive oil. Add beef, season with salt and pepper, and mix well. Add bay leaf, clove, and mushrooms (first soaked in warm water for 30 minutes, then squeezed and chopped). After a few minutes, sprinkle with half a glass of white wine, and let wine evaporate. Add the strained tomato and continue cooking over low heat.

To make the filling, chop up onion, bologna, and *prosciutto,* and sauté in butter and two tablespoons of olive oil. Add the veal and sausage and brown well. At this point pour in half a glass of white wine, let it evaporate, then add the bouillon cube, diluted in a little warm water. Season with salt and pepper, and cook until the mixture is good and thick. Remove from heat, add the Parmesan cheese and, after a few minutes, add the egg and a pinch of nutmeg. Use dough and filling to make *ravioli,* as described on p. 77. Boil in salted water, drain, and dress, in layers, with the meat sauce and Parmesan.

Ricotta ravioli

- **Yield: 4 servings**
- **Time needed: 2 hours**
- **Difficulty: ***

Pasta and filling ingredients: Pasta dough made with 3½ cups flour and 6 eggs; 14 oz. *ricotta* cheese, 3 oz. (about ¾ cup) grated Parmesan cheese, 1 egg and 1 egg yolk, pepper, salt.
Sauce ingredients: ½ cup butter, ¼ tsp. sage, a little grated Parmesan cheese.

To make the filling, force the *ricotta* cheese through a sieve or food mill·into a bowl, add the grated Parmesan cheese, a whole egg and the yolk of another egg, and a little salt and pepper. Mix the ingredients well, until smooth and creamy.

Use the dough to make *ravioli,* as described on p. 77. Boil, drain, and dress, in layers, with melted butter, sage, and Parmesan.

Tortelli twist

- **Yield: 4 servings**
- **Time needed: 2 hours**
- **Difficulty: ****

Pasta and filling ingredients: Pasta dough made with 3½ cups flour and 6 eggs; 2 lbs. spinach, 9 oz. *ricotta* cheese, 2 oz. cream cheese, 1 oz. (about ¼ cup) grated Parmesan cheese, 1 egg, pepper, salt.
Sauce ingredients: Homemade tomato sauce flavored with basil, 5 tbsp. butter, 3 tbsp. grated Parmesan cheese, salt.

Boil, drain, squeeze-dry, and finely chop the spinach. Force the *ricotta* through a sieve and mix thoroughly with the cream cheese, Parmesan cheese, egg, and pinches of salt and pepper.

Place mounds of filling 3 to 3½ inches apart on a sheet of dough. Fold the dough over the filling (1) and cut the strip of stuffed pasta with a cutting wheel (2). Press the dough firmly all around the filling (3) and cut the strip into long rectangles (4). Twist the ends of the rectangles (5 and 6). Boil the *tortelli,* drain a few at a time, dress with butter and Parmesan. Serve sauce separately.

1 Place mounds of filling on dough. Fold dough over filling.

2 Use a pasta cutting wheel to cut the strip of filled dough from the rest of the sheet.

3 Press down on dough all around filling, to seal it tightly...

4 ...use the cutting wheel to cut the stuffed dough into long rectangles...

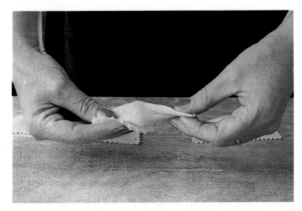

5 ...seal the dough and twist the longer ends...

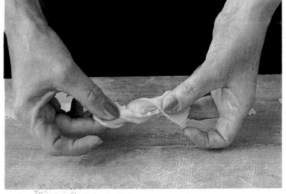

6 ... just like a candy wrapper, then spread the *tortelli* over the work surface to dry.

Chard tortelli

■ **Yield: 4 servings**
■ **Time needed: 2 hours**
■ **Difficulty: ****

Pasta and filling ingredients: Pasta dough made with 3½ cups flour and 6 eggs; 1½ lbs. Swiss chard or spinach, 10 oz. *ricotta* cheese, ¼ lb. cooked chicken, ¼ lb. boiled ham, 1 oz. (about ¼ cup) grated Parmesan cheese, 1 egg, nutmeg, pepper, salt.
Sauce ingredients: 7 tbsp. butter, 3 oz. (about ¾ cup) grated Parmesan cheese, ¼ tsp. sage.

To make the filling, chop the chicken and ham, then mix in the boiled, squeezed, and finely chopped greens, the *ricotta* (forced through a food mill or sieve) (1), the cheese, egg, and a bit of salt, pepper, and nutmeg. Place mounds of filling on the dough, about 2¼ inches apart (2). Fold the dough over the filling, and press down all around the mounds of filling to seal the two layers tightly (3). Use a pasta cutting wheel to cut half-moon or rectangular *tortelli* (4).

Boil the *tortelli*. Brown the butter with the sage. Drain the *tortelli* a few at a time (5), dress with butter and cheese (6).

1 After chopping up the greens, ham, and chicken, put the *ricotta* through a food mill or a strainer.

2 Place mounds of filling on dough, about 2¼ inches apart.

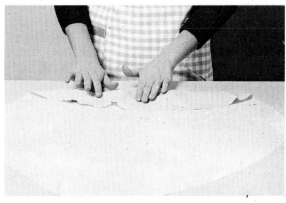

3 Fold dough over filling and press down all around each mound to seal filling in.

4 With a pasta cutting wheel, cut out half-moon or rectangular *tortelli*.

5 After boiling the *tortelli*, drain them gently, a few at a time. Place them in a bowl and...

6 ...dress them in layers with melted butter flavored with sage and lots of Parmesan cheese.

Agnolotti piedmont style

■ Yield: 4 servings
■ Time needed: 2 hours
■ Difficulty: **

Pasta and filling ingredients: Pasta dough made with 3½ cups flour, 3 eggs, and 6-8 tbsp. water, about 9 oz. braised beef, ¼ lb. roast pork, about 2 oz. sausage, ¼ lb. calf brains, 2 tbsp. butter, 10 oz. spinach (or cabbage leaves or endive), 1 egg, 3 tbsp. grated Parmesan cheese, nutmeg, pepper, salt.
Other ingredients: 7 tbsp. butter, grated Parmesan cheese, juice or gravy from roast or braised meat, degreased beef broth.

Cut up all the browned meat, then add the spinach or other vegetable (boiled, squeezed dry, chopped, cooked in butter, and seasoned with a few tablespoons of grated Parmesan cheese, salt and pepper, and lots of nutmeg), and bind together with the egg. The mixture should be thick and soft. Divide the dough into two parts and place hazelnut-sized balls of filling on one of these about 1½ inches apart. Cover the other sheet of dough and press down with two fingers between the mounds of filling. Cut out square *agnolotti* with a cutting wheel or a mold. Boil in lots of broth, drain while still a bit *al dente,* and dress with butter, the juice or gravy of a roast or braised meat, and cheese. Warm in pan before serving.

Pumpkin tortelli

■ Yield: 4 servings
■ Time needed: 2½ hours
■ Difficulty: **

Pasta and filling ingredients: Pasta dough made with 3½ cups flour and 6 eggs; 4½ lbs. pumpkin or butternut squash, 5 oz. Cremonese mustard fruits or any spicy pickled fruit, ¼ lb. macaroons, 5 oz. (about 1¼ cups) grated Parmesan cheese, 1 lemon, 1 tablespoon sour cherry jam, nutmeg, pepper, salt.
Sauce ingredients: 7 tbsp. butter, 3 oz. (about ¾ cup) grated Parmesan cheese, ¼ tsp. sage.

Cut up the pumpkin or squash and cook it in a hot oven in its shell. When tender, put it through a food mill or strainer and mix in the crumbled macaroons, jam, fruit pickle, Parmesan cheese, generous pinches of nutmeg, salt, and pepper, and grated lemon peel. The mixture should be fairly dry; if not, add a few more macaroons and a little Parmesan. Let the filling rest in the refrigerator for 24 hours.

Roll out half the dough and dot with mounds of filling 4-5 1½ to 2 inches apart. Cover with the remaining dough and cut out rectangular *tortelli.* Boil, drain, and dress, in layers, with melted butter flavored with sage, and Parmesan cheese.

Potato ravioli

■ Yield: 4 servings
■ Time needed: 2 hours
■ Difficulty: **

Pasta and filling ingredients: Pasta dough made with 3½ cups flour and 6 eggs; 1 lb. potoatoes, 10 oz. spinach or Swiss chard, 2 tbsp. butter, ¼ lb. fresh *crescenza* or cream cheese, 2 egg yolks, 1 oz. (about ¼ cup) grated Parmesan cheese, nutmeg, pepper, salt.
Sauce ingredients: 7 tbsp. butter, 3 oz. (about ¾ cup) grated Parmesan cheese, ¼ tsp. sage.

Boil, peel, and mash potatoes. Boil and squeeze dry the spinach, and mix with the potatoes, butter, *crescenza* or cream cheese, 2 egg yolks, Parmesan cheese, nutmeg, and pinches of salt and pepper. Use a round mold to cut the dough into circles. Place a mound of filling in the center of each, then fold the circles in half and firmly press the edges together. Boil, drain, and dress ravioli, in layers, with melted butter flavored with sage, and Parmesan cheese.

Fish ravioli

■ Yield: 4 servings
■ Time needed: 2 hours
■ Difficulty: **

Pasta and filling ingredients: Pasta dough made with 3½ cups flour, 3 eggs, and as much water as necessary; 10 oz. baked or poached fish, 1 lb. spinach or Swiss chard, ¼ lb. *ricotta* cheese, 3 oz. (about ¾ cup) grated Parmesan cheese, 1-2 eggs, pepper, salt.
Sauce ingredients: 1 cup chopped parsley, ½ tsp chopped garlic, 1 tsp. basil, 1 chopped onion, ½ tsp. thyme, ½ tsp. marjoram, a little olive oil, 2 tbsp. butter.

To make the filling wash and boil spinach or other greens; squeeze dry, chop, and mix with chopped fish (without bones or skin), *ricotta* cheese, Parmesan cheese, eggs, salt and pepper. Prepare *ravioli* as shown on p. 77 and boil. Sauté finely chopped herbs, garlic, and onion in olive oil and butter until tender. Drain and dress in layers, with sauce.

Casonsei brescia style

■ Yield: 4 servings
■ Time needed: 1½ hours
■ Difficulty: **

Pasta and filling ingredients: 3½ cups flour and 6 eggs; 10 oz. sausage, about 1 cup grated Parmesan cheese, the soft part of 1 roll (or 2 slices bread, without crusts), milk, salt.
Sauce ingredients: 7 tbsp. butter, 4 oz. (about 1 cup) grated Parmesan cheese, ¼ tsp. sage, salt.

For the filling soak the soft part of a roll in milk, squeeze dry, and place in a bowl. Add chopped sausage, cheese, salt, and pepper, if desired, and mix.

Knead dough with eggs and salt (1) and roll it out. Cut rolled dough into 3- x 4½-inch rectangles (2). Place filling on dough (3), fold over the long way (4), press dough together around filling (5), and fold down the corners (6).

Boil *casonsei,* drain, dress with butter flavored with sage and Parmesan.

1 Knead together flour, eggs, and a pinch of salt to make dough.

2 Roll dough paper thin and cut into 3-x 4½-inch rectangles.

3 Place filling, prepared beforehand, in the middle of the rectangles of dough.

4 Fold rectangles over filling the long way.

5 Press down all around filling to seal dough tightly.

6 Turn down corners to give *casonsei* their characteristic shape.

Casonsei from Val Camonica

■ Yield: 4 servings
■ Time needed: 2 hour
■ Difficulty: ***

Pasta and filling ingredients: Pasta dough made with 3½ cups flour and 6 eggs; 14 oz. potatoes, 1¼ lbs. (2 10-oz. bags), Swiss chard or spinach, 4 oz. sausage, 4 oz. bologna, 4 oz. (about 1 cup) grated Parmesan cheese, 1 tbsp. chopped parsley, 1 leek, 2 oz. bacon, 2 tbsp. bread crumbs, 1 egg, olive oil, pepper, salt.
Sauce ingredients: 7 tbsp. butter, 4 oz. (about 1 cup) grated Parmesan cheese, ¼ tsp. sage, salt.

First prepare filling for *casonsei*. Wash potatoes, boil in their skins in salted water, peel, mash, and place in a bowl.

Boil spinach, squeeze out moisture, chop, and sauté in just a little oil with leek, bacon, and parsley. Add to the mashed potatoes. Add to this mixture crumbled sausage, bologna chopped into large pieces (1), Parmesan cheese, bread crumbs, pepper, and salt, and bind the ingredients together with the whole egg (2).

Combine flour, eggs, and salt to make basic pasta dough. Using the palms of your hands roll dough into rods about one inch in diameter, then cut the rods into smaller pieces (3). Use a special implement (which resembles a spindle) or a small rolling pin to roll each piece of dough into a circle about 3 inches in diameter (4). Place a bit of filling in the middle of each circle of dough (5), and fold dough over filling (6). Pull on the joined edges of the circle, covering the filling completely, stretching the dough to form a "tail" and making little overlapping folds (7-8). Break off any excess dough when you have finished (9).

Boil the *casonsei* in salted water, bearing in mind that they do not cook as rapidly as ordinary potato *gnocchi;* therefore, do not drain them as soon as they bob to the surface. After about ten minutes drain them with a slotted skimmer. Dress, in layers, with melted butter flavored with sage leaves, and with cheese.

1 Mix mashed potatoes, spinach, sausage, and chopped bologna in a bowl.

2 Add remaining ingredients and bind them together with a whole egg.

3 Form dough into one-inch rolls and cut into small pieces.

4 Roll into circles 3 inches in diameter, using a small rolling pin.

5 Place a bit of filling in the middle of each circle of dough.

6 Fold dough over filling, pulling lightly.

7 Pull the edges of the circle over the filling, stretching the dough at the same time...

8 ...cover the filling completely, forming overlapping folds as you do.

9 If you have dough left over when you have finished, eliminate the excess.

Pansoti

- **Yield: 4 servings**
- **Time needed: 2 hours**
- **Difficulty: ****

Pasta and filling ingredients: Pasta dough made with 3½ cups flour, white wine, a few tablespoons water, and salt, 2¼ lbs. (4 10-oz. bags) spinach or Swiss chard, ½ lb. borage or other greens, 5 oz. *ricotta* cheese, 3 oz. (about ⅜ cup) grated Parmesan cheese, 1 clove garlic, 2 eggs, pepper, salt.
Sauce ingredients: 5 oz. walnut meats, 8 oz. (¾-1 cup) sour cream, 2 oz. pine nuts (optional), bread, 1 clove garlic, a few tablespoons olive oil, salt.

First make the filling. Wash all vegetables, boil in just a little water, squeeze, chop fine, and turn into a bowl. Add finely chopped garlic, eggs, Parmesan cheese, *ricotta* (1), salt, and pepper. Mix until evenly blended (2).

Now make the dough. Form flour in a mound on your work surface and make a depression in the middle. Add salt and work in a little white wine (3), then as much water as it takes to bring the dough to the right consistency. Roll out and cut into triangles 2½ to 3 inches to a side (4). Keep them covered with a cloth once they have been cut out. Place a little filling on each triangle (5), and fold over, sealing the edges tightly (6).

Before cooking the *pansoti* prepare the sauce. Cover the walnuts with boiling water, and let stand 2 minutes. Drain and put the nuts in a mortar or in a blender or food processor with 2 slices of crustless bread (soaked in water and squeezed dry), pine nuts, a few pinches of salt, and garlic. Grind or blend to a paste. If necessary, force through a sieve or strain (7), dilute with just enough sour cream to make a semi-thick sauce (8), and stir in olive oil (9).

Boil *pansoti* and dress with nut sauce.

1 Prepare filling by mixing cooked vegetables, garlic, eggs, Parmesan cheese, and *ricotta*.

2 Stir with a wooden spoon until smooth and fairly thick.

3 Prepare dough by working first a little white wine, then water, into the flour.

4 Roll dough into a thin sheet and cut into triangles about 2½ inches to a side.

5 Put a bit of filling, prepared beforehand, onto each triangle.

6 Fold dough over filling and seal edges tightly.

7 Grind walnuts, bread, pine nuts, and garlic, then force through a strainer into a bowl.

8 Dilute the nut mixture with sour cream until smooth and creamy.

9 Add olive oil a little at a time, stirring constantly.

Pansoti

Ofelle Trieste style

- Yield: 4 servings
- Time needed: 2½ hours
- Difficulty: **

Pasta and filling ingredients: 2¼ lbs. potatoes, about 2 cups all-purpose white flour, 1 egg, 1 tsp. baking powder, salt, 1¾ lbs. spinach or Swiss chard, 5 oz. ground veal, ¼ lb. pork sausage, 1 onion, chopped parsley and garlic (to taste), 2 tbsp. butter, salt.
Sauce ingredients: 7 tbsp. butter, 4 oz. (about 1 cup) grated Parmesan cheese, salt.

First prepare the filling. Wash spinach (or other greens), boil, drain, squeeze dry, chop and place in a bowl. Add crumbled sausage, veal, and a little salt. Finely chop onion and cook in butter until transparent. Add contents of bowl and cook for a few minutes over low heat, stirring occasionally. Remove from heat and cool. Add as much chopped garlic and parsley as you like.

Now prepare the dough. Boil potatoes in salted water, drain, peel, and mash. Turn onto working surface and add egg, flour, salt, and baking powder (1). Knead dough until it is like that used for making potato *gnocchi,* but a little firmer.

Working quickly and sprinkling your work surface with flour from time to time, roll dough paper thin, using a rolling pin sprinkled with flour (2). Sometimes the damp dough will stick to the work surface; to detach it, lift from time to time with long metal spatula sprinkled with flour. Cut dough into 2½- to 3-inch squares. Place filling on half the squares (3), and cover with the remaining squares (4). Lastly, press firmly around the filling (5) to seal the edges tightly.

As your prepare *ofelle* space them apart on a cutting board sprinkled with flour. This way the dough won't stick together.

Boil *ofelle* in lots of salted water (or broth), drain, place in a bowl and dress with melted butter and Parmesan cheese.

Serve hot.

1 Knead together flour, mashed potatoes, baking powder, salt, and eggs to make *ofelle* dough.

2 Roll dough, which should resemble potato *gnocchi* dough, paper thin.

3 Place filling, which has had time to rest, on half of the squares of dough.

4 Cover with the remaining squares, making sure they overlap perfectly.

5 Press firmly around filling and set *ofelle* aside not too close together.

Turteln

- **Yield: 4 servings**
- **Time needed: 1½ hours**
- **Difficulty: ***

Ingredients: 4⅓ cups light rye flour, 2 tbsp. butter, 1 egg, about ½ cup milk, pinch salt, 1 tsp. cumin seeds, 2 lbs. spinach, plenty of lard or oil (preferably peanut oil).

According to the traditional recipe, *turteln* filling was made of boiled spinach, with no additional seasonings. To make it tastier it is advisable to flavor the spinach with butter or to warm it briefly with chopped garlic and parsley, and to add a handful of grated Parmesan cheese.

Trim, wash, and boil spinach with a pinch of salt. Drain, squeeze out excess water, and chop.

Form flour in a mound on work surface and make a depression in the middle. Pour in salt, softened butter in small pieces, egg, and sufficient milk to make a basic *tagliatelle* dough (1). Work dough with your hands until perfectly smooth. Roll it fairly thin (2) and sprinkle surface with cumin seeds (3). Use a pasta cutting wheel to cut dough into 2½-inch squares (4) filling in the middle of half the squares (5), cover with the remaining squares (6), and press dough around filling to close. To seal more tightly

1 Put all the ingredients of the dough together on your work surface and slowly add milk.

2 Roll dough—which should resemble *tagliatelle* dough—into a thin sheet.

3 Sprinkle the surface with cumin seeds, spreading seeds around evenly.

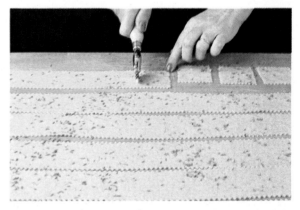

4 Use a pasta cutting wheel to cut dough into 2½-inch squares.

and to make the *turteln* more even, trim with a cutting wheel all around the edges.

Heat 3 inches lard or oil in a pot fitted with a wire basket for deep-frying. Add *turteln* a few at a time (7). When pasta is golden brown, lift out basket and drain (8). This way your finished *turteln* will all have the same golden tone.

If you don't have a basket, drain with wire skimmer (9).

Place *turteln* on a piece of paper toweling to draw off grease, then arrange on a plate and serve hot. If not served right away, keep *turteln* in a warm oven.

5 Place small portions of filling in the middle of half the squares of dough.

6 Cover with remaining squares, taking care to match up perfectly.

7 Place *turteln* in a special pot for deep-frying.

8 When *turteln* are golden brown lift out basket and drain all at once.

9 If you don't have a basket for deep-frying, use a wire skimmer.

Chestnut cappellacci

- **Yield: 4 servings**
- **Time needed: 2½ hours**
- **Difficulty: ***

Pasta and filling ingredients: Pasta dough made with 3½ cups flour and 6 eggs; 9 oz. dry-packed chestnuts (soaked for 30 minutes in water), 10 oz. sausage, about ¾ cup grated Parmesan cheese, 1 egg, olive oil, pepper, salt.
Sauce ingredients: 10 oz. sausage, about ¾ cup grated Parmesan cheese, 2 tbsp. butter, 9 oz. drained canned tomatoes, olive oil, salt, pepper.

Boil the chestnuts and mash while hot. Add 10 ounces sausage, crumbled and browned in a little oil. Add Parmesan cheese, egg, and pinches of salt and pepper. If the mixture is too soft, add bread crumbs. Cut the dough into circles 2 inches in diameter (1). Place a bit of filling in the middle of half of the circles and cover with those that remain (2). Press the edges of the dough (3). Bring together the opposite ends by twisting around the index finger and overlapping slightly (4). Sauté remaining sausage in butter and oil, add drained canned tomatoes, salt and pepper, and cook until thick. Boil, drain, and dress with the sauce and cheese.

1 After preparing dough, cut out a number of circles about 2 inches in diameter.

2 Place a bit of filling in the middle of half of the circles and cover with the ones that remain.

3 Firmly press the edges together with your fingers to seal them to prevent the filling from seeping out.

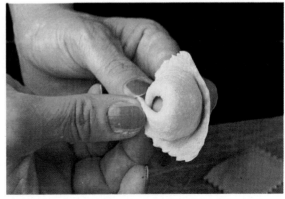

4 Bring together the two ends of the *cappellaccio* by closing them around the index finger.

Green tortelloni

- Yield: 4 servings
- Time needed: 2 hours
- Difficulty: **

Pasta and filling ingredients: Pasta dough made with 3½ cups clour, 4 eggs, and ½ lb. spinach, boiled and squeezed dry, 12 oz. *ricotta* cheese, 1 lb. boiled spinach, ¼ lb. baked ham, 1½ oz. (about ⅓ cup) grated Parmesan cheese, 1 egg yolk, nutmeg, pepper, salt.

Sauce ingredients: 14 oz. drained canned tomatoes, 2 tbsp. butter, 1 small onion, a few leaves of fresh basil or ¼ tsp. dried basil, olive oil, 1½ oz. grated Parmesan cheese, 4 oz. sliced mozzarella, pepper, salt.

Prepare homemade green pasta dough by kneading flour with eggs and chopped and squeezed spinach; roll into a thin sheet.

To make filling, mix chopped spinach with *ricotta* (forced through a strainer), chopped ham, Parmesan cheese, egg yolk, and pinches of nutmeg, salt, and pepper.

Cut the dough into 2-inch squares using a stamp (1) or a pasta cutting wheel. Place filling on each square (2), and fold dough over filling, joining the

two opposite corners to form a triangle (3). Press down around each mound of filling, and form the triangle into a large *cappelletto* by bringing together the opposite sides (4).

Prepare the tomato sauce separately. Sauté chopped onion in two tablespoons of olive oil, add the drained canned tomatoes, basil leaves, and pinches of salt and pepper, and cook until the sauce thickens.

Boil the *tortelloni,* drain when *al dente,* and toss with melted butter. Spread a layer of *tortelloni* in a baking dish, sprinkle with a bit of Parmesan cheese (5), and moisten with tomato sauce (6). Add another layer of *tortelloni* (7), and dress as before.

Place the sliced mozzarella (8) on top, spread with tomato sauce and with more grated Parmesan cheese, and bake for a few minutes in a hot oven.

1 Roll out the dough with a pasta rolling pin and cut into 2-inch squares.

2 Place a bit of filling, prepared beforehand, on each square of dough.

3 Fold each square of dough over the filling to form a triangle.

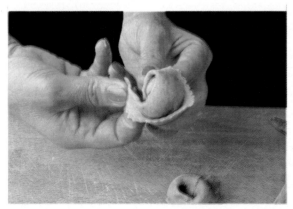

4 Form the triangle into a large *cappelletto* by bringing the opposite corners together

5 Place a layer of *tortelloni* in a baking dish, cover with plenty of grated cheese...

6 ...and then moisten with tomato sauce, prepared beforehand, spreading sauce evenly over the pasta.

7 Place another layer of *tortelloni* in the baking dish and dress as before.

8 Lastly, cover the *tortelloni* with slices of mozzarella.

Cialzons

- ■ **Yield: 4 servings**
- ■ **Time needed: 2 hours**
- ■ **Difficulty: ****

Pasta and filling ingredients: 3½ cups hard-wheat flour (semolina), 6 eggs, 1 lb. potatoes, 2 tbsp. sugar, 5 tbsp. butter, small bunch parsley, a few leaves fresh or ¼ tsp. diced mint, 1 small onion, ½ cup cognac or brandy, a few pinches nutmeg, ground cinnamon, broth, pepper, salt.
Sauce ingredients: 7 tbsp. butter, 4 oz. (about 1 cup) grated Parmesan cheese, salt.

Knead the flour with the eggs for about fifteen minutes, then form the dough into a ball and let it rest, wrapped in cellophane. Boil the potatoes in lightly salted water. Peel and mash, placing mashed potatoes in a bowl. Add chopped parsley and mint, sugar, and cognac. Season with salt and pepper, and add pinches of nutmeg and cinnamon.

Slice the onion and sauté it in butter, then discard onion and add the flavored butter to other filling ingredients, mixing well.

Roll pasta into a thin sheet, cut out 2-inch circles, place a bit of filling on each, and close. Boil *tortelli* in broth, drain, and dress with melted, lightly browned butter and grated Parmesan cheese.

Potato and onion tortelli

- ■ **Yield: 4 servings**
- ■ **Time needed: 2 hours**
- ■ **Difficulty: ****

Pasta and filling ingredients: Pasta dough made with 3½ cups flour and 6 eggs; 1 lb. potatoes, 3 oz. chopped bacon, 2 medium-sized onions, 2 tbsp. grated Parmesan cheese, 1 tbsp. parsley chopped together with ½ clove garlic, 1 egg yolk, 2 tbsp. olive oil, pepper, salt.
Sauce ingredients: 6 tbsp. butter, 2 oz. (about ½ cup) grated Parmesan cheese, salt.

For the filling, boil potatoes, peel, mash, and mix with chopped onions that have been sautéed with bacon and oil, add the parsley, garlic, Parmesan cheese, one egg yolk, and pinches of salt and pepper.

Use a stamp to cut the dough into circles about 2 inches in diameter. Place filling on half of the circles and cover with others. Press firmly with fingertips around edges to seal, and put aside to rest. Boil *tortelli* in salted water. Drain and dress, in layers, with lightly browned butter and Parmesan.

Beef marrow ravioli

■ **Yield: 4 servings**
■ **Time needed: 1½ hour**
■ **Difficulty: ***

Pasta and filling ingredients: Pasta dough made with 1¾ cups flour and 3 eggs; ¼ lbs. beef marrow, 2 oz. ham, 1½ oz. (about ⅓ cup) grated Parmesan cheese, nutmeg, pepper, salt.

Other ingredients: 1½ quarts beef broth, 2-3 tbsp. grated Parmesan.

Scald the marrow in boiling water. Put Parmesan cheese, eggs, finely chopped ham and drained marrow in a bowl (1), adding pinches of salt, pepper, and nutmeg and enough bread crumbs to make a soft mixture. Stir thoroughly with a wooden spoon (2). Knead flour with eggs (3) and roll dough into a paper-thin sheet (4). Spread the prepared filling over half the dough (5). Fold over the rest of the dough (6), taking care to make the edges meet (7). Then press lightly with a rolling pin; the two layers of dough should stick together (8). Use a cutting wheel to cut the dough first into ¾-inch strips (9), and then into squares, cutting the strips in the other direction (10). Cook in boiling broth and serve in a soup bowl; pass the Parmesan separately.

1 In a bowl, mix chopped ham, Parmesan cheese, eggs, and drained marrow...

2 ...with bread crumbs, salt, pepper, and nutmeg. Stir the mixture to blend thoroughly.

3 Prepare basic pasta dough firmer than usual, kneading together flour and eggs.

4 Roll into a thin sheet using a pasta rolling pin lightly dusted with flour.

5 Spread the filling, prepared earlier, in a uniform layer over half the dough

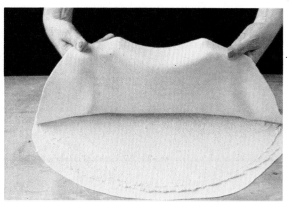

6 Fold the rest of the dough over the filling.

7 In enclosing the filling try to make the edges of the dough meet.

8 Gently press the two layers of dough together with a pasta rolling pin.

9 Use a pasta cutting wheel to cut the dough into long, parallel strips ¾-inch wide...

10 ...and cut the strips the other way to make little ¾-inch squares.

Marubini

- **Yield: 4 servings**
- **Time needed: 1½ hour**
- **Difficulty: ***

Ingredients: **Pasta dough made with 3½ cups flour and 6 eggs; 1 piece stewed beef weighing about ½ lb., ¼ lb. roast veal, ¼ lb. roast loin or leg of pork, ¼ lb. boiled beef brain, 3 oz. (about ¾ cup) grated Parmesan cheese, 1-2 eggs, nutmeg, pepper, salt.**

This is a traditional dish of Cremona.

To make the filling, chop up all the meats and place in a bowl. Add the Parmesan cheese, season with pinches of salt, pepper, and nutmeg, and bind together with a whole egg (add part or all of the other egg if the mixture is too thick; add some bread crumbs if it is too thin).

Divide the dough into two equal parts, roll out each piece, and place mounds of filling 1 inch apart on one of the sheets of dough (1). Cover with the other sheet, pressing down with fingertips around the mounds of filling (2). Cut out *marubini* with a stamp (3), then lift up the surrounding dough to free the pasta shapes (4).

From the leftover dough you can make *maltagliati* to cook in a savory vegetable or bean stock.

Marubini should be cooked in the finest quality beef broth and served with lots of Parmesan cheese.

1 Roll dough into two sheets of the same size. Place small mounds of filling on one of the sheets.

2 Cover the mounds of filling with the other sheet of dough, pressing down between the mounds to seal.

3 Cut out *marubini* with a round stamp dipped from time to time in flour.

4 Lift leftover dough, which can be used to make *maltagliati*.

The Cannelloni Family

Cannelloni are little rolls of dough wrapped around a filling. To make them all you need do is to cut dough into large squares or rectangles. These are then stuffed and baked with a white sauce, tomato sauce, or even a meat sauce. Whereas the shapes we mentioned in the preceding chapter are all northern Italian "inventions," many kinds of *cannelloni* can be found in central and southern Italian cookery. A stuffed roll is like a large *cannellone*, and it is quicker to make than other stuffed pastas. A single sheet of dough is covered with filling, and then rolled up and sealed at the ends like a package. The roll is wrapped in a cheese cloth, tied and cooked in gently boiling water. It is served in slices. Depending on what it is filled with, it may be dressed with melted butter and cheese, with a sauce made of stewed meats, or even with a simple tomato sauce flavored with basil. It is a hearty main dish.

Mascarpone cannelloni

- Yield: 4 servings
- Time needed: About 2 hours
- Difficulty: *

Pasta and filling ingredients: Pasta dough made with 3½ cups flour and 6 eggs, 12 thin slices *fontina* cheese, ½ lb. *ricotta* cheese, ½ lb. *mascarpone* or cream cheese, 3 oz. grated *fontina* cheese, 10 oz. spinach or Swiss chard, 3 tbsp. butter, freshly ground pepper, salt.
Sauce ingredients: 1 cup heavy cream, 3 tbsp. flour.

Boil, squeeze-dry, chop the spinach. In a bowl, mix the spinach, *ricotta*, *mascarpone* or cream cheese, freshly ground pepper, and salt. Melt 2 tbsp. of the butter add flour and salt. Slowly pour in cream. Simmer 1 minute, stirring. Remove from heat and stir in half of the grated *fontina* cheese.

Cut the dough into twelve 5-inch squares (1). Boil in salted water, drain, dry, and cover with the slices of cheese (2). Place a bit of filling in the center of each square (3) and spread evenly with a spatula (4). Tightly roll squares over filling (5). Place *cannelloni* seam-side-down in a buttered baking dish. Cover with white sauce (6), sprinkle with *fontina* cheese, and dot with a tablespoon of butter. Brown in a 375-degree oven.

1 Cut dough into five-inch squares and separate slightly.

2 Place boiled dough on a clean towel and cover with slices of cheese.

3 Place a bit of vegetable-and-cheese filling, prepared beforehand, in the middle of each square.

4 Spread the filling evenly, using a metal spatula.

5 Roll each square of dough tightly over filling.

6 Place *cannelloni* in a buttered baking dish and cover with white sauce.

Meat cannelloni

- **Yield: 4 servings**
- **Time needed: 2½ hours**
- **Difficulty: ***

Pasta and filling ingredients: 12 squares homemade egg dough (see page 10), 5 oz. ground beef, 3 tbsp. butter, 5 oz. ground veal, 5 oz. sausage, 1 cooked chicken breast (or other cut of chicken), ¼ tsp. sage, ½ cup dry white wine, pepper, salt.
Sauce ingredients: ¾ oz. dried boletus mushrooms, 3 tbsp. butter, 6 tbsp. flour, ½ cup brandy, 2 cups beef broth, ½ cup heavy cream, 3 tbsp. grated Parmesan cheese, pepper, salt.

To make the filling, lightly brown 3 tablespoons butter in a saucepan with sage. Add beef, veal, crumbled sausage, and ground chicken. Mix well, season with salt and pepper, moisten with wine, and let wine evaporate. Continue cooking for half an hour, adding a tablespoon of water or broth from time to time. Boil the squares of dough in lots of salt water, drain when half done, and lay out on a towel to dry.

Meanwhile, prepare the sauce. Soak dried mushrooms for 30 minutes in warm water to cover, then drain, chop, and sauté in 3 tablespoons butter. Moisten with brandy. After ten minutes, add flour and mix well. Off heat, add hot broth a little at a time, stirring constantly. Cook the sauce until thick. Add cream, salt, and pepper, bring to a boil, and remove from heat. Spread the meat filling over the squares of dough, roll up the squares, and arrange them in a buttered baking dish. Cover with sauce and Parmesan cheese, and brown in a 375-degree over for about 20 minutes. Serve hot.

Giblet cannelloni

- **Yield: 4 servings**
- **Time needed: 2¼ hours**
- **Difficulty: ***

Pasta and filling ingredients: 12 squares homemade egg dough (see page 10), 6 oz. chicken gizzards, 5 oz. chicken livers, 4 oz. cream cheese, 4 oz. *ricotta* cheese, 3 oz. (about ¾ cup) grated Parmesan cheese, 3 tbsp. butter, 2 egg yolks, 1 small onion, 1 handful parsley, ½ cup dry white wine, 1 lemon, pepper salt.
Sauce ingredients: 2 cups milk, 5 tbsp. all-purpose white flour, 3 tbsp. butter.

Peel and cook gizzards until tender in boiling water with a little butter and lemon juice. Sauté chopped onion in 2 tbsp. butter. Add chopped chicken livers and chopped gizzards, season with salt and pepper, moisten with wine, and continue cooking, adding chopped parsley just before removing from heat. In a separate bowl, mix the *ricotta* (forced through a strainer or mashed with a fork), cream cheese, half of the Parmesan cheese, and the giblets. Season with salt to taste.

Boil the squares in lots of salted water. Drain when half-cooked and set out on a cloth to dry. Place a bit of filling on the squares, spread evenly with a spatula, and roll up.

Melt 3 tablespoons butter in a saucepan. Stir in the flour, and, off heat, slowly add the hot milk, stirring constantly. Season with salt and pepper. Simmer sauce a few minutes, then remove from heat and add the remaining grated Parmesan cheese and the two egg yolks, one at a time.

Arrange *cannelloni* seam-side-down in a buttered baking dish, cover with white sauce, and brown in a hot oven (375° F) for about 20 minutes. Serve hot.

Ricotta cannelloni

- **Yield: 4 servings**
- **Time needed: 2 hours**
- **Difficulty: ***

Pasta and filling ingredients: 12 squares homemade egg dough (see page 10), ½ lb. mozzarella, ¼ lb. baked ham, 8 oz. sieved or mashed *ricotta* cheese, 2 eggs, nutmeg, pepper, salt.
Sauce ingredients: 14 oz. drained canned tomatoes, 4 tbsp. butter, 1 small onion, 1 stalk celery, 1 carrot, chopped basil leaves, or ½ tsp. dried basil, 4 tbsp. Parmesan cheese, olive oil, pepper, salt.

In a saucepan, sauté chopped onion, carrot, and celery in a few tablespoons of oil. Add the drained canned tomatoes. Season with salt and pepper, and cook over low heat for half an hour, stirring and adding a little water or broth if necessary.

Boil the squares of dough, a few at a time, in lots of salted water. Drain when half cooked, and dry on a cloth.

Meanwhile prepare the filling. Chop the mozzarella and ham and mix in a bowl with sieved or mashed *ricotta*. Add the beaten eggs, and pinches of nutmeg, pepper, and salt..

Place the mixture on the squares of dough, spread with spatula, roll up the squares, and arrange seam-side-down in a buttered baking dish. Spread tomato sauce over the top, and sprinkle on the basil, Parmesan, and the remaining butter, cut in pats. Brown at 375° F for 20 minutes.

Spinach roll

- ■ **Yield: 4 servings**
- ■ **Time needed: 2 hours**
- ■ **Difficulty: ***

Ingredients: Pasta dough made with 1¾ cups flour and 3 eggs, about 2¼ lbs. spinach, 8 oz. sieved or mashed *ricotta* cheese, 7 tbsp. butter, 3 oz. (about ¾ cup) grated Parmesan cheese, ¼ tsp. sage, pepper, salt.

Boil the spinach. Drain, squeeze out excess water, chop, and sauté in 2 tbsp. butter. Remove from heat and stir in sieved or mashed *ricotta* (1). Add a little Parmesan cheese (2) and pinches salt and pepper. Roll the dough into a rectangle about 10 inches wide and 20 inches long (3). Spread the filling over the dough with a spatula (4), leaving a little dough uncovered around the edges. Roll up the dough tightly (5-6), then wrap the roll in cheesecloth (7) and tie it at the ends and at several points in between (8). Place the roll in an oval pot (a fish poacher, for example) with lots of boiling water and boil gently for about 40 minutes.

Drain the roll (9), unwrap it from the cloth (10), and cut into ½-inch slices. Melt the remaining butter with the sage and pour over the slices.

1 Place *ricotta* in a bowl and add boiled spinach sautéed in butter.

2 Season with salt, pepper, and Parmesan cheese, and mix well.

3 Roll dough into a thin sheet and sprinkle with flour.

4 Cover with filling, spreading evenly with a long metal spatula.

5 Tightly roll dough over filling, taking care that filling doesn't spill out.

6 Press the roll lightly with both hands so that dough and filling stick together.

7 Wrap the roll of dough in a large, thin white cloth or in a double thickness of cheesecloth.

8 Tie the roll at the ends, then in several points in between, using white kitchen string.

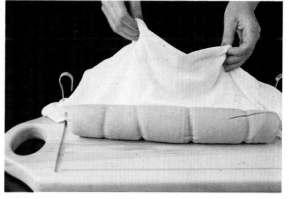

9 After boiling roll in lots of water, drain carefully (do not bend).

10 Cool for a few moments on a cutting board, then unwrap.

Crêpes

How to make crêpes

Crêpes are a kind of pancake, thin as paper, which can be sweet or savory. The savory ones, which we will deal with in this chapter, are filled with different fillings made with meat, spinach, *ricotta* cheese or vegetables. They are prepared with white sauce or tomato sauce or with butter and Parmesan cheese, lightly browned in the oven, and served as a first course.

To make crêpes, a batter is prepared with milk, eggs, and flour, which is then cooked by being poured with a small ladle into a pan that has been lightly buttered and heated (1). The pan is then swirled gently so that the batter spreads out evenly (2). When the crêpe is cooked on one side, it is flipped over (3) and cooked on the other side. The temperature of the pan should be moderate. If it is too hot the crêpe will burn, and if it is too cold it will not cook fast enough. The batter is cooked in these small amounts until it is all used up.

The best pan for making crêpes is a no-stick pan with a diameter of about 8 inches; you can also use an iron frying pan. Another handy kitchen item for making crêpes is a nonbending plastic bowl with a spout which allows you to pour the batter directly into the pan.

Crêpes prepared in the traditional way as described above tend to stick to the pan if it is not buttered before forming each crêpe. It is easier to make crêpes if you use one of the crêpe-making skillets on the market (see page 125). A round shallow bowl comes with them in which you keep the batter (4). When the skillet is good and hot, it is inverted and dipped into the batter in the plate (5), then lifted up (6), turned at a 90-degree angle (7), and finally turned completely upright. The heat will leave a thin film of batter on the skillet (8). After a few minutes the crêpe will be cooked and you take it off with the spatula that comes with the skillet and put it on a plate. You continue doing this until all the batter is used up.

1 Pour a small amount of batter into an iron pan that is about 8 inches in diameter.

2 Lift the pan from the heat and swirl it gently so that the batter is evenly distributed.

3 As soon as one side is lightly browned, cook it on the other side until it too is golden brown.

4 Pour a little of the crêpe batter into the shallow bowl that is packed with the appliance.

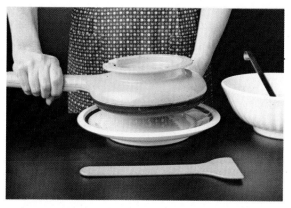

5 Dip the electric skillet, which you have heated ahead of time, into the batter in the shallow bowl.

6 After a few seconds, lift the skillet up (don't leave it any longer or else the crêpe will be too thick).

7 Turn the skillet at a 90-degree angle. A thin film of batter will have stuck to it.

8 Turn the skillet over completely and let the crêpe cook a few seconds more.

9 Lift the crêpe off with the special spatula and place it on a plate.

Asparagus crêpes

- **Yield: 4 servings**
- **Time needed: 1½ hours**
- **Difficulty: ****

Crêpe ingredients: ¾ cup all-purpose white flour, 4 "large" eggs, a bit of milk or water (optional), salt. **Filling and sauce ingredients:** ¾ cup Swiss cheese cut into very thin pieces, 1½ oz. (about ⅓ cup) grated Parmesan cheese, a bunch of asparagus, 2 tbsp. flour, 1 cup milk, 7 tbsp. butter, nutmeg, pepper, salt.

Make the crêpes. Beat the eggs in a bowl. Add the flour little by little, beating all the while to make the batter smooth, then add salt and thin the batter to the consistency of medium cream with milk or water, mixing well. Using an iron skillet or a no-stick pan, make many thin crêpes in the following way. First, heat the skillet and spread a thin film of butter in it. Pour a small amount of batter into the pan, lift the pan from the heat, and swirl it so that the batter spreads out evenly. As soon as one side of the crêpe has cooked, turn it over with a spatula and cook the other side. Keep doing this till all the batter is used up. (See p. 124).

To make the filling, cut off the woody part of the asparagus stems; then wash the asparagus, boil, and drain the stalks while slightly underdone. Briefly sauté the stalks in a pan with 2 tablespoons butter to give them flavor and drain them (1). Force through a sieve or purée into a blender or food processor. Melt 4 tablespoons butter, add the flour, stirring constantly so there will be no lumps, add a bit of salt, then add the boiling milk very slowly. Let the sauce come to a boil over low heat, and simmer, stirring continuously, for 5 minutes. Then take the pan off the heat. Set aside one quarter of the sauce; stir the rest of it into the puréed asparagus (2). Add a little nutmeg and the Parmesan cheese to the asparagus filling and mix together. Spread the crêpes out on a table and put a little filling on each one (3). Spread the filling evenly with a spatula (4). Place a very thin slice of Swiss cheese on each crêpe (5). Fold the crêpes first in halves, then in quarters (6-7), place in a butter oven dish (8), spread the rest of the sauce over the crêpes (9), and brown in a 375-degree oven.

1 Force the boiled and butter sautéed asparagus through a sieve or purée in a blender.

2 Add three quarters of the white sauce to the puréed asparagus and mix thoroughly.

3 Spread the crêpes out and put a little of the filling on each one.

4 Using a spatula, spread the asparagus filling evenly, without going all the way to the edges of the crêpes.

5 Place a very thin slice of Swiss cheese on each crêpe, or else cut the cheese into cubes.

6 Fold the crêpes in half, making sure the edges line up and the filling does not leak out, then...

7 ...fold the crêpes in quarters so that they look somewhat like little fans.

8 Arrange the crêpes in a circle in a buttered oven dish.

9 Last, pour the rest of the white sauce evenly over the crêpes.

Gorgonzola crêpes

■ Yield: 4 servings
■ Time needed: 1 hour
■ Difficulty: **

Ingredients: 16 crêpes (see recipe for Asparagus Crêpes on p. 126), 5 oz. sweet *Gorgonzola* cheese, 1½ oz. (about ⅓ cup) grated Parmesan cheese, 5 tbsp. butter, 1 tbsp. flour, 7 cup milk, nutmeg, pepper, salt.

Melt 2 tablespoons of the butter in a saucepan and add the flour, mixing well. Add the hot milk a little at a time, stirring constantly. Add the salt, pepper, and nutmeg and cook the white sauce for a few minutes until it thickens and becomes smooth. Remove from the heat, add the *Gorgonzola* cheese, cut up in pieces, and half the Parmesan cheese and mix well. Fill the crêpes with the filling, roll them up, and place them in a lightly buttered baking dish. Spoon 3 tablespoons melted butter and the remaining Parmesan cheese over the top of the crêpes and bake in a 375-degree oven for a few minutes till they brown.

This dish can be made ahead of time and kept in the refrigerator, leaving only the baking and browning for the last minute.

Truffle crêpes

■ Yield: 4 servings
■ Time needed: 1½ hours
■ Difficulty: **

Ingredients: 16 crêpes (see recipe for Asparagus Crêpes p. 126), 7 oz. lean ground pork, 7 oz. ground beef, ½ lb. mozzarella, 1 oz. dried boletus mushrooms, 1 small truffle, grated, 6 tbsp. butter, 3 tbsp. flour, 1 cup stock, 1 piece of onion, nutmeg, pepper, salt.

To make the filling, sauté the diced onion in 2 tablespoons of butter, then add the pork and beef. Add the mushrooms, previously soaked in water for 30 minutes, drained, and chopped in thin pieces. Add salt and cook, stirring constantly, for several minutes. If necessary, add 1 or 2 tablespoons of stock. In the meantime, melt 2 more tablespoons butter in another saucepan, add the flour, stir to blend, and add the boiling stock little by little, stirring constantly. Cook the sauce for a few minutes, then add a few tablespoons of the meat mixture (which should be quite soft). Add the finely diced mozzarella cheese, a little of the grated truffle, and pinches of nutmeg, pepper, and salt.

Fill the crêpes with the meat mixture. Roll them up and place them in a buttered baking dish. Pour the sauce over the crêpes. Spread the remaining optional truffle shavings and dots of butter over the crêpes. Bake in a 375-degree oven for a few minutes until the crêpes brown.

Ham crêpes

■ Yield: 4 servings
■ Time needed: 1 hour
■ Difficulty: **

Ingredients: 16 crêpes (see recipe for Asparagus Crêpes p. 126), 16 slices *fontina* cheese (or Swiss cheese), 3 tbsp. butter, 8 slices ham, 2 tbsp. grated Parmesan cheese, 1 egg yolk, 1 tbsp. flour, 1 cup milk, nutmeg, salt.

Melt 2 tablespoons of the butter, add the flour, mix well, and stir in the hot milk little by little. Season with salt and a pinch of nutmeg and simmer the sauce, stirring, for a few minutes. Remove from the heat and add the Parmesan cheese and the egg yolk. Blend together. First place a slice of cheese on the crêpes, then a half slice of the ham. Roll up and place in a buttered baking dish. Cover the crêpes with a thin layer of white sauce. Dot with remaining tablespoon butter. Place in a 375-degree oven to brown.

Mushroom crêpes

■ Yield: 4 servings
■ Time needed: 1 hour
■ Difficulty: **

Ingredients: 16 crêpes (see recipe for Asparagus Crêpes p. 126), 10 oz. fresh mushrooms, 4 oz. ham, 7 tbsp. butter, 1 tbsp. flour, 1 cup milk, a few pinches nutmeg, pepper, salt.

Clean the mushrooms, slice them thinly, and sauté in 2 tablespoons of the butter. Add a pinch of salt and pepper. Remove from the heat and let cool. Melt 2 additional tablespoons butter, add the flour, and slowly add the boiling milk. Add salt and cook the white sauce for a few minutes. Remove from the heat and add the nutmeg. Let the sauce cool slightly and add the mushrooms and thin strips of ham. Fill the crêpes with the filling, roll them up, and place them in a buttered baking dish. Pour the remaining butter, melted, over the crêpes and place in a 375-degree oven to brown.

PASTA SAUCES

How to Make a Sauce

How many kinds of sauces are there for pasta, boiled rice, ravioli or *gnocchi?* There are many, many sauces and each one has different variations. They can all turn a first course into a delicious meal-in-itself. The sauces can be cooked or uncooked with tomatoes or without them, with meat or without it. This chapter will deal with honest-to-goodness sauces, sauces that are made with many different ingredients, yet the end results are smooth and well-blended. There are also meat sauces, cooked slowly over low heat with other ingredients—sometimes with vegetables, when the recipe calls for them. These recipes may seem informal, but they are actually the result of an artful blending of flavors—vegetables, cheeses, and herbs all mixed together. And lastly, we can't forget the tasty fish and seafood sauces, or the "white" sauces, which are the most delicate sauces of all.

If we look back in the past, we can find sauces that were used with pasta though perhaps they were different from the sauces we use today. The Romans ate a kind of *tagliatelle* which they tossed with pepper and *Apicius liquamen*, which is a liquid obtained from the fermentation of salted raw fish, to which herbs are added. We find sauces mentioned by Boccaccio, who writes about macaroni and ravioli cooked in capon stock, drained, and tossed with butter and Parmesan cheese. In the Renaissance, pasta was usually tossed with spices, sugar or honey, and grated cheese—and this way of eating pasta lasted for centuries. In those times, no one thought of tossing pasta with the gravies from roasts or stews, though braised-meat dishes were very common then. When the tomato arrived from America, in the early 1600s, pasta sauce changed a lot. At the same time fragrant natural herbs replaced many of the strong spices as a basic ingredient.

How to make pasta sauces

Here we will consider the various ingredients that are used in nearly all pasta sauces.

Fats — Since all fatty substances are easier on the digestion when they are uncooked rather than cooked, when we must cook with them we are confronted with the problem of which to use: olive oil, one of the many vegetable oils, margarine, butter, pork fat, lard, or bacon?

Unless a recipe specifies which fat to use, it is best to stick with olive oil, especially unrefined olive oil. This contains up to one percent acidity, has no chemical additives, and its vitamins have been completely preserved. If you want an oil that is less nutritious and less tasty but certainly cheaper, you have to use a vegetable oil. This could be made from corn, peanuts, sunflowers, and so on. Stick margarine, which is made of vegetable oils (peanut oil, palm oil, cottonseed oil, and coconut oil), is easy to digest for people who have stomach problems. The beneficial qualities of the vegetable oils are lost in industrial production when it gets hardened. In this case, it is better to use an easy-spreading tub of margarine. As far as the animal fats are concerned, butter is without a doubt the best one to use from a nutritional standpoint. However because of its cholesterol, it is not recommended for certain people.

A word of caution about pork fats. These fats, as well as those from other animals, take longer to digest. They should be used in moderation by people who have stomach problems and liver problems. Lastly, it is important to remember that all the fats have more or less the same caloric value, about 240 calories per ounce.

Herbs and spices — Very few people know that herbs and spices are medicinal plants, plants that influence the body in certain ways. They are therefore used not only to make sauces taste good and smell appetizing, but also to make them wholesome and digestible. Among the aromatic herbs, the one that is most frequently used in sauces is basil, which originated in India but has adapted perfectly to the Mediterranean climate. Basil may be torn by hand, but it is even better to snip it with a scissors to keep all of its wonderful fragrance.

Indigenous to Europe, parsley was used by the ancient Greeks and Romans. This herb too is added after the cooking is over and is almost always finely chopped before use with a rocker or other chopping device.

Another aromatic plant that is widely used is oregano. It is very common in dishes from southern Italy. It is well known because it is used on pizza, but it is also indispensable for certain tomato sauces and fish sauces. It is one of the few aromatic plants that does not lose its smell even when it is dried. A pinch is all you need, because too much will overpower other flavors. Sauces also may be enhanced by the addition of marjoram, thyme, and, in some instances, mint. The most widely used of all spices, pepper, can be either white (sharp and spicy) or black (fiery and aromatic). It is always best to use whole peppercorns and to grind them as needed.

Another spice that is often used is red pepper, with its very spicy flavor. This can be added fresh, dried, or in ground form.

Lastly, let's not forget nutmeg, with its special taste and strong aroma. Because of its potency, nutmeg is grated and used a pinch at a time.

Vegetables for sautéeing — The starting point for nearly all sauces is a *soffritto*, a mixture of chopped vegetables and aromatic herbs, sautéed in one of the fats mentioned above. In addition to carrots, which add sweetness, and celery, which lends character, all *soffritti* contain either onion or garlic. There are many kinds of onions, but the ones most often used are yellow globe onions, which have a golden outer skin and a rather strong taste. Purple-skinned onions, which are even stronger, may also be used. Finally, white onions are preferred by some because they are sweeter and more delicate than other types. If you want to tame the pungent flavor of an onion, cut it in pieces and let it sit in cold water for about 15 minutes before using it. Be careful not to brown the onion too much before adding the other ingredients or it will turn bitter and ruin the sauce. The part of the garlic plant that is used is the bulb. The bulb is separated into cloves that impart a strong flavor and aroma to sauces. Like onion, garlic should not be overcooked in the *soffritto*. To make it more digestible, sauté garlic with the skin on, then, mash it lightly with a fork, and take it out, when the sauce is cooked. To give your sauce a garlic flavor, you may also rub the inside of the saucepan with a cut clove.

A few rules for saucing pasta — The different shapes, weights, sizes, and surface areas of different kinds of pasta function in special ways to hold and blend with sauces and sauce ingredients. Generally speaking, long-shaped pasta goes well with uncooked sauces (*pesto*, fresh tomatoes, etc.), with quick, light sauces (oil, garlic and red pepper, clams, etc.) or with white sauces (cream sauces, cheese sauces, white sauces, etc.). Short, thick pasta goes well with various meat sauces, with sauces that require long slow cooking, or with vegetable sauces.

Once the pasta is cooked it should be drained immediately and tossed in a heated bowl. You can even toss the pasta in a pan. To do this, first put the sauce in the pan, then add the pasta, and toss over low heat a few times. If the pasta is really *al dente*, you can add a few spoonfuls of the water the pasta was cooked in to prevent the pasta from absorbing too much of the sauce, thereby losing texture and flavor. You never use cheese with fish sauces or with sauces based on fresh raw tomatoes, and you use very little with vegetable sauces.

Some useful advice

—To make a good *soffritto* cook the mixture of aromatic vegetables till pale golden with pork fat or, when called for, with bacon or prosciutto.

As soon as the sauce begins to simmer, lower the heat. Partially cover and stir often. The sauce is cooked when the fat comes to the surface.

If the sauce tends to stick to the bottom of the saucepan, merely drop in two colored glass marbles, which will absorb part of the heat.

When you use fresh tomatoes, scald them in boiling water for 30 seconds before adding them to the sauce. Peel them and remove the seeds. Cut into pieces. If they are watery, drain them in a colander.

In the summer, when tomatoes are very tasty and ripe, you can prepare a simple sauce by combining raw tomatoes with a little basil and salt.

When you make meat sauce let each kind of meat brown well before adding the other ingredients. Some recipes call for the vegetables and the bacon used in the *soffritto* to be forced through a sieve, while others don't.

For fish sauces that call for a long cooking time, it is a good idea to add hot water or stock before you add the tomatoes, which are added when the sauce is half cooked. If you need to thicken a sauce in a hurry, don't bother raising the heat. Just add a teaspoon of flour or cornstarch, mixed with butter.

To remove acidity from tomato sauces, add a teaspoon of sugar when the sauce is half cooked.

Spices are added before the sauce is cooked. Aromatic herbs are added toward the end of cooking and ground herbs at the very end.

Kitchen equipment

A word about the best pots for making sauces. Nearly all the sauces require a long cooking time over low heat. The choices are between traditional small copper pans, earthenware pots, or the modern stainless steel pots that have a thick base reinforced by copper. Earthenware pots are ideal, especially for meat sauces, because in addition to conducting heat evenly, they heighten the flavor and the smell of the sauce. (But they must be able to withstand a direct flame.) All these pots must have their own covers. To prevent sauces from burning, it is a good idea to have a heat diffuser. Besides holding the heat and conducting it evenly, they save energy, since you can keep the heat to a minimum without interrupting the simmering. A wooden spoon to stir the sauces is imperative. Wood is an ideal material because it does not absorb heat and consequently does not withdraw heat from the sauce; nor does it change the flavor. You will also need a ladle with a spout to pour the sauce into a container. It's handy to have various kitchen utensils that dice and chop vegetables. The halfmoon-shaped rocker is one. The crank-operated parsley-chopper that chops parsley right into the pot is another. The onion-chopper with a spring handle is yet another. There are hand-operated vegetable-choppers and electric ones that have attachments to squeeze tomatoes. There are also little knives used to peel tomatoes and sieves designed to purée and strain pulp. The old marble mortar and pestle are used to make *pesto*. The modern electric blender saves time and energy and can be used instead of one of the hand gadgets.

To clean the fish and seafood used in making sauces, you will need a pair of scissors, a sharp knife, and a stiff metal brush that can be used to clean mussel shells.

A last note about what you'll need for making sauces: large earthenware pots with covers, a large spaghetti fork, an electric or a hand-held cheese grater, and a sauce boat of ceramic, stainless steel, or pyrex.

Preserving sauces

Almost all the sauces in this book can be prepared in larger quantities than the recipes call for and stored for later use. To keep a sauce for four or five days, put it in a closed container, cover with a layer of oil, and refrigerate. When you want to use the sauce, take out the amount you need and warm it over very low heat until it comes to a boil. You may also warm it in a double boiler. If you want to keep sauces for an even longer period, you should freeze them. The sauce should be transferred to small containers that hold the amount you'll need for a meal. Ice cube trays (see photo on this page) do the job nicely. So do yoghurt containers, which you can cover with tin foil or cellophane. When you fill the containers, leave about an inch at the top, because liquid and semi-liquid substances expand when they are frozen. When you use frozen sauce, let it thaw at room temperature, then heat as described above. You can even refrigerate or freeze the *soffritto* in the same way. To keep tomato sauce for a long time you can even sterilize it and freeze it. More about this on p. 140.

1 Pour the tomato sauce, cold, into an ice cube tray that has an removable cube divider...

2 ...or into individual cube containers and put in the freezer to harden. You will have...

3 ...many tiny cubes of sauce that you can wrap in tin foil and keep in the freezer.

4 If you want to freeze a large amount of sauce, put the cubes in a plastic bag.

Tomato Sauces

The tomato, which is indispensable for many sauces, originated in Peru, where it was widely cultivated and constituted one of the basic ingredients in the native foods. It was brought to Europe by the Spanish conquistadors after the discovery of America and for two centuries was not simply ignored but actually considered harmful and inedible. Only towards the end of the 17th century did it begin to be cultivated in southern Italy, and used in different foods. The tomato, which flourishes in the summer, is an annual. It is very rich in vitamins A, B, and C and in minerals, especially calcium and phosphorus. The best tomatoes for making sauces are the ones of the highest quality, very juicy (not watery), unblemished, and completely vine-ripened. The strain most often used are plum tomatoes. All other kinds of tomatoes are too watery for sauces. First of all, tomatoes should be carefully washed in running water to remove any traces of soil or insecticides. Then you can begin to make the sauce. There are different ways of doing this. You can cut the tomatoes into small pieces and put them through a food mill, or you can cook them in a small amount of water for 15 to 20 minutes, put them through a food mill, and cook again. Another way, which is more time-consuming, is to scald them for a half a minute in boiling water, which allows you to peel them easily. Then you cut them open, remove the seeds, cut them into small pieces, and put them back in the saucepan to cook.

Once they have been put through a food mill, the tomatoes should be added to the *soffritto*, which is usually made with onions. The sauce should be cooked over very low heat for many hours. Some people say for two hours. Some say four. The pot should be covered, but not tightly. The sauce will be ready when it is thick and fats come to the surface.

How to use raw tomatoes—In the summer, when tomatoes are delicious and full of pulp, you can even make sauces with raw tomatoes. Wash them well under running water. Remove the skins with a sharp knife, remove the seeds, and chop the pulp finely. Add whatever herbs you desire (chopped basil or parsley, oregano), garlic, pure olive oil (of course) and, if necessary, salt.

How to can and freeze tomato sauce—There are so many ways of canning and freezing tomato sauce at home that we can practically say that every Italian housewife has her own patent. The commonly used methods differ from one region of Italy to another. In the north, where tomatoes are "imported" from the south of Italy, the sauce, either raw or cooked is put into bottles with a pinch of salicylic acid. Alternatively, when it is still hot, sauce can be poured into airtight jars and sterilized for 20 to 30 minutes in a special pot filled with boiling water. The same method is used to preserve whole tomatoes that are to be used for sauces. Another good method is to put containers of tomato sauce, raw or cooked, right in the freezer until you need them. Just remember to take them out a day ahead of time and put them in the warmest part of the refrigerator. In the south of Italy, on the other hand, tomatoes are preserved by being cooked for hours and hours, until they become the famous *conserva* (paste), dark and very thick. Or else they are cut into pieces or put through a food mill and then into airtight bottles. These are then wrapped in a cloth and boiled two or three at a time (many more can be boiled at one time if you use the huge pots that are used in the province of Naples) until they have been completely sterilized. The choice of tomatoes is of the utmost importance in canning and freezing them. They must be perfectly ripe and be picked at the peak of the season.

If you don't have time to can or freeze tomatoes at home, you can buy them in cans at the stores—whole, in pieces, or puréed. The best kind of canned whole tomatoes for sauces are plum tomatoes with the skins removed. These have a lot of pulp with very little water. They are ideal for all recipes that call for whole tomatoes. Chopped tomatoes in a can are slightly inconvenient if you want a smooth purée because the seeds have not been removed, but this product does save time when you're making sauces. You can also find tomato purée and tomato paste on the market. Ready-to-use tomato purée is a big help because it saves a lot of time. Tomato paste is tomato purée that has been cooked down to remove most of the water. It is sold in tubes as well as in cans. Tomato paste in tubes can be used a little at a time and it keeps well, when closed, in the refrigerator.

Tomato sauce

■ **Yield: 4 servings**
■ **Time needed: 45 min.**
■ **Difficulty: ***

Ingredients: 18 oz. whole plum tomatoes (or 1 14-oz. can plum tomatoes), 1 clove garlic, ½ onion, 1 small carrot, 1 stalk celery, bunch parsley, a small bunch basil, 2 tbsp. butter or oil, pinch sugar (optional), pepper, salt.

Trim the vegetables. Wash them. Drain them and chop them with a rocker (1) or chef's knife. Cut the tomatoes into big pieces (2). Put the onion, carrot, celery, and parsley in a saucepan (made of copper or earthenware, if possible) with some oil or butter (3). Cover and cook the sauce over medium heat for a few minutes, stirring every now and then.

Add the cut-up tomatoes (4), the bunch of basil and the whole clove of garlic (5). Cover and cook over very low heat for about 15 minutes. Then add the salt, sugar (if you want to), and a pinch of freshly ground pepper. When it is done, put the sauce through a food mill (6) or purée in a blender or food processor. Any kind of pasta or *gnocchi* can be tossed with this sauce.

1 Trim the carrot, celery, onion, and parsley and chop them all finely using a rocker or knife.

2 Wash the tomatoes and, without removing the skins or seeds, cut them into good-sized pieces.

3 Put the oil and butter in a saucepan over medium heat and add the finely chopped vegetables.

4 When the vegetables have wilted and are a light gold color, add the tomatoes.

5 When the tomatoes fall apart, add the basil and the clove of garlic.

6 When the tomato sauce gets very thick, put it through a food mill.

Tomato sauce with basil

- **Yield: 4 servings needed**
- **Time needed: 45 min.**
- **Difficulty: ***

Ingredients: 18 oz. plum tomatoes, 2 tbsp. butter, 1 small onion, a bunch basil, oil, freshly ground pepper, salt.

Sauté the onion in the butter and a tablespoon of oil until it is pale gold in color. Add the tomatoes, peeled, seeded and forced through a sieve. Season with salt and pepper. Cook for 30 minutes over moderate heat, stirring every now and then. When you use this sauce, add the basil leaves, chopped coarsely. This sauce is good tossed with homemade egg pasta as well as any shape dry pasta.

Tomato sauce with mint

- **Yield: 4 servings**
- **Time needed: 45 min.**
- **Difficulty ***

Ingredients: 18 oz. whole plum tomatoes, a small sprig very fresh mint, 1 clove garlic, salt.

Peel and seed the tomatoes and chop into chunky pieces. Put the tomatoes in a strainer or colander and let their water drain out. In the meantime, chop the mint leaves and the clove of garlic together finely. Pour the chopped tomatoes into a saucepan. Add the chopped mint and garlic mixture, add salt, and bring to a simmer. Stir from time to time. Let the sauce simmer for 10 minutes.

This is a very good sauce and a quick one to make. When it's time to toss the pasta, just add a little olive oil. As a savory touch, add 4 to 8 ounces mozzarella cut up in pieces.

Tomato sauce with herbs

- **Yield: 4 servings**
- **Time needed: 20 min.**
- **Difficulty: ***

Ingredients: 18 oz. whole plum tomatoes, 1 sprig basil, 1 sprig parsley, ¼ tsp. sage. large pinch oregano, clove garlic, ¼ tsp. rosemary, salt.

Peel and seed the tomatoes, and chop coarsely. Put the tomatoes in a strainer or colander and let their water run out. Meanwhile, chop together the basil, parsley, sage, rosemary, oregano, and garlic. Put the chopped tomatoes in a saucepan. Add salt. Add the herbs and bring sauce to a simmer, removing the scum and stirring continually. Let it simmer for about 5 minutes.

Tomato sauce with oregano

- **Yield: 4 servings**
- **Time needed: 45 min.**
- **Difficulty: ***

Ingredients: 18 oz. of whole plum tomatoes, 1 clove garlic, ¼ tsp. oregano, olive oil, pepper, salt.

Remove the skins of the tomatoes, take the seeds out, and chop finely. Mince the garlic clove (or crush it with the side of a knife, if you intend to take it out later) and place the garlic in a saucepan with 2 tablespoons oil. Heat the oil slowly and when the garlic begins to fry (don't let it brown) add the tomatoes, a pinch of salt, and pepper. Cook slowly until the sauce is nicely thickened.

Remove the sauce from the heat, discarding the garlic if you wish . Season with oregano, crumbled up into bits.

This sauce can be tossed with spaghetti or with *trenette* or *linguine.* Adding cheese is not recommended.

Uncooked tomato sauce

- **Yield: 4 servings**
- **Time needed: 1 hour**
- **Difficulty: ***

Ingredients: 18 oz. ripe garden tomatoes, 1 onion, bunch basil, 1 clove garlic, 1 small carrot, a few tablespoons olive oil, salt.

Wash the tomatoes, cut them into pieces, and put them in a saucepan. Add the onion, sliced, the whole carrot, the clove of garlic, the washed basil, and the salt. Place the saucepan over moderate heat and let the sauce cook for about three-quarters of an hour. Stir from time to time. When the water from the tomatoes has nearly evaporated, remove the garlic and the basil and force the sauce through a sieve or purée in a blender or food processor. Let the sauce cool and pour a few tablespoons of olive oil over the top. This is an ideal sauce for spaghetti *trenette.*

Amatriciana sauce

- **Yield: 4 servings**
- **Time needed: ½ hour**
- **Difficulty: ***

Ingredients: ¼ lb. salt pork cut into cubes, ¼ lb. peeled, seeded, and juiced tomato pulp, 1 small piece onion, 1 small piece hot red pepper, oil, salt.

Put 4 tablespoons oil into a pan and place over moderately high heat; when the oil is hot, add the salt pork (1). Turn the cubes so they brown all over (2). When the salt pork is golden brown, remove it with a slotted spatula (3), put it on a plate, and keep warm. Add the finely chopped onion and the red pepper to the fat in the pan (4). When the onion begins to brown, add the tomato pulp, cut into pieces (5). Add salt and cook for 5 to 6 minutes, stirring continually. Finish the sauce by adding the reserved pieces of browned salt pork (6).

This sauce can be tossed with *bucatini* or with spaghetti, in the following way. Let the sauce cool and pour a few tablespoons olive oil over the top. This is an ideal sauce for spaghetti or *trenette*. Pour the pasta, previously boiled in salted water and drained while *al dente,* into the sauce pan. Stir.

1 Put about 4 tablespoons oil in a pan and when the oil gets very hot, add the salt pork.

2 Brown the salt pork over high heat, continually stirring the pieces with a wooden spoon.

3 When the pieces are golden brown and crispy, take them out of the fat.

4 Add the finely chopped onion and the red pepper to the bacon fat.

5 When the onion begins to turn brown, add the tomato pulp, which should be well drained.

6 Finish the tomato sauce by adding the pieces of bacon that were cooked before and set aside.

Frankfurter sauce

- **Yield: 4 servings**
- **Time needed: 45 min.**
- **Difficulty: ***

Ingredients: 3½ oz. bacon, 1 small onion, 1 8 or 9-oz. can tomato purée, frankfurters, 1 hot red pepper, a few tbsp. oil, pepper, salt.

Cut the bacon into strips. Chop the onion finely. Slice the frankfurters into rounds (1). Put the chopped onion in a pan with a few tablespoons oil and sauté it just until it wilts. Add the bacon and cook until it browns lightly (2). Then add the frankfurters (3) and the red pepper, whole (4). Mix well and add the tomato purée (5). Season with salt and pepper. Cover and cook for about half an hour. This sauce is good to toss with shells or even with big ribbed macaroni. Add grated Romano cheese or Parmesan cheese if you want to.

When it is time to serve the pasta, pour the pasta, already boiled and drained *al dente,* into the pan containing the sauce (6), and stir together for a few minutes.

1 Cut the frankfurters into rounds.

2 Sauté the onion in oil, then add the bacon and cook until it browns nicely.

3 Continually stirring with a wooden spoon, add the frankfurters, cut into rounds...

4 ...and stir them to brown nicely all over; then add the whole red pepper.

5 Add the tomato purée, salt, and pepper, stir, and cover the pan.

6 When it is time to toss the pasta, cooked *al dente*, pour the pasta right into the pan of sauce.

Ciociara sauce

■ **Yield: 4 servings**
■ **Time needed: ½ hour**
■ **Difficulty: ***

Ingredients: 18 oz. whole plum tomatoes, 5 oz. mozzarella cheese, 3 tbsp. grated Romano cheese, about 6 tbsp. olive oil, oregano to taste, freshly ground black pepper, salt.

Cut the mozzarella first in slices and then in cubes (1). Wash the tomatoes, dry them, and cut them into pieces, discarding the seeds. Put them in a saucepan, preferably earthenware, together with a few tablespoons oil (2). Add the mozzarella (3) and stir until the cheese begins to melt (4). Add the Romano cheese (5), and season with salt, freshly ground pepper, and oregano to taste, crumbled with your fingers (6). Cover the pan and cook over rather high heat for about 15 minutes, stirring continuously with a wooden spoon.

This sauce can be used with spaghetti or *fusilli*. Drain the pasta while it is still *al dente* (7). Toss it with the sauce (8). Pour it into a baking dish (9) and bake it in a 400-degree oven until the top browns.

1 Slice the mozzarella and cut it into cubes.

2 Put an earthenware pot over moderate heat and add a few tablespoons oil and the tomato pulp.

3 When the tomatoes begin to soften, add the mozzarella cubes...

4 ...stirring with a wooden spoon until the cheese begins to melt.

5 Add the Romano cheese, stirring rapidly with a wooden spoon.

6 Flavor with salt and pepper and finish the sauce by adding a good amount of crumbled oregano.

7 Pour the pasta, boiled and drained while still *al dente*, in a warmed mixing bowl.

8 Immediately cover the pasta with the boiling sauce, mixing it quickly with two wooden forks.

9 Pour the sauced pasta into a baking dish and put it in a hot oven to brown.

Broccoli sauce

- Yield: 4 servings
- Time needed: ½ hour
- Difficulty: *

Ingredients: 1⅓ lbs. peeled, seeded, and juiced tomato pulp, 3 oz. raisins and pine nuts, 1 bunch of firm broccoli, 2 cloves garlic, 1 tbsp. chopped parsley, ½ cup oil, salt.

Soften the raisins in cold water. Boil the broccoli in salted water, drain it while it is still crisp-tender, and break it into pieces. Cook the garlic in oil until it turns brown. Add the chopped tomato pulp, season with salt, and cook for around 10 minutes. Then add the broccoli, the raisins, chopped, and the pine nuts. Cook for five minutes. Stir in the parsley just before you remove from heat.

Southern sauce

- Yield: 4 servings
- Time needed: ½ hour
- Difficulty: *

Ingredients: 14 oz. peeled, seeded, and juiced tomato pulp, 2 oz. large black olives, pitted, 1 tbsp. capers, 4 flat anchovy fillets, 2 well-drained, small sour pickles, 2 cloves garlic, 1 tbsp. chopped fresh basil or, 1 tsp. dried basil, pinch oregano, ½ cup oil, pepper, salt.

Chop the anchovy fillets together with the pickles. Sauté the garlic in the oil until it turns brown. Add a dash of pepper, the chopped anchovies and pickles, add the capers, and the olives, cut into slices. Add the tomato pulp, chopped. Season with salt and cook for about 15 minutes. Finish the sauce by adding basil and oregano.

Puttanesca sauce

- Yield: 4 servings
- Time needed: ½ hour
- Difficulty: *

Ingredients: 5 oz. large black olives, 3 tbsp. butter, 4 flat anchovy fillets, well drained, 2 cloves garlic, 1 tbsp. capers, a few tomatoes, oil.

Brown the garlic, sliced, with the anchovies chopped, in the butter and a few tablespoons of oil. Then add the olives, pitted and sliced, the capers chopped, and the tomatoes, cut in pieces. Cook for 15 minutes.

Meat Sauces

At one time meat sauces were "only for Sunday," especially for poor people. Sunday was the only day when people had enough time to prepare these sauces and were willing to disregard the extra expense of buying meat. No doubt the meat they used, far from choice, was simply a scrap piece taken from a large cut of meat. The meat was cooked with the sauce to give it flavor and then served as a main course. In fact, if you look at cookbooks from the last century, you'll find recipes for meat sauces that specify this way of cooking, that is braising the meat in the sauce, until all the flavors have blended together. Even today, in central and southern Italy, meat sauce is never made from ground beef, but from a large piece of meat that slowly comes apart as it cooks. However, most people today use ground beef because it's much easier to work with and because it presents a way of using up end pieces of large cuts.

There are two kinds of meat sauces: red meat sauce, which calls for tomatoes in the list of ingredients, and white meat sauce, which has no tomatoes in it. The meat sauces that are the best known and the most widely used are those made from beef cooked together with sausage and vegetables. Sometimes the beef is completely or partially replaced by veal or pork. The best cuts of beef to use are the ones that have both lean and fat, such as rump, chuck, and the leaner parts of the breast and flank.

Pork products, which are always used along with ground beef, make the sauce moister and gives it a stronger taste. Pork sausage, which must be very fresh and not too fatty is often used. *Prosciutto* which is both lean and fatty, can also be added. Different kinds of bacon may be used. The vegetables that are added are the basic ones used in cooking: onion, celery, carrots, and parsley. Some recipes call for mushrooms, garlic, basil, sage, bay leaf, etc. Meat sauces can be made just from pork or from pork products combined with vegetables. The leg is the best cut of pork to use, and if it's in one whole piece all the better. The Neopolitans cook whole pork leg very slowly over low heat until it is completely done and has formed a nice thick sauce. The pasta is tossed with the sauce and the meat is eaten as a main course. Lastly, meat sauce can also be made with chicken giblets, sometimes mixed together with a small amount of ground meat. The chicken parts used in Italy include the livers, cock's combs, wattles, unlaid eggs, and gizzards. Mushrooms go nicely with this kind of sauce, and appropriate seasonings include rosemary, sage, and bay leaf.

So far, we have only mentioned meat sauces that you can make with beef, veal, pork, and chicken giblets, but you can make also delicious sauces even using other kinds of meat and poultry. Duck cooked with a *soffritto* of ham and vegetables, lots of nutmeg, and tomatoes becomes a mouth-watering sauce used in tossing *pappardelle all'aretina*, a time-honored dish mentioned in Boccaccio. An equally famous variation of this famous recipe is made with hare. Even rabbit, the poor cousin of the hare, makes an excellent meat sauce if highly seasoned. In Abruzzi, lamb is cooked with herbs, mushrooms, and tomatoes to make a wonderful meat sauce that is tossed with guitar macaroni.

How to make meat sauces—Put the meat in a casserole dish or pot that is large enough to hold about a quart of liquid. Add the *soffritto* made with onion, garlic, and vegetables that have been sautéed in oil and butter. Put a flame-control device under the pot, and cook over moderate heat. To prevent the sauce from sticking to the bottom of the pan during the long cooking time, stir often with a wooden spoon. From time to time, you'll have to add liquids. A cup of good full-bodied red wine or even white wine (which goes well with a meat sauce containing mushrooms and pork) may be used. Instead of wine, you can add degreased meat stock or a broth made from bouillon cubes or canned broth. Even the liquid from a can of whole tomatoes can be added, if the recipe calls for tomatoes. To meat sauces made with pork or with pork and mushrooms, you can even add milk or cream during cooking. When you have a sauce made with chicken giblets and chicken livers, use sweet wines such as Marsala or Vin Santo.

Bolognese sauce

■ Yield: 4 servings
■ Time needed: 2 hours
■ Difficulty: *

Ingredients: 7 oz. ground beef, ¾ oz. dried boletus mushrooms, 1 oz. pork fat, 1½ tbsp. butter, 2 chicken livers, ½ onion, ½ carrot, 1 stalk celery, bunch parsley, 2 tbsp. tomato paste, ½ cup white wine, pinch sugar (optional), pinch nutmeg, pepper, salt.

Soak the mushrooms in a little warm water for 20 minutes. Chop the onion, carrot, and celery finely. Chop the parsley. Slice the pork fat and beat it with the blade of a knife that has been warmed in boiling water, until it is reduced to a paste (1). Put the pork fat, butter, and chopped vegetables in a saucepan (2). Cover and cook over moderate heat for about 10 minutes, stirring often.

Add the meat at this point (3) and cook it until it colors lightly. Add the wine (4) and the chopped parsley (5), and after a few minutes, add the tomato paste, diluted in 2 ladles of hot water (6). Season with salt, pepper, and nutmeg. Add the sugar. Add the mushrooms, cut into good-size pieces, (7) and the chicken livers, cut in pieces (8). Cover and bring to a boil. Lower the heat and cook the sauce for about an hour, stirring from time to time and keep the cover ajar to let the steam escape. At this point, add the water the mushrooms soaked in, strained (9), and, if you want, a little cream. Continue cooking, uncovered, until the sauce has thickened to your taste.

Use this meat sauce with any kind of pasta, especially *fettuccine* and egg lasagna, homemade if possible. This meat sauce is made in Emilia, capital of homemade pasta.

Some people make this sauce with two different meats, that is, with equal parts of red beef and pork; for extra flavor, tiny cubes of *prosciutto* are added. Instead of white wine you can use a full-bodied red wine. And instead of tomato paste you can use 10 ounces of ripe tomato purée.

1 Beat the pork fat to a paste with the blade of a knife dipped every so often in boiling water.

2 Sauté the vegetables in the pork fat and butter until they wilt, stirring continuously.

3 When the vegetables have softened and become translucent, add the ground meat...

4 ...and let it sauté until it colors lightly.

5 At this point, add the wine. When it has completely evaporated, add the parsley and mix well.

6 Add the tomato paste, diluted in two ladles of hot water...

7 ...add the mushrooms drained of their soaking water, chopped coarsely...

8 ..and lastly, add the chicken livers, carefully cleaned and cut into small pieces.

9 After about an hour of cooking, add the mushroom-soaking water, strained, to the meat sauce.

Bolognere sauce

Romagna sauce

■ Yield: 4 servings
■ Time needed: 1½ hours
■ Difficulty: *

Ingredients: 9 oz. beef, ground coarsely, 10 oz. whole tomatoes, (or 4 oz. tomato purée), 3 oz. chopped chicken giblets, 4 tbsp. butter, 2 oz. pork fat or bacon, 1 small onion, ½ stalk celery, ½ bay leaf, ½ cup robust red wine, pinch nutmeg, a little stock, pepper, salt.

Chop the lard or bacon together with the vegetables and sauté them in 1½ tablespoons butter. Add the ground meat and the bay leaf. Season with salt, pepper, and nutmeg and cook until the meat has browned nicely, stirring continually. Add the wine, let it evaporate completely over high heat, and then add the chopped whole tomatoes. Cook over moderate heat with the cover on for at least an hour. Add some stock if it needs it, and stir frequently, especially towards the end of the cooking. When the sauce is done, remove the bay leaf and add the chopped chicken parts, previously sautéed in the remaining butter. Do not cook the sauce too long or the chicken livers will harden.

This meat sauce goes well with any kind of pasta, especially egg pasta.

Sausage and mushrooms sauce

■ Yield: 4 servings
■ Time needed: 1 hour
■ Difficulty: *

Ingredients: 10 oz. whole tomatoes, 7 oz. sausages, 10 oz. *porcini* mushrooms or ordinary fresh mushrooms, 3 tbsp. butter, 1 onion, 1 carrot, 1 bay leaf, marjoram, a little stock, oil, pepper, salt.

Clean the mushrooms and slice them. Chop the onion and carrot finely and sauté in a saucepan with the butter and a few tablespoons of oil. Add the bay leaf, the sausage, thinly sliced, and the mushrooms, and brown nicely. Add the whole tomatoes, first forced through a sieve. Season with salt and pepper and mix all together. Add a few tablespoons stock and continue cooking over moderate heat. Cover the pot and cook until the sauce is reduced.

Before you remove the sauce from the heat add marjoram to taste and stir carefully.

This sauce can be used with *rigatoni, penne,* or *torciglioni.*

Finanziera sauce

■ Yield: 4 servings
■ Time needed: 1 hour
■ Difficulty: *

Ingredients: 4 chicken livers, 3 chicken gizzards, ½ carrot, ½ onion, ½ stalk celery, ¾ oz. softened dried boletus mushrooms, 3 tbsp. butter, ½ cup dry white wine, 2 ladles of stock, 1 tsp. flour, salt.

Trim the chicken livers, dry, and cut into pieces. Peel and wash the gizzards, then chop them finely.

Trim and wash the vegetables. Chop them finely and put into a saucepan together with 2 tablespoons butter. Let them cook over moderate heat until they wilt. Then add the gizzards. When they are nearly cooked, add the chicken livers and mushrooms, squeezed and chopped finely. Let everything brown nicely for a few minutes, mixing continuously with a wooden spoon. Pour in the wine and when it has half evaporated, add the hot broth. Add salt, cover, and bring to a boil. Then lower the flame and simmer the sauce for about 30 minutes, stirring often. When the sauce is done add the remaining butter and the flour mixed to a smooth paste. Stir continually, without bringing the sauce to a boil, until the sauce thickens.

This meat sauce is especially good on ravioli and *tortellini.*

Ground pork sauce

■ Yield: 4 servings
■ Time needed: 2 hours
■ Difficulty: *

Ingredients: 9 oz. ground pork, 2 oz. bacon, 1 10-oz. can whole tomatoes, 1 carrot, 1 onion, 1 tbsp. each parsley and basil chopped finely, red wine, oil, salt.

Cut the bacon up and chop the vegetables finely. Pour a little oil into a saucepan, add the bacon, and fry it lightly. Add the vegetables and the herbs and cook them until they wilt. Add the ground pork, and season to taste with salt and pepper. When the meat begins to brown, add a glass of wine and let it evaporate. Then add the tomatoes, first forced through a sieve. Cover and cook over very low heat, stirring from time to time. While the sauce is cooking, thin it out a bit by adding a little boiling water, or better yet, water and a bouillon cube. Toss this meat sauce with *maccheroni* or *penne.*

Meatball sauce

- Yield: 4 servings
- Time needed: 1½ hours
- Difficulty: *

Ingredients: 7 oz. ground beef, 3 tbsp. butter, a stale roll, 2 eggs, one hard-boiled and one raw, 1 cup heavy cream, a few tbsp. milk, bunch parsley, 2 tbsp. grated Parmesan cheese, 1 tsp. chopped pickled pepper, ¼ tsp. sage, 1 tbsp. oil, salt.

Soak the inside part of the roll in a little milk. Squeeze it, shred it, and mix it with the ground meat. Add the Parmesan cheese, the chopped parsley, the oil, a hard-boiled egg, chopped up, the pickled pepper, and a pinch of salt. Add the raw egg to bind the mixture (1) and combine all the ingredients well (2). Form the mixture into balls the size of large olives (3).

Melt the butter in a pan and add the sage. Cook briefly and add the meatballs. Let them brown for a few minutes, turning each one carefully (4). Lastly, add the cream and 2 tablespoons milk (5). Simmer the sauce for several minutes to thicken slightly.

Use this recipe with wheels (6) or other pasta like shells or *bucatini*.

1 In a bowl, mix the meat, bread, cheese, parsley, pepper, the hard-boiled egg, and the raw egg.

2 Combine all the ingredients until they are well blended using a wooden spoon.

3 Form the mixture into round balls the size of olives or a bit bigger.

4 Brown the meatballs in the butter and sage for a few minutes, turning them to brown evenly.

5 When the meatballs are nearly done, add the cream and milk. Cook briefly.

6 Toss this meatball sauce with wheels, shells, or *torciglioni*.

Fish and Seafood Sauces

Many superb fish sauces come from the southern coasts of Italy and the islands off the mainland. The exquisite taste of these sauces depends on the right choice of ingredients.

All kinds of fish and shellfish are used in these sauces, including octopus, squid, mussels, clams, hake, sardines, anchovies, and other small fish. The fish must be very fresh. You can make sure it is by examining the gills, which must be vivid red, and the eyes, which should be clear and not filmy. The fish should smell like the sea and not like ammonia. To be sure shellfish is fresh, see that the shells are closed tightly or just slightly opened. If a slightly opened shellfish is alive, it will close immediately if you touch it. In place of fresh fish or shellfish you can use canned or frozen seafood.

Preparation of seafood—Slit the belly of whole fish to remove the insides and wash the fish under running water. Scrape the scales off from head to tail with a little knife, and cut off the fins with a scissors. Squid must also be cleaned by removing the backbone, the viscera, and the ink sac. The eyes and mouth of octopus must be cut away. Shellfish has to be scraped well with a small, sharp knife or brushed hard before being put into a pan and left to open over medium heat.

Advice for making sauces—For all fish sauces and seafood sauces a *soffritto* is indispensable. It is always made with oil, garlic, or onion. Olive oil, is of course, the best oil to use. Vegetable oil is not recommended because it doesn't have enough flavor. Butter and margarine are not compatible with fish sauces. The garlic should be finely chopped or added whole after being flattened with the side of a knife. The onion should be cut into thin rings. Garlic and onion should be removed from the pot when they get dark. Fish and seafood sauces also call for herbs and spices. The herbs most often used are parsley, basil, oregano, mint, and thyme. The spices most often called for are white and black pepper, red pepper, paprika, and nutmeg. Herbs and spices are added to the sauce following the addition of the seafood if the dish requires a lot of cooking, and before if the dish is cooked quickly. When you thin out the sauce, use dry white wine or the broth produced from the opening of the clams or mussels, strained first. As far as adding salt is concerned, wait until the last moment to see if the sauce needs it. Generally speaking, you don't add salt because the juice from the clams and mussels is already salty enough. Tomatoes, if needed, are added after the wine. Shellfish needs very little cooking; squid, octopus, and other fish need longer cooking time.

Mussel sauce

■ Yield: 4 servings
■ Time needed: 1½ hours
■ Difficulty: *

Ingredients: 2½ lbs. mussels, 10 oz. whole tomatoes, 2 oz. black olives, 2 oz. green olives, 1 clove garlic, 2 tsp. anchovy paste, chopped parsley, a little fish stock, or bottled clam juice, olive oil, pepper, salt.

Brush the mussels well (1), wash them several times in running water, and place over high heat in a large pan with 2 tablespoons oil and one tablespoon parsley. Leave them over the heat until they open (2). Remove the mussels from the shells (3), place them in a bowl, and add a little of the broth that was produced when they were cooked.

Place a pan over moderate heat and add a few tablespoons oil and a clove of garlic. Add the anchovy paste, the olives, pitted and either whole or cut in pieces (4), salt, and pepper. Stir well and add the tomatoes, cut into pieces or forced through a sieve (5). Cook the sauce for about 10 minutes. Add about ¼ cup fish stock or clam juice and let the sauce reduce a little over medium heat. A few minutes before taking the sauce off the heat, add the mussels (6). Finish the sauce by adding a little chopped parsley.

This sauce can be tossed with bucatini or spaghetti.

1 Wash the mussels under running water and brush them with a hard-bristle brush to clean them.

2 Place them in a large pan with oil and parsley and heat them until they open.

3 As soon as they open, take the mussels out of the shells.

4 Heat some oil and garlic, then add the anchovy paste and the pitted olives, whole or in pieces.

5 Let the sauce brown for a few minutes, then add the cut up tomatoes.

6 Add the stock, reduce over medium heat, and then add the mussels.

7 Finish the sauce by adding the chopped parsley *just* before you take the sauce off the heat.

Fisherman's sauce

■ **Yield: 4 servings**
■ **Time needed: 1 hour 15 min.**
■ **Difficulty: ***

Ingredients: 1 lb. different varieties fish (preferably some shellfish) cleaned, sprig parsley, 1 large onion, 1 stalk celery, 1 clove garlic, 1 bay leaf, 1 lemon, 1 carrot, 1 cup canned tomato sauce, ½ cup dry white wine, oil, pepper, salt.

Prepare a *court-bouillon* with 2 cups water, the carrot, bay leaf, a little parsley, ½ onion, sliced, the celery, broken up, and a little salt. Add the lemon juice (1) and the wine. Bring to a boil and add the fish, gutted and washed (2). Cook the fish and then drain well (3) Force it through a sieve or grind in a blender or food processor. Chop the remaining onion together with the garlic and a little parsley. Put the mixture in a pot with some oil (4) and let it cook until the vegetables wilt. Add the tomato paste (5), thinned with a half ladle of strained fish stock (6). Reduce the sauce over moderate heat. Add the ground fish (7) and some freshly ground pepper (8). Toss this sauce with spaghetti and *fettuccine* (9-10).

1 Make a *court-bouillon* with water, vegetables, salt, lemon juice, and wine.

2 Bring to a boil, then add the various fish, gutted and cleaned.

3 Let the fish simmer over low heat, then drain by lifting the rack of the fish poacher.

4 Sauté a mixture of onion, garlic, and parsley in olive oil until the vegetables wilt.

5 As soon as the vegetable mixture begins to brown, add the tomato sauce.

6 As the sauce cooks, thin it with a half ladle of the fish stock, strained.

7 Boil the sauce until it reduces, then add the ground fish.

8 When the sauce has cooked, season it with freshly ground pepper.

9 Boil the pasta in salted water, drain it when it is *al dente*, and pour it directly into the sauce.

10 Let the pasta cook for a few minutes, tossing it often with two wooden forks.

Sardine sauce

■ Yield: 4 servings
■ Time needed: 1½ hour
■ Difficulty: *

Ingredients: ½ lb. very fresh sardines or fresh frozen smelts, 2 cloves garlic, 1 tbsp. raisins, some bread crumbs, 1 tbsp. chopped parsley, ½ cup olive oil, salt.

Soften the raisins in cold water. In the meantime, clean and gut the sardines. Pull back the head with two fingers in such a way as to release the skeleton and the viscera that cling to it (1). In a pan, fry the garlic, flattened with the side of a knife, in oil, add the fish (2) and the parsley (3), and let it cook over moderate heat. Add salt to taste. Add the raisins, previously drained (4), and a tablespoon bread crumbs (5). Let the sauce finish cooking, shaking the pan every now and then (6).

This sauce is excellent with *maccheroncelli*, spaghetti, and *bucatini*. Before serving the pasta let it rest in the serving bowl for a few minutes so that it will absorb the flavor of the sauce. You can also add some toasted fennel seeds and a tablespoon of pine nuts to this sauce.

1 Pull back the head of the sardine in such a way as to release the skeleton and the viscera.

2 Fry the flattened garlic in oil, adding the sardines after a few seconds.

3 Stir the sardines gently in the pan and toss in the chopped parsley.

4 When the sardines have absorbed the flavor of the oil, add the raisins, drained.

5 Sprinkle bread crumbs evenly over the fish.

6 Finish the cooking by gently shaking the pan without turning the fish again.

Squid sauce

- ■ **Yield: 4 servings**
- ■ **Time needed: 2 hours**
- ■ **Difficulty: ***

Ingredients: 1 lb. squid, 14 oz. whole tomatoes, 1 to 2 cloves garlic, 2 tbsp. chopped parsley, 1 tbsp. chopped onion, several hot peppers, ½ cup dry white wine, 3 tbsp. oil, salt.

Clean the squid, eliminating the backbone (1), the hornlike beak in the center of the tentacles, and the ink sac. Pull the tentacles from the body (2). Squeeze the body to remove entrails and scrape the skin from both parts with a knife. Slice the tentacles thinly and cut the body into thin rings (3). Pour the oil into a saucepan. Add half the parsley, the garlic, chopped up, and the onion (4). Sauté till translucent. Add the squid (5); stir. Then add the wine, the tomatoes, forced through a sieve, lots of red pepper (6), and some salt, if necessary. Continue cooking over moderate heat until the squid is very tender (if necessary, add a little water). Just before you take the sauce off the heat, add the rest of the parsley. You can use this sauce with spaghetti or with *bucatini*.

1 First, eliminate the backbone of the squid by pulling it through the body sac opening.

2 Pull the tentacles from the body sac and scrape the skin from both parts with a knife.

3 Cut up the tentacles and cut the body sac into thin rings.

4 Sauté the garlic and parsley in oil and add the onion, chopped finely.

5 After the onion browns, add the squid.

6 Add the red pepper or a healthy pinch of ground red pepper and, lastly, salt.

Vegetable Sauces

When we talk about vegetable sauces we have to distinguish between sauces made with vegetables and sauces like *pesto* that are made with herbs. Many of these recipes are traditional, originating centuries ago and refined by long experience and common sense. Have you ever thought what a marvelous meal-in-itself pasta with eggplant *alla Siciliana* is? Or pasta with broccoli? Such dishes present a perfect nutritional balance between the carbohydrates of the pasta, the vitamins of the vegetables, and the protein of the cheese that is sprinkled on top. The vegetables you choose must be fresh and of the best quality. We advise you to buy them during the peak of their season because they have the richest flavor and the highest vitamin content. If possible, you should buy organically grown vegetables, which are available at special stores in big cities. Some recipes call for the vegetables to be cooked by themselves, others together with the pasta.

For all the recipes you must trim the vegetables before cooking. Brush off clinging soil and remove any bad parts or tough stringy parts. Take off the outer leaves or the skin. Wash the vegetables under running water, let the water drip off, and, if necessary, dry.

Some vegetables require special preparation before you cook them. *Artichokes*, for example, have to be put into water acidulated with vinegar or lemon juice, after the removal of the tough outer leaves and the thorns. Then just before they are used they are dried and, to prevent them from turning brown, cut into slices before adding them to the sauce. *Chick-peas* and *lentils* have to be soaked for at least 12 hours, then rinsed and cooked in liquid until tender. *Pinto beans* have to be soaked like chick-peas if they are dry; if they are fresh, they have to be shelled and cooked in lots of liquid. *Fava beans* are handled like other beans: they have to be cooked in lots of water and then they are nearly always forced through a sieve. *Fresh peas* that are to be added to a sauce are first cooked in just a tiny amount of water along with a bit of onion, a piece of bouillon cube, and a pinch of sugar, which makes them tastier and more delicate. *Wild mushrooms* should never be washed, because they too readily absorb liquid. Rather, scrape off dirt with a knife, then wipe with a damp cloth and rub with half a lemon. Mushroom sauce can also be made with ordinary cultivated mushrooms, washed quickly under running water. Dried mushrooms have to be soaked in warm water for at least 20 minutes, then drained and squeezed delicately. The water used for soaking the mushrooms is never thrown away, but left to settle, strained through a piece of cheesecloth and used in the sauce to enrich the flavor. *Eggplant* is cut into thick slices, spread out on a plate, and sprinkled with salt so that its bitter liquid will be exuded. It is then covered with another plate that has a weight put on it. Before you fry the eggplant slices rinse them in water to remove the salt and then dry them very carefully with a clean cloth or with paper towels. *Peppers* have to be charred over a gas flame or under a hot broiler in order to remove the skin easily. (The skin is unpleasant to eat and hard to digest.) Cut the peppers in half, and remove the white ribs, the seeds, and the core before adding them to the sauce.

When we talk about vegetable sauces, we can't forget the ones that are made with *herbs*. The queen of herb sauces is without a shadow of doubt, *pesto alla genovese*. According to the original recipe, the basil, the main ingredient, must be a special variety that has unusually small leaves. It must have a strong aroma, and therefore it must be grown in Liguria, where the soil and climate conditions are just right. If we continue by the book, the basil should be pounded in a marble mortar until it is bright green and creamy. Nowadays it's much faster to use a blender or a food processor.

Excellent sauces can be made from other fresh herbs, such as sage, rosemary, oregano, thyme, mint, and marjoram. These herbs can be mixed together or added to capers, black olives, and pine nuts. And let's not forget parsley, which is added to all herb sauces. The same herbs, when dried, can make quick fragrant sauces if combined well with other ingredients and used in the right quantity. Lastly, let's include *capers*, which are not an herb, but the buds of the plant of the same name. To make a good sauce with capers, shop around for the ones that are preserved in salt (try a gourmet food shop), because they are much tastier than brine-packed capers. Salt-packed capers may be soaked in cold water and rinsed well, thus removing the salt entirely. Brine-packed capers can be used but the vinegary taste is impossible to wash out.

Vegetable sauce

- ■ **Yield: 4 servings**
- ■ **Time needed: 1½ hours**
- ■ **Difficulty: ***

Ingredients: 1 onion, 3 zucchini, 1 small eggplant, 5 oz. bacon, 5 tbsp. butter, 1 lb. ripe tomatoes, bunch basil, 2 cloves garlic, olive oil, pepper, salt.

Peel and chop the onion finely. After first removing the stem, peel the eggplant and cut it into cubes. Cut the zucchini into cubes too (1). Dice the bacon. Peel the tomatoes after scalding them first in boiling water (2).

Now take a saucepan and add the butter, 3 tablespoons oil, the bacon, and the chopped onion (3). Let the mixture sauté gently, then add a clove of garlic. When the mixture turns brown, add the zucchini and the eggplant (4). Season with salt and pepper and cook until the vegetables are soft and all the flavors have blended together nicely. Add the tomatoes, crushed with a fork (5). Cook briefly. Before removing the vegetable sauce from the heat, sprinkle it with a mixture of chopped basil and garlic (6).

1 Peel and cut the eggplant into cubes; cut the zucchini into cubes too.

2 Scald the tomatoes a few seconds in boiling water and peel them: the skin will come off easily.

3 Sauté the bacon in oil and butter, then add the chopped onion.

4 As soon as the onion wilts and browns lightly, add the eggplant and the zucchini.

5 When the vegetables have softened, add the crushed tomatoes.

6 Before you remove the sauce from the heat, sprinkle chopped basil and garlic over the sauce.

Vegetable sauce

Bean sauce

■ **Yield: 4 servings**
■ **Time needed: 3 hours**
■ **Difficulty: ***

Ingredients: 1 lb. fresh pinto beans, shelled or ⅓ lb. dried pinto beans, previously cooked, 3 oz. bacon, 1 carrot, 1 onion, 1 stalk celery, 1 tbsp. chopped parsley, 1 clove garlic, 1 beef bouillon cube; 1 lb. ripe tomatoes (or 1 can 10-oz. tomatoes), oil, pepper, salt.

Lay out all the vegetables on the counter (1).

Finely chop the bacon with the carrot, celery, garlic, and onion (2). Put the mixture in a large saucepan, with a few tablespoons oil (3). Let the vegetables wilt, then add the beans (4) and, when the beans have absorbed flavor from the vegetables, add the tomatoes, peeled, seeded, and crushed tomatoes (5) or substitute whole canned tomatoes with their juice.

After a few minutes add a cup of boiling water with a bouillon cube dissolved in it (6). Add salt and pepper and simmer, covered, over low heat, stirring occasionally. If too much water evaporates, add more boiling water or stock. Let the sauce simmer until cooked. Before removing from heat, add parsley.

Use this bean sauce with ribbed *ditaloni*. Before you add the sauce, add a big pat of butter to the pasta; finish the dish with Parmesan.

1 Lay out all the vegetables for the sauce: fresh beans and various aromatic vegetables.

2 Chop the bacon finely together with the carrot, garlic, celery, and onion.

3 In a saucepan, heat a few tablespoons oil and then add the mixture of chopped vegetables.

4 Allow the vegetables to wilt, stirring continually, then add the beans.

5 When the beans have absorbed the flavor of the vegetables, add the crushed tomatoes...

6 ...and a cup of stock made from diluting a bouillon cube in hot water.

Bean sauce

Puréed bean sauce

■ Yield: 4 servings
■ Time needed: 1½ hours
■ Difficulty: *

Ingredients: 10 oz. fresh shelled pinto beans or ⅓ lb. dried pinto beans previously cooked, 1 small white onion, 2 carrots, 1 bay leaf, 2 stalks celery, 3 oz. smoked bacon, 3 tbsp. butter, 2 tbsp. olive oil, 3 tbsp. grated Parmesan cheese, pepper, salt.

If using fresh beans boil them in a large amount of water with the onion and bay leaf. Add salt towards the end of the cooking. Trim the carrots and celery and cut them into cubes. Dice the bacon in oil in a saucepan and brown it. Add the carrot and celery to the bacon and brown over low heat.

When the beans are cooked, drain them while still very hot and put them through a food mill or purée in a blender or food processor. Add this purée to the browned vegetables along with a few tablespoons of the water the beans cooked in if necessary. Add the butter, in pieces, and flavor the sauce with the cheese and a lot of freshly ground pepper. Use this sauce with spaghetti, *trenette,* and *fettuccine.*

Fava bean sauce

■ Yield: 4 servings
■ Time needed: 1 hour
■ Dificulty: *

Ingredients: 10 oz. cooked fava beans, 2 oz. *prosciutto,* ½ onion, a little stock, olive oil, pepper, salt.

Over moderate heat sauté the chopped onion in a few tablespoons oil until it turns deep yellow. Add the beans, moisten them with a little stock, and heat them, adding more stock if necessary. Season with salt and pepper. Just before removing the beans from the heat, add the ham, cut in strips and stir.

This sauce can be used with *fettuccine, bavette,* and *trenette.* Add butter and grated Parmesan cheese at the last minute.

Artichoke sauce

■ Yield: 4 servings
■ Time needed: 45 min.
■ Difficulty: *

Ingredients: 4 artichokes, 6 tbsp. butter, 3 tbsp. cream, 2 tbsp. grated Parmesan cheese, 1 tbsp. finely chopped parsley, a bit of meat stock, freshly ground pepper, salt.

Trim the artichokes, removing the tough outer leaves, the thorns, and the fuzzy chokes. Wash them, dry them, and cut into thin slices. Cook the artichoke slices in a saucepan over low heat with half the butter. Add a few tablespoons stock a little at a time. Season with salt and freshly ground pepper.

Just before you remove the sauce from the heat, add the rest of the butter, cut up in pieces, the Parmesan cheese, the cream, and the parsley. Stir well. This is a dry sauce. If it seems too dry to you, add more cream to taste.

You can use this sauce with *maccheroni, penne,* and *rigatoni.*

Cacciatora sauce

■ Yield: 4 servings
■ Time needed: 1 hour
■ Difficulty: *

Ingredients: 1 slice bacon ½-inch thick, 1 small onion, 1 stalk celery, 1 clove garlic, 1 bay leaf, 1 2½ oz. slice *prosciutto,* 1½ oz. dried boletus mushrooms, 2 tbsp. brandy, ½ cup heavy cream, 5 tbsp. oil, pepper, salt.

Wash the dried mushrooms. Put them in a bowl, cover with warm water, and let them soak for about a half hour.

As soon as the vegetable mixture browns, add the bacon, cut into cubes, and let it brown over rather high heat, stirring continuously. Season with salt and pepper. Pour in the brandy and let it evaporate. Then add the prosciutto, cut into tiny cubes, the bay leaf, and the mushrooms, drained, squeezed and cut up coarsely. (Reserve the water the mushrooms soaked in. Let it settle, strain it, and add it to the sauce about halfway through the cooking time.)

Stir again and let the sauce simmer over low heat for about 15 minutes. Then add the cream. Stir well and simmer 10 minutes longer to reduce. Before you use the sauce, remove the bay leaf.

This sauce is good with small macaroni, spaghetti, *bucatini, fettuccine,* and *fusilli.* Instead of using dried mushrooms, you can make this sauce with fresh *porcini* mushrooms or cultivated mushrooms. In this case, cook the sauce longer to let the water in the mushrooms evaporate and just before you take the sauce off the heat, add a tablespoon finely chopped parsley and garlic.

Syracuse sauce

- **Yield: 4 servings**
- **Time needed: 1 hour**
- **Difficulty: ***

Ingredients: 2½ lb. whole plum tomatoes, 1 oz. pitted black olives, 12 flat anchovy fillets, well drained, 3 cloves garlic, peeled and left whole, 1 large eggplant, 1 green pepper, 1 tbsp. capers, bunch parsley, ½ cup olive oil, pepper, salt.

Pit the olives using an olive pitter (1) or a knife. Char the pepper over a gas flame (2), turning it as you do it; peel.

Pour the oil into a saucepan, brown the cloves of garlic, and then remove them. Add the eggplant, cut in cubes, and the tomatoes, crushed (3), and boil for about 10 minutes, stirring continuously. Then add the pepper, skinned and cut in pieces (4), the capers, the olives, the anchovies, cut in pieces, the chopped parsley, salt, and pepper. Cook for a few minutes. This sauce is good with *fusilli* or spaghetti, *bucatini, linguine* or *torciglioni*.

1 Get all the ingredients ready. Pit the olives with the olive pitter or a knife.

2 Char the green pepper over a gas flame to make removing the thin outer skin easier.

3 Add the eggplant, cut in pieces, and the crushed whole tomatoes to the sautéed mixture.

4 Add the peppers, peeled and cut up, and then add the rest of the ingredients.

Syracuse sauce

Pesto

■ **Yield: 4 servings**
■ **Time needed: 1 hour**
■ **Difficulty: ***

Ingredients: A big handful of very fresh basil leaves (about 1½ cups), 3-4 cloves garlic, 3 oz. (about ¾ cup) grated strong Romano cheese, 1 tbsp. pine nuts, ⅓-½ cup olive oil, pepper, salt.

Wash the basil leaves gently. Let the water drain off, then put the leaves in a mortar (1), made of marble if possible. Add a pinch of salt (which helps the basil keep its nice green color), the whole cloves of garlic, and the pine nuts (2). Begin to pound the mixture with a pestle for a few seconds (3). Thin out the pesto with a bit of oil, poured in very very slowly (4). To obtain a creamy texture, push the pestle down hard against the bottom and sides of the mortar. Add the cheese (5). Continue adding the oil, a little bit at a time (6). Add a dash of pepper. Of course, the mortar and pestle today is often replaced by the blender which also works well.

Many people add a bit of marjoram and use half Romano and half Parmesan cheese.

This is an ideal source for *trenette* and spaghetti.

1 Wash the basil and drain it well; remove the leaves and put them in a mortar.

2 Add a pinch of salt to keep the basil green, 3 or 4 cloves of garlic, and the pine nuts.

3 Pound all the ingredients in the mortar with the pestle...

4 ...add a little olive oil to thin out the sauce, pouring it in little by little.

5 Pound the mixture until it is creamy and smooth, then add the grated Romano cheese.

6 Add more oil until the sauce has the right consistency, blending well, and season with pepper.

Uncooked pepper sauce

■ **Yield: 4 servings**
■ **Time needed: ½ hour**
■ **Difficulty: ***

Ingredients: 3 large ripe tomatoes, 1 red pepper, 1 yellow or green pepper, bunch basil, 1 tbsp. mustard, a few drops of Worcestershire sauce, 6 tbsp. olive oil, 1 lemon, salt.

Scald the tomatoes in boiling water for a second. Peel them (1), halve them, remove the seeds, and cut them into small pieces or strips (2). Char the peppers over a gas flame and rub them with a cloth to remove the thin outer skin. Remove the seeds and whitish ribs (3) and cut the peppers into small cubes (4). Pour the lemon juice in a cup and beat together with pinch of salt (5). Add the oil (6), the mustard, and the Worcestershire sauce (7). Use this sauce with the spaghetti.

To prepare the pasta, drain while still *al dente*, rinse under cold running water, and pour in a bowl. Add the peppers (8), add the tomatoes (9), and then add the sauce you prepared (10). Season with salt, sprinkle with chopped basil. Let stand for an hour.

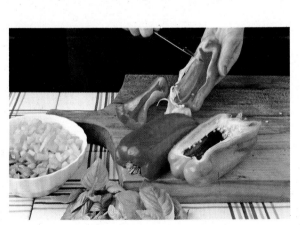

1 Scald the tomatoes in boiling water for a second so that you'll be able to peel them easily.

2 Remove the seeds and cut the tomatoes in pieces or in strips.

3 Carefully clean the inside of the peppers, removing the seeds and whitish ribs.

4 Cut the peppers into strips and the cut the strips into dice.

5 Squeeze the lemon, pour the juice in a cup, add salt, and beat with a fork.

6 Add 6 tablespoons olive oil to the lemon juice, beating continually...

7 ...add a tablespoon mustard and a few drops of Worcestershire sauce.

8 Boil the pasta until it is *al dente*. Drain it and run cold water over it. Add the peppers to it.

9 Add the tomatoes, cut up in pieces, and stir well...

10 ...add the sauce and toss the pasta well with the sauce so that the flavors blend nicely.

Cream Sauces

What do we really mean by the term "cream sauces." The term refers to all the sauces that are more or less white because they are made with cream. Butter, milk, cheese and eggs also have an important role in these sauces. On the other hand, with a few exceptions, herbs are prohibited. Likewise oil is banished from these sauces, replaced by butter. Cream sauces sometimes contain unusual ingredients, such as strong liquors or fruits, and spices such as pepper, curry mixtures, and nutmeg are sometimes used to make the flavor stronger, at times even a little sweet. Some cream sauces even require pork, especially the special sauces that grew out of local traditions. Rigid gourmets think that adding milk or cream is downright taboo. They are quick to state that these ingredients were never included in the old recipes passed down from one generation to another. But today they are used a great deal—and with good reason. Besides being natural delicious foods, milk and cream mprovide a dish of pasta with precious nutritional substances.

The freshness and high quality of the ingredients can be assured if you know what to look for. Most cheeses can be used. Fresh cheeses, like mozzarella, *ricotta* and cream cheese have to be chosen carefully and stored properly. Remember, for example, that *ricotta* cheese keeps for only about a week in the refrigerator. Aged cheeses like *gorgonzola* and *taleggio* should be good brands. You should buy a whole piece of Parmesan rather than Parmesan that's already been grated. It's important to protect cheeses like *fontina* and Swiss cheese from air by wrapping them in cellophane. This should keep them from drying out. In the country, people say that a fresh egg is a real find and those of us who live in cities know just how true this is. In fact, in all phases of cooking fresh eggs are of utmost importance, and this is even more true

if the eggs are used in a sauce. To check the freshness of an egg, put it up to a light bulb and look at it. The light should shine evenly through the egg, without any shaded areas, and clearly showing the form of the egg inside the shell. Milk, which is repeatedly used in cream sauces (even if it's rarely the main ingredient), must be very fresh and it must be whole milk. The cream that is used in sauces must also be very fresh, without any trace of spoilage.

To have these sauces come out well—and they are actually very easy to make—the first rule is, as we have said, to make sure the ingredients are fresh and pure. The second rule is to use the ingredients correctly. Warm milk before using it to thin out cheese over heat or in a double-boiler; otherwise the cheese will not melt easily. Eggs that are used in a sauce—for example, in making *"carbonara,"* —have to be beaten in a bowl before being added to the pasta, and they should be at room temperature. Cream should be added to sauces only at the last minute, to avoid thickening; otherwise it will not blend with all the other ingredients. Soft and semi-soft cheeses should always be cut into pieces before being added to a sauce; hard cheeses should be shredded or grated. This way the cheese can be melted over very low heat or, even better, in a double-boiler. Butter should nearly always be warmed with herbs such as sage and marjoram. All the cream sauces, since they are very delicate, are excellent with green pasta like spinach *tagliatelle* and *paglia e fieno* (hay and straw) and with pasta filled with vegetables, such as ravioli and *tortelloni*.

Sometimes instead of using a cream sauce, pasta is tossed with bechamel sauce seasoned with nutmeg and pepper and often enriched with eggs and cheese. The resulting sauce will be lighter because it contains less fat.

Curry sauce

- **Yield: 4 servings**
- **Time needed: 1 hour**
- **Difficulty: ***

Ingredients: 4 oz. sliced onion, 2 tbsp. butter, 3 tbsp. flour, 1 tbsp. spicy ("Madras") curry powder, 1 lemon, ½ bay leaf, a mixture of ¼ cup chopped parsley and ¼ cup diced celery, pinch thyme, a bit of mace or grated nutmeg, 2 cups stock, ½ cup heavy cream, salt.

Sauté the onion in butter until it turns pale yellow (1) and immediately add the mixture of chopped parsley and celery, thyme, bay leaf, and mace (2). Sprinkle in the flour (3), stir, and add the curry (4). Blend all ingredients well. Cook slowly for several minutes. Then add the stock (5). Stir and bring to a boil. Add salt. Cook for about 40 minutes, then strain through a cheesecloth-lined sieve (6). Return sauce to the heat, bring to a simmer again, and add the cream (7) and a few drops of lemon juice (8).

This sauce is good with ribbed pasta (like ribbed macaroni) as well as with spaghetti, *vermicelli, linguine, bucatini* and *tagliatelle*. If you want to add an "exotic" touch add half a banana, forced through a sieve, to the finished sauce. Garnish the dish with slices of bananas sautéed in butter.

1 Slice the onions and sauté them until golden.

2 Add the chopped parsley and celery, the thyme, bay leaf, and mace.

3 Sprinkle a little flour over the chopped vegetables; mix well...

4 ...add a tablespoon spicy curry powder, to give the sauce a nice curry flavor.

5 Let all the ingredients cook briefly and then add the stock, stirring continuously.

6 After the sauce has cooked for about 40 minutes, put it through a sieve lined with cheesecloth.

7 Return the sauce to the heat and bring it to a simmer, add the cream...

8 ...and lastly, add a few drops of lemon juice.

Mascarpone sauce

■ **Yield: 4 servings**
■ **Time needed: ½ hour**
■ **Difficulty: ***

Ingredients: 3-4 oz. *mascarpone* or ordinary American cream cheese, 7 tbsp. butter, 1 cup heavy cream; 2 egg yolks, 4 oz. Swiss cheese, pepper, salt.

Place a large pan over moderate heat and melt the butter in it. Add the cream (1) and let it reduce for a few minutes. Then add the Swiss cheese, shredded (2), and stir over moderate heat until the cheese melts (3).

In a bowl, soften the *mascarpone* or cream cheese with a wooden spoon. Add the egg yolks one at a time (4) and continue to beat until the mixture is smooth and creamy (5). Add salt and pepper. Now the sauce is ready to toss with macaroni.

Pour 1 pound ribbed macaroni, boiled and drained when *al dente,* into the pan (6). Toss with the cheese sauce for a few minutes. Remove from the heat, add the *mascarpone* mixture, and mix vigorously. Serve immediately while the cheese is still creamy and soft.

1 Melt the butter in a large pan, pour in the cream, and let it reduce.

2 Add the shredded Swiss cheese ...

3 ...stir, and let the cheese melt slowly over moderate heat.

4 In a bowl, soften the *mascarpone* with a wooden spoon and add the yolks one at a time.

5 Combine well and beat until smooth and creamy.

6 Pour the macaroni, drained when *al dente*, into the pan and mix with the sauce.

Mascarpone sauce

Vodka sauce

- **Yield: 4 servings**
- **Time needed: ½ hour**
- **Difficulty: ***

Ingredients: 3 tbsp. butter, 1½ oz. (about ⅓ cup) grated Parmesan cheese, 3 tbsp. tomato paste, 1 hot red pepper, 1 tbsp. Vodka, 1 tsp. brandy, 1 cup heavy cream.

Melt the butter in a saucepan and add the red pepper and the tomato paste, diluted in hot water (1). Cook for a few minutes. Pour in the cream (2). As soon as the sauce comes to a boil, add the vodka and the brandy. Remove the red pepper. Add the cheese to the sauce (3). Stir continuously with a wooden spoon until the sauce thickens. Toss this sauce with *penne, rigatoni,* or *torciglioni* (4). Remember cook the pasta in lots of salted water and drain it when it is still *al dente*. Carefully let all the water drain off and pour it right into the pan containing the sauce. Stir quickly so that the pasta "takes in" all the sauce, and bring to the table right away.

1 Pour the tomato paste diluted in a little hot water, into the saucepan.

2 Let the sauce simmer for a few minutes, then pour in the cream, stirring continuously.

3 Add the grated Parmesan cheese to the sauce, stirring until it blends in well with the sauce.

4 Pour the pasta, cooked *al dente*, into the pan with the sauce, and combine all the ingredients well.

Carbonara

■ **Yield: 4 servings**
■ **Time needed: ½ hour**
■ **Difficulty: ***

Ingredients: 4 oz. salt pork or smoked bacon, 1½ oz. (about ⅓ cup) grated Parmesan cheese, 4 eggs, a few tbsp. cream (optional), olive oil, pepper, salt.

Heat the oil in a saucepan, add the salt pork cut in small pieces, and cook until golden brown (1). Beat the eggs just enough to mix the yolks and whites well (2). (You may also use the yolks alone.) Add the grated cheese, a pinch of salt, and pepper, and continue stirring. Add a few tablespoons cream, if you want to. After the pasta is boiled and drained, pour it into a large bowl. Add the salt pork (3) and the beaten eggs and cheese and mix everything together very quickly (4). Bring right away to the table good and hot.

This sauce is especially good with spaghetti or *bucatini*.

1 Brown the salt pork, cut into small pieces, in a saucepan in a little oil.

2 Place the whole eggs or egg yolks if you want, in a bowl and beat with a whisk.

3 Pour the boiled pasta into a bowl, toss with the browned salt pork...

4 ...pour in the beaten eggs and cheese, mix everything together and serve at once.

Carbonara

Rice, Risotti and Rice Desserts

Rice Appetizers

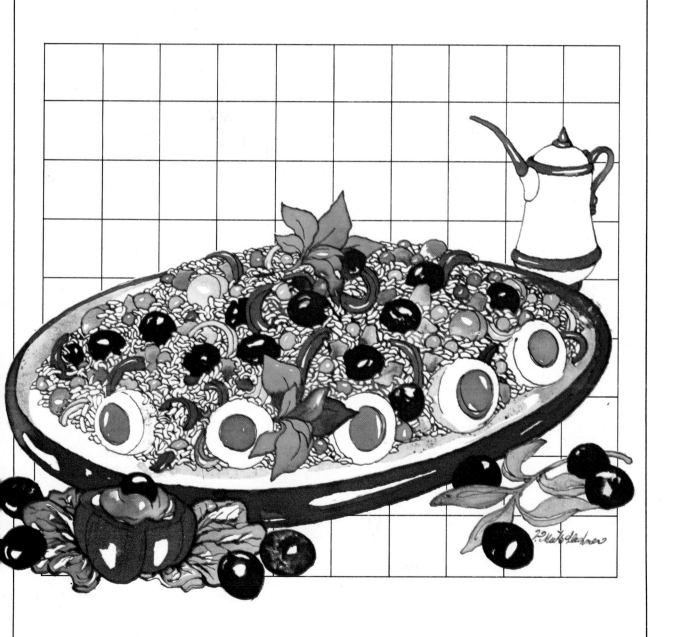

After wheat, rice is the most widely consumed cereal in the world. Its use as food on the Asian continent goes back to prehistoric times, when wild rice was gathered; later, but still thousands of years before Christ, the cultivation of rice spread from India to all of southwest Asia and beyond, where rice became the basic ingredient of many people's diets. This cereal was introduced to Europe by the Arabs and arrived at first as an ingredient of the so-called *"pane di mistura'* (a bread made from a combination of different flours derived from various cereals) or for use in aristocratic desserts (in fact, for a long time rice was considered a luxury good comparable to the spices coming from the Orient). Finally, in the 15th century (when the Sforza family was in power), rice cultivation began in Italy too, spreading throughout the water-rich northern regions, and more specifically in the Novara, Pavia, Vercelli, and Lomellina areas. Today, Italy is the leading producer of rice in Europe, but the quantity of rice consumed in the country is scandalously low compared to the consumption of pasta, despite the fact that rice is an excellent food—healthful, easily digested, and as nutritious as pasta or bread. Rice is, in fact, rich in carbohydrates and mineral salts, especially phosphorous, and it is almost totally without fats and cellulose, which is what accounts for its digestibility. It also contains proteins rich in indispensable elements, the so-called essential amino acids. Four ounces of rice have about 400 calories, about the same as pasta, though naturally the amount of calories increases if the rice is accompanied by substantial sauces or ingredients rich in fats.

Let us consider rice appetizers first, appetizing and nourishing enough in themselves to fully satisfy even the hungriest person. There are a thousand ways of using rice in appetizers, including rice salads, small, tasty croquettes, and rich, savory fillings. In all these preparations the imagination will suggest the right combination of a wide assortment of ingredients to create dishes that may be traditional or original, familiar or unusual, but always good.

Isabella salad

Rice salads & appetizers

Rice salads — —Few dishes are as practical, economical and easy to prepare as rice salads. Even though rice salads are usually served as savory and fresh appetizers, they can also be nourishing whole meals in themselves because they are so rich in nutritious ingredients that they satisfy even the heartiest appetites.

A rice salad should be made with hard-grained rice with a low starch content, whose grains will not stick together during cooking; this type of rice has long, somewhat transparent grains and in Italy comes in fine and very fine grades. Converted rice, which has been steamed under pressure so that it will hold its shape after cooking and maintain a good part of its original iron and vitamin B content, is also very suitable for rice salads. Converted rice is ivory-yellow in color, costs a bit more than other types of rice, but never becomes sticky or overdone, and yields 20% more cooked rice by volume than normal rice.

The simplest and most common cooking method is to boil the rice in water. The rice is poured into plenty of boiling salted water, stirred with a wooden spoon, and cooked in an uncovered pan. The cooking time depends on the type of rice, but is usually about 15 minutes. It should be kept in mind that rice to be used in a salad should never be overcooked and soft; and after cooking it should be poured into a strainer and briefly rinsed under cold water.

The ingredients added to rice to make a salad usually consist of raw vegetables: sweet peppers, tomatoes, green beans, mushrooms, and young zucchini, in summer; artichokes, carrots, celery, and in winter, lettuce. Often cheeses (mozzarella, Swiss cheese, Parmesan), hard-boiled eggs, tuna fish, ham and hot dogs are added as well. To make a really complete dish containing all the nutritious components, pieces of cooked chicken, pork, or boned fish can be included. Then there are the more unusual salads which include nuts or exotic fruits such as walnuts, almonds, pine nuts, avocados, pineapple, kiwi, etc., and the more expensive ones with ingredients such as smoked salmon, caviar, and wild mushrooms. Finally, for an added pleasantly sharp flavor, anchovies, mustard, and pickled vegetables are often included. A rice salad should be seasoned with the dressing that best suits its ingredients: from a simple vinaigrette (oil, lemon juice, salt, and pepper) to a mayonnaise flavored with mustard and Brandy; from an Aurora sauce (a pink combination of white sauce and tomato sauce) to sauces made with cream and yogurt, which are clearly Asian in origin and are often made spicy by adding curry. These salads should be served in glass or crystal bowls through which can be seen the colors of the different ingredients, making the table inviting and cheerful.

Other cold rice appetizers — Aside from salads, boiled rice can be used to make other tasty cold appetizers such as rice-and-shrimp cocktails served in individual cups, an inviting gelatin aspic, or a refined cold dish garnished with truffles—all especially suited to an elegant meal. For simpler appetizers one can make little pastry boats filled with a tuna and rice salad or omelets made with rice, cheese, and vegetables, served cold and sliced, or tomatoes stuffed with rice and other ingredients. Finally there are all kinds of raw vegetables that can be stuffed with rice; though very good when hot, these dishes are often even better when served at room temperature.

Hot appetizers with rice — Starting with stuffed vegetables like sweet peppers, tomatoes, and eggplant, which make wonderful containers for rice combined with other ingredients, there are numerous recipes for hot rice appetizers that will make your mouth water: small rice custards with Swiss cheese and truffles hot from the oven; a delicate rice and milk soufflé; little balls or croquettes made with leftover *risotto* rolled in bread crumbs and deep-fried; disks of leftover *risotto* enclosing a piece of *fontina* cheese and then deep-fried; and crêpes stuffed with rice. A special favorite of children are the marvelous little fritters made with rice cooked in milk, flour, egg yolks, and stiffly beaten egg whites. And finally we are reminded of those delicious little fried croquettes that are called *supplí* in Rome and *arancini* in Sicily, a name given them because of their resemblance to oranges. The *supplí* are stuffed with a variety of fillings—chicken giblets or veal liver and sweetbreads; fillings made of Parmesan, *prosciutto,* eggs, and parsley; a Roman filling of a meat-flavored tomato sauce and mozzarella; or a filling of mozzarella and ham or sausage rolled in flour and fried.

Savory rice salad

- **Yield: 4 servings**
- **Time needed: ½ hour**
- **Difficulty: ***

Ingredients: 1 cup rice, 1 can tuna fish in oil, 1 slice ham weighing about 3½ oz., ¼ lb. hot dogs, sweet pickles, 3 tbsp. stuffed olives, sliced roasted sweet red pepper, 3½ oz. Swiss cheese, fresh or frozen peas, 1 lemon, oil, salt, pepper.

Cook the rice in boiling salted water, drain it when grains are still firm, and rinse it under cold running water (1). Drain it well and pour it onto a dish towel, spreading it out well. Pour the rice into a bowl and stir it with a fork to separate the grains (2).

Now prepare all the other ingredients. Boil the peas and drain them. Dice the ham and Swiss cheese. Cut the hog dogs, simmered in water until plump, into rounds and flake the tuna into small pieces. Thinly slice the pickles, the stuffed olives, and the red pepper (3).

Prepare a dressing by mixing a pinch of salt and pepper with some lemon juice in a small bowl (4); slowly add oil in a thin stream (5), beating the mixture with a fork to blend the ingredients.

Now add the pickles, the olives, the diced ham (6), the cooked peas (7), and all the other ingredients to the rice. Stir and add the prepared dressing (8) to the salad. Continue stirring gently until the salad is well mixed (9) and keep in a cool place until ready to serve.

If you wish, you can decorate the salad with slices of firm red tomato. For a more amusing presentation serve the rice salad in six medium-ripe tomatoes. Prepare the tomatoes in the following manner: after having removed the tops of the tomatoes, spoon out their pulp, sprinkle with salt and pepper, and let drain upside-down for about 20 minutes. Fill them to the brim with the rice salad and cover with the tops removed previously. Arrange the tomatoes on a serving dish and decorate with sprigs of parsley.

1 Boil the rice, drain it while still firm, and rinse under cold water to stop it from cooking further.

2 Pour the rice into a bowl and stir with a fork to separate the grains.

3 Dice the ham and the Swiss cheese, slice the hot dogs, olives, and the roasted pepper.

4 Prepare a dressing by combining salt, pepper, and lemon juice in a small bowl...

5 ...and adding the oil in a thin stream while beating the mixture with a fork to blend the ingredients.

6 Now add the pickles, peppers, sliced olives, diced ham...

7 ...the cooked peas, and all the other ingredients, and stir well.

8 Pour the dressing over the rice...

9 ...and stir again gently with two forks until all the ingredients are well coated.

Rice salad contadina

■ **Yield:** 4 servings
■ **Time needed:** 1 and ½ hours
■ **Difficulty:** *

Ingredients: 4 large white onions, 1 cup rice, ⅓ cup shelled peas, ⅓ cup green beans, 2 ripe tomatoes, 1 celery heart, ¼ lb. fresh mushrooms, 2 oz. salami, 6 oz. cooked white chicken meat, 1 lemon, curly parsley, olive oil, pepper, salt.

Boil the whole onions in lightly salted water. Drain them when tender but still in one piece, then let cool. Cut a slice off the top (1) and remove the interior sections with a small knife (2). Boil the rice, drain it while still firm, and spread it on a plate to cool (3). Cook the peas and green beans in boiling water, drain, and let cool. Chop the green beans, the celery, the salami and the chicken (4). Peel the tomatoes and slice them. Clean the mushrooms, slice them, and sauté them in the olive oil. Combine all the ingredients except the mushrooms in a large bowl and dress with olive oil, lemon juice, salt, and pepper (5). Fill the onions with the rice mixture (6). Arrange onions on a plate and decorate with the mushrooms and parsley.

1 After having boiled the onions whole, cut a slice off the tops.

2 Remove the interiors with a pointed knife so that you have four small cups.

3 Boil the rice, drain it while still quite firm, and spread it out on a plate to cool.

4 Chop the boiled beans, the celery, the salami, and the cooked chicken meat.

5 Combine all ingredients in a bowl and dress with the olive oil, lemon juice, salt, and pepper.

6 Fill the onions with the rice salad and arrange them on a serving dish.

Rice salad contadina

Tomatoes capriccio

■ Yield: 4 servings
■ Time needed: 1 hour
■ Difficulty: *

Ingredients: 4 large medium-ripe tomatoes, 1 cup rice, 1 egg yolk, 4 tablespoons ketchup, ¼ cup olive oil, 1 tablespoon white wine vinegar, 1 tablespoon brandy, salt.

Cook the rice in boiling sated water and drain it while still quite firm. Rinse it in cold water to stop it from cooking further (1) and drain it again. Make a mayonnaise by mixing the egg yolk with the vinegar and a pinch of salt and slowly adding the oil a drop at a time. Mix the mayonnaise, ketchup (2), and the brandy and toss the rice with this dressing (3). Wash the tomatoes, cut off the bottoms (4), and remove the seeds and some of the pulp (5). Salt the tomatoes and leave to drain for half an hour. Fill the tomatoes with the rice (6) and serve.

Decorate the tomatoes, if you wish, with a crown of olive rounds and garnish the platter with sprigs of curly parsley. Serve the stuffed tomatoes as an appetizer or as the main dish of a summer lunch.

1 Cook the rice in boiling salted water, drain it while still firm, and plunge it into cold water.

2 With the egg yolk, vinegar, oil, and a pinch of salt make a mayonnaise and mix in the ketchup...

3 ...and a tablespoon of brandy and dress the cold rice with this sauce.

4 Wash the tomatoes, dry them with a cloth, and cut a slice off the bottom.

5 Empty the tomatoes of some of their pulp, salt them, and drain them on a rack.

6 Fill the tomato shells with the rice and serve.

Tomatoes capriccio

Mozzarella croquettes

■ **Yield: 4 servings**
■ **Time needed: 1½ hours**
■ **Difficulty: ***

Ingredients: 1¾ cups rice, 2 tbsp. butter, ½ lb.
mozzarella cheese, 2 eggs, 1 thick slice of ham, 4
tablespoons grated Parmesan cheese, 4 cups stock,
bread crumbs, oil, pepper, salt.

Melt the butter in a casserole over low heat, add
the rice, and let it brown for a few minutes, stirring
with a wooden spoon. Add the boiling stock (1) and
cook the rice for about 15 minutes or until all the
stock has been absorbed and the rice is quite dry.
Then add the grated Parmesan cheese, season with
salt and pepper, and pour the *risotto* out onto a large
plate or marble counter (2) so that it will cool
quickly.

In the meantime mince the mozzarella and the
ham. When the rice is cold pour it into a wide bowl,
add one beaten egg and mix well (3). Roll the rice
in your hands to make little balls the size of an egg
(4), make a depression in the middle of each
croquette with your finger (5), and fill it with some
minced ham and mozzarella (6). Enclose the filling
with rice so that it can't leak out (7). First dip the
croquettes in the remaining egg, beaten (8), and
then roll them in the bread crumbs (9), with the
help of two forks. Heat plenty of oil in a skillet and,
when it begins to smoke, add the croquettes (10).
Turn them gently until golden on all sides, remove
them from the oil with a slotted spoon (11), drain
them, and lay them on paper toweling to rid them of
excess oil. Pile the croquettes into a little mound on
a plate, decorate with a few sprigs of parsley, and
serve.

These croquettes should be eaten very hot; if you
wish they can be served as a hot appetizer or as an
accompaniment to a plate of roast meat or fried
seafood. These cheese croquettes can also be made
with leftover rice dishes such as rice with butter,
Parmesan *risotto,* or *risotto* with saffron. If you
serve the croquettes with a tomato sauce on the side
they can even be considered an entrée.

1 After having cooked the rice for a few minutes in
the butter, add the boiling stock.

2 When the rice is done and the stock has evaporated,
mix in the cheese and spread the rice out on a place.

3 As soon as the rice has cooled, turn it into a wide
bowl and add a beaten egg, mixing well.

4 Roll the rice between the palms of your hands to form the croquettes.

5 Use your finger to make a depression in the middle of each croquette.

6 Fill the hole with some of the minced cheese and ham.

7 Enclose the filling with rice so that it will not leak out during cooking.

8 Beat another egg with a pinch of salt and dip the croquettes in egg one at a time.

9 Using two forks, roll the croquettes in the bread crumbs coating them well.

10 Heat plenty of oil in a deep skillet, and when it is hot immerse the croquettes.

11 Turn them in the hot oil so they will brown uniformly, and then drain them.

Mozzarella croquettes

Giblet croquettes

■ Yield: 4 servings
■ Time needed: 1 and ½ hours
■ Difficulty: *

Ingredients: 1 cup rice, 2 tbsp. butter, 1 gizzard and 2 chicken livers, ⅓ lb. mozzarella, 2 eggs, 1 teaspoon tomato paste, ½ small onion, 2 cups stock (approximately), ½ cup white wine, some flour, bread crumbs, plenty of oil for frying, pepper, salt.

Finely chop the onion and sauté until soft in a saucepan with half of the butter. Add the rice and let it brown lightly, stirring. Add the wine, letting it evaporate, season with salt and pepper, and cook the rice by adding the boiling stock ½ cup at a time, pouring in more stock only when the stock already added has been absorbed by the rice.

Melt the remaining butter in a frying pan and sauté the chopped chicken gizzard for 10 minutes. Add the chopped chicken livers, sauté briefly, and then add the tomato paste, diluted in a bit of stock. Season with salt and pepper and reduce the liquid.

Remove the rice from the stove when it is tender and quite dry, and mix in the giblets. Add the mozzarella, diced, and an egg yolk, mix well, and pour the *risotto* onto a plate and let it cool. Form the rice into balls the size of an egg, roll them in flour, then in the remaining beaten egg, and finally in the bread crumbs.

Heat plenty of oil in a deep skillet. When it is good and hot immerse the croquettes and fry them until uniformly golden, turning them with a fork. Remove them with a slotted spoon to paper toweling so that the excess oil will be blotted up. Finally, arrange the croquettes on a serving dish and serve them very hot. They make an excellent appetizer.

Swiss cheese fritters

■ Yield: 6 servings
■ Time needed: 1 hour
■ Difficulty: *

Ingredients: 1⅛ cups rice, 3½ oz. (almost 1 cup) shredded Swiss cheese, 3 eggs, some flour, bread crumbs, 4 cups milk, plenty of oil for frying, salt.

Pour the milk into a saucepan, add a bit of salt, and bring almost to a boil. Add the rice and stir continuously with a wooden spoon until the rice has absorbed all the milk and is quite dry. Remove from the stove, mix in the Swiss cheese, and let the rice cool a bit. Add two egg yolks one at a time, saving the whites. Beat one of the egg whites with a pinch of salt until stiff and stir gently into the rice. Beat the other egg white on a plate with the remaining whole egg and add salt.

Shape the rice into many small balls and flatten them between the floured palms of your hands. Dredge both sides of the fritters in flour, then dip in the beaten egg and finally in the bread crumbs. Heat plenty of oil in a deep skillet, immerse the fritters, and fry them until golden on both sides, turning them carefully with a spatula. Drain the fritters on paper toweling to blot up excess oil and serve hot as an appetizer.

Isabella salad

■ Yield: 4 servings
■ Time needed: 1 hour
■ Difficulty: *

Ingredients: 1 cup rice, 3½ oz. (about ½ cup) shelled peas, 3½ oz. ham, 2 medium-ripe tomatoes, 1 sweet red pepper, 1 sweet green or yellow pepper, some sweet pickles, 1 lemon, 1 clove garlic, a few basil leaves, oregano, oil, salt.

Cook the rice in boiling salted water, drain it when three-quarters done, and turn it out onto a clean dish towel to dry it.

Boil the peas in lightly salted water. Scorch the peppers over the flame of a gas stove or under a broiler and rub off the skins. Cut the peppers and the ham into very thin strips. Thinly slice the pickles lengthwise; slice the tomatoes, letting them drain well to rid them of some of their water. In a bowl, combine the cold rice, the peppers, the ham, and the peas, and stir to blend all the ingredients.

In a separate small bowl beat the juice of the lemon with a pinch of salt, add 4 or 5 tablespoons of oil, and continue to beat with a fork to emulsify all the ingredients. Add salt and pepper, and flavor the dressing with a bit of mashed, pressed, or finely chopped garlic. Pour the dressing on the rice, mix well, and keep the rice salad in the refrigerator until ready to serve. Before bringing it to the table, give it more flavor by stirring in some minced fresh basil and a big pinch of oregano. Garnish with tomato slices alternated with the sliced pickles.

You can vary the vegetable in this excellent summertime dish, as you please, using rounds of fresh young onions, white or navy beans, green beans, celery, etc. A photograph of this salad is on page 196.

Risotti, Timbales
and Sartù

For these splendid first-course dishes, the choice of the right kind of rice is fundamental. let us consider the classification of the different types given by the *Ente Risi Italiano*—(the Italian Rice Society). Rice is broken down into four groups, according to the appearance of the grain: *'superfino'* with long, big grains, *'fino'* with long, tapering grains, *'semifino'* with rounded grains of medium length, and *'originario'* or *'comune'* with small, round grains.

The most typical Italian dish prepared with this precious cereal is *risotto*. The etymology of this word goes back to a contraction in Latin of *"risus optimus,"* or "great rice," a phrase that was spoken by a pleased diner when a plate of yellow *risotto* was served him in the 6th century at the court of the Dukes of Milan. Legend confirms the Lombard origins of the *risotto* to the city of Milan where a certain Valerio of Flanders, who worked as a painter on the stained-glass windows of the Cathedral, happened to spill some saffron (then used only as a color) into some rice that was cooking, turning it into the traditional Milanese dish that we know.

Timbales and *sartùs* are southern dishes. In fact, in the Kingdom of Naples, rice dishes inspired by the classic French school were made by cooks who worked for a small group of nobles. Elaborate new inventions resulted from the combination of refined French culinary ideas with typical local ingredients and customs: the very name "sartù" derives from the French *"surtout"* (above all) connoting that the rice sits on top of a fantastic filling.

Preparing risotto

The ingredients and quantities — The success of a good *risotto* depends in the first place on the choice of the appropriate rice, which should have an average starch content so that it will remain intact when cooked but will also uniformly absorb the seasoning. The *'fino'* rice types belong to this category. The right quantity of rice per person is about 4 ounces for ½ cup, an amount that can be increased if large portions are desired, or diminished if other ingredients like legumes, vegetables, meat, and so on are cooked with the rice. The second basic ingredient for a *risotto* is the stock, preferably a good strong chicken or meat stock or, as a substitute, a vegetable stock or a stock made with bouillon cube. The most important thing, however, is that the stock should always be kept simmering, because the addition of a lukewarm or cold liquid will irrevocably compromise the success of the *risotto*. The amount of stock recommended is of about a cup for every ½ cup rice (or 1 serving), but accounting for evaporation, it is always better to have a greater quantity available.

Cooking the risotto — The first step is to carefully pick over the rice, removing any blemished grains, grit, or small stones. Do not, however, wash the rice. The rice is then put in a heavy saucepan in which some finely chopped onion or sometimes garlic or shallots have been sautéed in oil or butter. It is then browned lightly in the oil or butter, and stirred with a wooden spoon. (Sometimes the sautéeing is eliminated to make the rice more easily digestible: in this case the rice is poured into a small quantity of boiling stock—as much as one thinks it will absorb—and is seasoned when cooked with a piece of butter and plenty of Parmesan cheese). When the rice has been browned in the butter or oil, one can add about half a cup of white or red wine. When this has evaporated, begin to add the boiling stock a ladle at a time, stirring steadily and waiting for the rice to absorb one ladleful before adding the next. When the rice is almost done, that is, after 15 to 18 minutes, the saucepan is removed from the stove and, if the recipe calls for it, a piece of butter and some light cream and plenty of Parmesan or other cheese are added; the *risotto* is mixed well. The rice should be *al dente* but still soft and smooth. It is advisable to let the *risotto* sit covered in the pan a few minutes before serving.

A great variety of ingredients can be added to this basic *risotto* recipe, since rice combines well both with meat, seafood, vegetables, and even with certain kinds of fruit. Thus we have an infinity of *risottos,* from the classic ones with mushrooms or saffron to the lesser known or unusual ones that call for grape juice, strawberries, or wild berries.

Rice pilaf — A close relative of *risotto,* pilaf is a dish of Turkish origin (*"pilaf"* in Turkish means rice). By now the word has come to mean a certain cooking method which is quite quick and delicious in its results: after the rice is browned in butter or oil, and other flavorings, it is covered with hot stock, brought to a boil, and placed in a 350-degree oven for 18 to 20 minutes. When the time is up, the rice will have completely absorbed the stock and the grains of the rice will not stick together. Before serving, butter is usually added, and the pilaf is stirred with a fork. For this dish one should choose a rice of the *"superfino"* variety (Arborio, Carnaroli) or even a converted rice.

Sartù and timbales of rice — In regional cuisines, especially in those of southern Italy, we find that a normal *risotto* can be enriched to the point of becoming a highly nutritious meal in itself, giving rise to two elaborate preparations—*timbales* and *sartùs*. These are made with *risotto* or boiled rice which is placed in layers in a greased mold lined with bread crumbs. The layers of rice are alternated with a wide variety of ingredients, including chicken giblets, peas, tiny meat balls, sausage, salami, mushrooms, slices of hard-boiled egg, and mozzarella cheese. All this is covered with a meat-flavored tomato sauce, a white sauce, and grated cheese. The *sartù* and *timbales* are cooked for about a half hour in a hot oven, and are left to set for a few minutes before being turned out of their molds onto a platter. Sometimes *timbales* can be covered with a pastry dough made of flour, butter, and eggs before cooking.

How to serve risotto — *Timbales* and *sartù* are considered one-dish meals *par excellence,* and even a simple *risotto* or rice pilaf, if properly combined with another dish, are no less nourishing. Rice pilaf is good with a veal stew or casseroled chicken and pork, and is at its best with shellfish cooked in creamy sauces.

Necessary utensils

To cook rice, one should have a number of different pots and pans suited to the cooking methods called for in the recipes. For boiled rice, an ordinary saucepan of a sufficiently large size is fine, although the special steamer with a basket inside is even more convenient. *Risotto* requires a heavy-bottomed pan or casserole for long, slow cooking, such as the classic stainless steel pan, preferably with a double- or triple-layered bottom that will conduct heat evenly and prevent sticking, or the traditional but now expensive copper pan lined with tin, which, if provided with a lid and short handles, is also very suitable for cooking pilaf. Rice pilaf and other rice dishes made in the oven can be cooked in porcelain or glass oven casseroles that can even be brought to the table if they are put on a metal trivet or straw pot holder.

Then there are a whole series of molds, small and large. There are those without a hole in the middle for *timbales* and *sartù,* and those with a hole in the center for molding both sweet and savory rice dishes into rings.

To fry croquettes, *supplí, arancini,* and fritters a deep skillet is needed or, even better, an electric frier. For serving rice, one can use a special tureen or a slightly concave platter.

Seafood risotto

■ **Yield: 4 servings**
■ **Time needed: 1½ hours**
■ **Difficulty: ***

Ingredients: 1¾ cups rice, 1 lb. mussels, 1 lb. clams, 3 tbsp. butter, 1 small onion, 1 tablespoon parsley chopped with 1 clove garlic, an additional clove garlic, oil, whole pepper, salt.
Fish stock ingredients: 2¼ lb. inexpensive fish or fish trimmings, 1 onion, 1 bay leaf, ¼ tsp. thyme, whole peppercorns, salt.

Scrub the mussels with a wire brush (1) and wash well under running water. Wash the clams and pour all the shellfish into a large frying pan in which you have sautéed a whole clove of garlic in some oil (2).

Place the pan on the stove, and as the shellfish open up remove from their shells (3), saving a few mussels in their shells to decorate the *risotto*. Strain the liquid that has collected on the bottom of the pan (4) and keep it warm. To prepare the fish stock, clean the fish if necessary, removing only the insides and leaving on the fins and heads. Wash the fish or fish trimmings and put them in a kettle, adding 1½ quarts of water. Put the kettle on the stove over low heat and bring to a boil. Remove the scum carefully from the surface of the stock, then add the onion, sliced into rounds, the bay leaf, the thyme, a few peppercorns, and a pinch of salt. Simmer for about 30 minutes, then strain the broth through a triple thickness of cheesecloth and keep the stock warm. Sauté the finely chopped onion in one tablespoon of butter and a little oil until soft, add the rice and stir (5), season with salt and freshly ground pepper, moisten with the liquid from the shellfish (6), and stir again.

Continue cooking, adding the boiling fish stock ½ cup at a time, waiting for one addition to be absorbed before adding the next. A few minutes before taking the *risotto* off the stove mix in the clams and mussels (7) and add the remaining butter and the chopped parsley-and-garlic mixture (8).

Serve on a round platter and garnish with the reserved mussels in their shells (9). For a quick *risotto* substitute frozen, pre-cooked shellfish for the clams and mussels.

1 Scrub the mussels well with a wire brush before washing them thoroughly under running water.

2 Turn the mussels and clams into a frying pan with a little oil and a clove of garlic.

3 Put the pan on the stove and remove the clams and mussels from their shells one by one as they open.

4 Strain the liquid collected on the bottom of the pan through a cheesecloth-lined sieve.

5 Sauté the finely chopped onion in the butter, add the rice, and stir.

6 After seasoning with salt and pepper, moisten the rice with the cooking liquid from the shellfish.

7 A few minutes before taking the rice off the stove, add the clams and mussels...

8 ...and finish with the remaining butter (in pieces) and the chopped parsley-and-garlic mixture.

9 When ready to serve, garnish the *risotto* with the whole mussels set aside for the purpose.

Seafood risotto

Milanese risotto

- ■ Yield: 4 servings
- ■ Time needed: 1 hour
- ■ Difficulty: *

Ingredients: 1¾ cups rice, 2 oz. beef marrow, 5 tbsp. butter, 2 oz. (about ½ cup) grated Parmesan cheese, pinch saffron, 1 small onion, ½ cup dry white wine, meat stock as necessary, pepper, salt.

Coarsely chop the beef marrow (1). Melt half the butter in a casserole, and add the marrow (2), the chopped onion and pinches of salt and pepper. When the onion is soft (but not browned) add the rice (3) and the white wine (4), letting it evaporate over high heat. Simmer for a few more minutes and add, very slowly, the necessary stock (5) and continue cooking, stirring with a wooden spoon. Halfway through the cooking add the saffron, dissolved in some stock (6). Take the *risotto* off the stove when *al dente* but cooked completely. Add the remaining butter, in pieces, and the cheese as the finishing touch. Let the rice sit in a corner of the stove for a few minutes. Often it is served so soft that it is called *all'onda,* or wavy.

1 Coarsely chop the beef marrow.

2 Melt half the butter in a casserole, and add the chopped marrow.

3 Add the chopped onion and pinches of salt and pepper. When the onion is soft, add rice.

4 After a few minutes add the wine, letting it evaporate over high heat.

5 Simmer for a few more minutes and very slowly add the necessary stock.

6 Halfway through the cooking add the saffron dissolved in some stock

Milanese risotto

Rice pilaf

■ **Yield: 4 servings**
■ **Time needed: 45 minutes**
■ **Difficulty: ***

Ingredients: 1¾ cups short-grained rice, 7 tbsp. butter, 1 onion weighing about 3 oz., 3¾ cups stock, salt.

Rice pilaf is a Turkish dish. Cooked in the oven, pilaf is served as an accompaniment to meat dishes such as casseroles, pot roasts or stews, or with poached or baked fish dishes.

Sauté the chopped onion in 4 tablespoons butter (1) until soft but not browned, add the rice all at once (2) season with a pinch of salt, raise the heat, and stir briskly for a few minutes so that the rice can brown in the butter and onions (3). Add all of the boiling stock (4), bring the mixture to a boil, cover the casserole (5), and put it into the oven. Bake the rice at 400° F, without stirring, for about 18 to 20 minutes or until all the liquid has been absorbed. Flavor the rice with the remaining butter, cut in pieces, stirring well; the rice should not come out sticky (6).

Rice pilaf with raisins

■ **Yield: 4 servings**
■ **Time needed: 45 minutes**
■ **Difficulty: ***

Ingredients: 1¾ cups short-grained rice, 7 tbsp. butter, 1 onion weighing about 3 oz., ½ cup raisins, 2 tbsp. pine nuts, 1 cup dry white wine, 3¾ cups stock, salt.

Soak the raisins in warm water. Sauté the finely chopped onion in 4 tablespoons of the butter and brown the rice as indicated in the previous recipe. Season with salt, moisten with the white wine, add the drained raisins and the pine nuts, and cover with the boiling stock. Bring the mixture to a boil on the stove, cover the casserole, and put it into a 400-degree oven for about 15 minutes.

Take the pilaf out of the oven, mix in the remaining butter in little pieces, stir, and serve immediately. This rice pilaf is a good accompaniment to pork cooked in a sweet-and-sour sauce or a stew of lamb made with yogurt or curry.

1 Finely chop the onion and let it soften in 4 tablespoons butter without browning.

2 When the onion begins to melt add the rice all at once, and stir.

3 Raise the heat and stir for a few minutes so that the rice will brown in the butter and onions.

4 Add the boiling stock and bring the mixture to a boil, stirring continuously.

5 Cover the casserole and put it into a hot oven.

6 After baking the rice should be nice and separate, not sticky.

Rice ring finanziera

■ **Yield: 4 servings**
■ **Time needed: 1 hour**
■ **Difficulty: ***

Rice ingredients: 1¾ cups rice, 7 tbsp. butter, 1 oz. beef marrow, 3½ oz. (about ¾ cup) grated Parmesan cheese, 1 small onion, ½ cup of dry white wine, 3¾ cups of stock, pepper, salt.
Finanziera **ingredients: 12 oz. chicken gizzards, hearts, and livers, 1 carrot, 1 onion, 1 rib celery, 1 bunch parsley, 2 tbsp. butter, oil, ½ cup dry Marsala or Madeira, ½ lb. mushrooms, salt, pepper.**

First prepare the *risotto*. Sauté the chopped onion and marrow in 3½ tbsp. of butter, add a good pinch of salt and pepper, and when the onion is quite soft, pour in the wine and let it evaporate. Add the rice, cook for a few minutes, stirring, and then continue cooking by adding the boiling stock a little at a time.

While the rice is cooking, clean the giblets. Chop the carrot, onion and celery. Grease a ring mold with a rounded base with a little oil (1). Sauté the chopped vegetables in a frying pan with 2 tbsp. butter and a little oil and add the gizzards and hearts cut in small pieces. Cook over low heat, and when almost done add the sliced livers. Mix well, pour in the Marsala or Madeira, season with salt and pepper, and sprinkle with chopped parsley.

Trim the woody ends from the mushrooms (2) and remove the outer skin (3) from the caps and stems. Slice the mushrooms thickly and keep them in water to which you have added a little lemon juice until you are ready to use (4). Sauté them in a skillet with a little oil and the rest of the chopped parsley (5). After they have cooked a few minutes, add a splash of Madeira (6) and cook a little longer, adding a dash of salt and pepper.

Add a little of the giblet sauce to the cooked rice, add the remaining 3½ tbsp. butter and the Parmesan (7). Stir well, and then fill the mold with the rice (8), pressing it down with a wooden spoon (9). Put the mold in the oven so the rice will stay hot. When ready to serve, turn the mold upside-down on a platter and remove. Spread half the mushrooms over the top of the mold. Fill the center of the ring with the giblet sauce, garnish with mushrooms.

1 Brush a ring mold with a little oil.

2 Trim the woody ends from the mushrooms.

3 With a sharp knife, remove the skin from the caps and stems.

4 Slice the mushrooms and keep them in water with a little lemon juice until ready to use.

5 Sauté them in a skillet with a little oil and chopped parsley.

6 Add a splash of Madeira to the mushrooms.

7 When the rice is cooked, take it off the fire and add a little giblet sauce and the cheese.

8 Fill the greased ring with the rice.

9 Press it down into the mold with a wooden spoon.

Rice casserole

■ **Yield: 4 servings**
■ **Time needed: 1½ hours**
■ **Difficulty: ***

Ingredients: 1¼ cups rice, 4 tbsp. butter, 1 small onion, 2½ oz. (about ⅔ cup) shredded Swiss cheese, ¼ lb. ham, 3 tbsp. flour, meat stock, ½ cup dry white wine, 2 cups milk, oil, pepper, salt.

First of all prepare a thin white sauce. Melt 2 tablespoons butter in a saucepan, add the flour, and stir well with a wooden spoon to dissolve any lumps. Let the mixture cook a bit, season with a pinch of salt, and, off heat, add the boiling milk a little at a time, stirring constantly. Let the sauce simmer for a few minutes, taking it off the stove when it appears thickened and smooth (1). Season it with a pinch of pepper, freshly ground if possible, and mix in the shredded Swiss cheese (2), stirring vigorously to make it melt.

Finely chop the small onion and sauté it in half the remaining butter and two tablespoons of oil. Add the rice and let it brown lightly, stirring with a wooden spoon. Pour in the wine, letting it evaporate completely, and then add the boiling stock, a little at a time, never forgetting to stir (3). Take the rice off the stove when still quite *al dente;* it will finish cooking in the oven. Generously butter a casserole (4) and cover the bottom with a layer of rice (5), spreading it evenly with a spatula or the back of a spoon. Cover it with some slices of ham (6) and a layer of white sauce (7), smoothing this well too. Continue layering in this way until all the ingredients are used up, ending with the white sauce (8). Dot the surface with the remaining tablespoon of butter (9) and put the casserole in a 400-degree oven until the surface is nicely browned.

Serve the rice hot, in the same dish in which it was cooked.

For an even tastier dish you can alternate the layers of rice with layers of sliced mushrooms prepared as follows: Sauté plenty of chopped parsley and garlic in 2 to 3 tablespoons of oil, add 10 ounces fresh mushrooms, sliced, season with salt, and sprinkle them with a bit of brandy. Add a few tablespoons of boiling stock in which you have dissolved half a bouillon cube and continue cooking.

1 With the butter, the flour, milk, and salt prepare a smooth white sauce.

2 Season the sauce with a bit of pepper, add the grated Swiss cheese, and mix well.

3 After browning the rice in the mixture of oil, butter, and onion, add the boiling stock.

4 Take a wide oven-proof casserole and generously butter the bottom and sides.

5 Cover the bottom of the casserole with a layer of rice and spread it evenly with a spatula.

6 Cover the surface of the rice with the ham cut into thin slices.

7 Pour a few spoonfuls of white sauce on the rice, spreading it with a spoon.

8 Continue layering, alternating rice, slices of ham, and white sauce.

9 Dot the surface of the casserole with butter and put it into the oven.

Layered rice casserole

Rice and dumplings

■ **Yield: 4 servvings**
■ **Time needed: 2 hours**
■ **Difficulty: ***

Ingredients: 1¼ cups rice, 2 cups cornmeal, 4 "large" eggs, 7 tbsp. butter, 4 oz. (about 1 cup) grated Parmesan cheese, 7 oz. *fontina* cheese, 4⅓ cups milk, salt.

Bring the milk to a boil with some salt and slowly sprinkle in the cornmeal, stirring constantly (1). Continue cooking, and stirring, for about half an hour (2). Take the *polenta* off the stove and let it cool a bit. Mix in the Parmesan cheese (3) and the eggs (4). Stir well to bind the mixture (5) and let it sit for half an hour. Cook the rice in plenty of salted water (6), drain it when a bit *al dente,* pour it into a bowl, and add the diced *fontina* cheese (7), stirring so that the cheese will melt (8). Then make the *polenta* into little balls about ¾-inch in diameter (9).

Grease an oven-safe casserole with some butter, arrange the *polenta* dumplings in it (10), cover with the rice (11), and pour on the remaining melted butter (12). The traditional recipe calls for a much greater quantity of butter than used here.

Put the casserole in a 400-degree oven, for five minutes before servings.

1 Sprinkle the cornmeal into the lightly salted boiling milk, stirring constantly.

2 Continue cooking and stirring the *polenta,* for about half an hour.

3 Take it off the stove, let it cool a bit, and mix in the cheese...

4 ...followed by the four whole eggs.

5 Continue to stir vigorously until the mixture is smooth...

6 Bring plenty of salted water to a boil in a pot and pour in the rice.

7 Drain the rice when *al dente*, pour it into a bowl, and add the diced *fontina* cheese.

8 Continue stirring so that the fontina will melt and blend with the rice.

9 Using your hands, make the *polenta* into little balls about ¾-inch in diameter.

10 Grease an oven-safe casserole with some butter and arrange the *polenta* dumplings in it.

11 Cover the layer of *polenta* dumplings with all of the rice, smoothing it on top.

12 Pour the remaining melted butter over the rice.

Rice and dumplings

Green timbales

- Yield: 4 servings
- Time needed: 2 hours
- Difficulty: *

Ingredients: 1¼ cups rice, 1 small onion, 10-oz. box frozen leaf spinach, 14 oz. veal or turkey cutlets, 5 tbsp. butter, 1 beef bouillon cube, 1 tablespoon parsley finely chopped with 1 clove garlic, dry Madeira wine or juice of 1 lemon, meat stock, flour, oil, pepper, salt.

Little rice *timbales* accompanied by a plate of veal or turkey cutlets can be served as a one-dish meal.

Melt 2 tablespoons butter with 2 tablespoons oil in a frying pan. Dredge the cutlets in flour and sauté (1), seasoning with salt and browning on both sides. When the meat has taken on a golden color, add the lemon juice (2) or ½ cup Madeira, and let evaporate completely. Stir a teaspoon of flour into the juices in the pan, then add the bouillon cube, and a little stock; if you have used Madeira, add a knob of butter as well. Let the sauce reduce for a few minutes.

Take the cutlets off the stove, flavor them with the chopped parsley-and-garlic mixture, and season with a little pepper. Keep the meat warm in a chafing dish. In another saucepan, sauté the onion until soft in 2 tablespoons butter and a little oil. Add the spinach, previously blanched, drained thoroughly and chopped (3), and warm it with the butter and onions. Finally add the rice (4) and stir.

Cook the rice-and-spinach mixture for a few minutes and then begin adding the stock, a little at a time, until the rice is done (5). Make sure to take it off the stove when *al dente*. Transfer the rice to four small fluted molds (6), which have been greased with the remaining melted butter, packing it with a spoon to make nice compact forms.

Invert the molds on to a serving platter (7), place a slice of meat on each (8), put the remaining cutlets in the middle of the plate and around the edges, and pour the hot pan gravy over them (9). Decorate the platter with boiled carrots cut into rounds or with mixed cooked vegetables.

1 Melt the butter in a frying pan with the oil and sauté the floured cutlets.

2 When the meat is lightly browned, add the juice of one lemon.

3 Add the blanched, drained, and chopped spinach to the sautéed onion...

4 ...let cook briefly, and add the rice.

5 After a few minutes add the stock, a little at a time, until the rice is done.

6 Transfer the rice with spinach to four buttered molds.

7 Invert the molds onto a warm serving plate...

8 ...and place a slice of meat on each one.

9 Put the remaining cutlets on the platter and pour the hot pan gravy over them.

Green timbales

Sartù

■ Yield: 4 servings
■ Time needed: 2 hours
■ Difficulty: **

Ingredients: 1¼ cups rice, ¾ oz. dried mushrooms, 7 oz. sausage, 7 oz. ground beef, 2 oz. (about ½ cup) grated Parmesan cheese, 1 thick slice *mortadella* or boiled ham, 1 large mozzarella cheese, 5 tbsp. butter, 1 onion, 1 lb. canned tomatoes, preferably peeled plum tomatoes, 1 carrot, 1 rib celery, 1 clove garlic, 1 tbsp. finely chopped parsley, 5 or 6 tbsp. bread crumbs, flour, 3 eggs, 1 tbsp. of bread soaked in milk, stock as needed, oil, salt, pepper.

First prepare the little meatballs. Put the ground beef in a bowl, add the bread after squeezing out the milk, the chopped *mortadella,* the parsley, one egg, salt, and pepper. Make the mixture into little balls about the size of a walnut. Flour the meatballs lightly, fry in a little butter, and drain. Sauté the dried mushrooms, which have been soaked in warm water for 30 minutes, drained, and chopped, in the same pan, seasoning with salt and pepper and adding the sausage in slices.

Chop the carrot, celery, and garlic and sauté them in a little oil. Season with salt and pepper and add the puréed tomatoes; cook for half an hour.

Heat four tablespoons of butter in a saucepan, add four tablespoons of the tomato sauce, and after a minute, add the rice. Let cook for a few minutes and then add the boiling stock, a little at a time, until the rice is almost done. After about a quarter of an hour the rice should appear quite dry. Take the pan off the stove, mix in the Parmesan cheese and an egg and then spread the rice mixture out on a board or table so that it will cool.

Mix the little meatballs, the sausage, and the mushrooms into the remaining tomato sauce. Grease a mold with tall, smooth sides and dust it with bread crumbs. Beat the remaining egg and pour half of it into the mold, dust again with bread crumbs, and pour in the rest of the egg, coating the sides of the mold with it. Dust with bread crumbs again. Pour all the rice except four tablespoons into the mold, packing it down with a spoon. Pour the prepared sauce into the mold, mix in the diced mozzarella, and cover with the remaining rice. Mix the remaining tablespoon melted butter with two tablespoons of bread crumbs and sprinkle over the surface of the rice. Bake the mold in a medium oven (350°F) for about 40 minutes, or until the surface is golden and has formed a hard crust. At this point take the mold out of the oven, and let the *sartù* cool a bit before unmolding it onto a platter and serving.

Paella

■ Yield: 8-10 servings
■ Time needed: 2 hours
■ Difficulty: *

Ingredients: 1 small frying chicken weighing about 2¼ lbs., 10 oz. lean pork meat, 10 oz. cubed veal, 3½ oz. *prosciutto* ham, 8 *chorizos* (or small pepper and garlic sausages), 30 cleaned snails (optional), 2¼ lbs. clams and mussels, 8 crayfish (or 2 small lobsters or 8 large shrimp), 10 oz. squid, cleaned, 3¾ cups rice, 1 onion, 2 sweet peppers, 2¼ lbs. ripe tomatoes, 3 artichokes, 10 oz. canned small white beans or flageolets, ¾ lb. fresh or frozen peas, 1 clove garlic, some parsley, 1 lemon, 1 small piece hot red pepper, pinch saffron, about 2 quarts stock, oil, salt.

Rinse the chicken and cut into small pieces along with the pork and the *prosciutto.* Scrub the clams and mussels and heat them in a pan. When the shells have opened, drain the mollusks, leaving them in their shells; strain the juices. Scorch the peppers, then peel and cut into pieces. Purée the tomatoes. Clean, trim the artichokes, slice, and put in a bowl of water and lemon juice.

Place the special *paelliera* (a large iron skillet with two handles) on the stove and pour in about ½ cup oil. When this is hot, add the chicken, the pork, the veal, and the sausages and let brown. Take the pan off the stove, remove the meats with a slotted spoon, and pour out the fat. Pour fresh oil into the pan and add a clove of garlic. Put the *paelliera* back on the stove, put the meats back in, and add the sliced onion, chopped squid, optional snails, crayfish, *prosciutto,* the peppers, artichokes, and beans. Season with salt, stir, and when the vegetables have become soft, stir in the puréed tomatoes and the juice from the clams and mussels; sprinkle with parsley. Pour in a little boiling stock, stir and continue to cook for about an hour altogether, adding the peas about halfway through the cooking. If needed, add more stock. When the mixture has cooked for an hour, put another pan on the stove with ¼ cup of oil. When this is hot add the rice, and let it brown lightly, stirring occasionally. Moisten the rice with a ladle of stock in which you have dissolved the saffron, add the hot red pepper, and season with a pinch of salt. After a few minutes pour the rice into the *paelliera* together with meats and vegetables and stir well.

Add enough stock to the *paella* to cook the rice *al dente,* cover and finish cooking. Three minutes before taking the *paella* off the stove, add the clams and mussels. Take the pan off the stove and put it in a 350-degree oven for 6 to 7 minutes.

Rice Desserts

In Italy, rice desserts are unusual, whereas in Anglo-Saxon countries, where one is always in search of a dessert which can worthily substitute for fruit, these desserts are well known and appreciated. In fact, most of the recipes for desserts made from rice come from Great Britain or the U.S. For example, there is Queen Anne's plum cake, a cake created by Queen Anne of England's personal cook at the end of the 17th century, in which rice together with sugar, eggs, lemon juice, cream, cream cheese, and dried and candied fruit becomes a delicate and delicious filling for a fragrant pastry shell. Rice cakes, which are served in America, usually for breakfast or as a substantial snack, and which are cooked over a red-hot grill, are another famous sweetened recipe using rice.

The rice usually used for these desserts is common cooking rice, the kind that breaks up and blends easily with the other ingredients. Depending on the recipe, the rice is cooked either in water or, more often, in milk, and it is nearly always flavored with sugar, eggs, and butter. Ideally, one should use sugar from fruit (fructose rather than ordinary table sugar), because it is drier and makes the desserts lighter. Also to make the dessert lighter and softer, one often adds stiffly beaten egg whites. The taste of sweet rice complements either fresh or dried fruit and thus there are many delicate and delicious fillings made of rice and fruit. For example, baked peaches and apples may be filled with rice that has been mixed with almonds, walnuts, raisins, pistachios and pine nuts. There is also a filling for delicate omelets made of rice, bananas, pineapple, and sometimes other exotic fruits. Then there are other desserts that call for rice to be mixed with canned fruit, prunes, or candied fruit, wrapped in pastry, bread dough, or sponge cake, and made into hearty and nourishing cakes. There are, furthermore, rice molds and puddings flavored with lemons, oranges and liqueurs. These can be served either hot or cold, with or without sweet sauces.

Rice pudding with dates

Rice cake

■ Yield: 4 servings
■ Time needed: 1½ hours
■ Difficulty: *

Ingredients: 1¼ cups rice, 10 tbsp. (½ cup + 2 tbsp.) sugar, 3½ oz. (about ⅔ cup) almonds, a few drops almond extract, 1 small piece of candied citron (optional), 2 oz. (about ⅓ cup) mixed candied fruit, 5 "large" eggs, 1 lemon, small amount of bread crumbs, 5 cups milk, ½ jigger dark rum, butter, pinch of salt.

Butter a spring-form pan or a 6- to 8-cup cake pan generously. Sprinkle it with bread crumbs, rotating it so as to cover all the surfaces, and then tip out the excess (1).

Heat the milk, add the sugar (2), salt, and grated lemon peel (3), and bring to the boil. Add all the rice at once (4) and let it cook until it has absorbed the milk (5). Pour the rice into a bowl and let it cool. Meanwhile, blanch and peel the almonds, if necessary and chop finely. Chop or cut into small pieces the optional citron and the other mixed candied fruit.

Add one egg yolk at a time to the rice (6), mixing thoroughly. Mix into this the almonds and candied fruit (7), the ½ jigger of rum, the almond extract, and last the stiffly beaten egg whites (8). Lightly blend so as not to deflate the egg whites until the ingredients are well mixed.

Pour this into the pan (9), levelling the mixture with the back of a spoon. Put the cake in the oven at 350°F for approximately 45 minutes. Remove it from the oven and let it rest in the pan for 5 minutes. Turn the cake out onto a round plate to cool at room temperature before serving.

You can also bake this mixture in a crust of sweet short pastry. For the pastry, mix 1½ cups flour with 7 tablespoons butter, a pinch of salt, ¼ cup of sugar and a whole egg. Roll out the pastry quite thin and line the buttered cake pan, pricking the pastry with a fork to stop it from buckling while cooking. Fill with the rice mixture. This cake is suitable for breakfast or for snacks.

1 Butter spring-form pan and sprinkle with bread crumbs.

2 Heat the milk, add the sugar, and slowly bring to a boil.

3 Just before the milk comes to a boil add the grated lemon peel.

4 Add the rice to the boiling milk, stirring continuously with a wooden spoon.

5 Slowly cook the rice until it has totally absorbed the milk.

6 Take the rice off the heat and add the egg yolks, one at a time, mixing thoroughly.

7 Add the almonds, blanched and chopped, and the candied fruit.

8 Flavor the mixture with the rum and almond extract and add the stiffly beaten egg whites.

9 Pour the mixture into the prepared cake pan and level it with the back of a spoon.

Rice cake

Rice Pudding

■ **Yield: 4 servings**
■ **Time needed: 1 hour**
■ **Difficulty: ***

Ingredients: 1 cup plus 2 tbsp. rice, 2½ oz. (about ⅓ cup) almonds, 1 cup plus 2 tbsp. sugar, 3½ tbsp. butter, 2 oz. (about ⅓ cup) candied citron, 2 oz. (about ⅓ cup) candied cherries, 4 "large" eggs, 4 cups milk, 1 vanilla bean or 1 tsp. vanilla extract, 14 oz. strawberries, 2 oz. (about ⅓ cup) candied orange peel, sweet Malaga wine (or other dessert wine), 1 lemon peel, cognac, kirsch, salt.

Peel the almonds by covering them with boiling water and pinch off the skins. Dry them in the oven, making sure they do not color, and then chop.

Heat milk with ½ cup sugar, the vanilla beans and the lemon peel. As soon as the milk begins to boil, add the rice and cook it slowly until it has absorbed all the milk. Take it off the heat, add 3 tablespoons of butter, cut in little pieces (1), the egg yolks (one at a time) (2), almonds, chopped candied citron (3), and two spoonfuls of cognac. Let the mixture cool.

In another bowl, beat the egg whites with a pinch of salt until stiff. Fold this into the rice mixture so as not to deflate the whites (4). Butter a fluted ring mold with remaining butter (5), and lay the candied orange peel and cut cherries on the bottom (6). Pour the rice mixture on top, levelling lightly with a spoon (7). Place the mold in a large pan three-quarters full of boiling water (8). Put the mold and the *bain marie* in a 350-degree oven for 30 minutes (the water should simmer).

Prepare the strawberry sauce. Bring ¼ cup sugar and 2 tablespoons water to a boil (9). Cook to the soft-ball stage (238°F), or until a drop of syrup between your thumb and index finger forms a small thread which breaks immediately (10). Pass the strawberries through a sieve (or purée in a blender). Add a dash of Malaga wine, then stir the strawberry mixture into the syrup with the remaining 6 tablespoons sugar (11). Cook the strawberry sauce until the last drops falling from the spoon are sticky (12) and remove from heat.

Take the rice pudding out of the oven and let it cool (it may flatten a little). Then turn it out on a dessert dish (13) and decorate with candied fruit.

Flavor the strawberry sauce with one or two jiggers of kirsch (14).

Serve the strawberry sauce in a sauceboat, or pour the sauce over the dessert (15).

1 Boil the rice in the sugared milk, remove it from the stove, and add the butter, cut in pieces...

2 ...add the egg yolks one at a time mixing in each one thoroughly...

3 ...then add the chopped blanched almonds, and the chopped candied citron.

4 Beat the egg whites until they are stiff and gently fold them into the rice mixture.

5 Butter a ring mold with a pastry brush.

6 Lay the candied orange peel and cherries (cut in half) on the bottom.

7 Pour the rice mixture on top, levelling it lightly with a spoon.

8 Place the mold in a larger pan three-quarters full of hot water.

9 Prepare a syrup by dissolving ¼ cup sugar in two tablespoons water...

10 . . . and cook it until it reaches the soft-boil stage.

11 Add the remaining sugar, the wine, and the puréed strawberries to this syrup.

12 Cook the sauce until the last drops falling from the spoon are sticky.

13 Take the pudding out of the oven, let it cool in its mold, and then turn it out onto a plate.

14 Flavor the strawberry sauce before serving with kirsch or any other liqueur of your choice.

15 Serve the fruit sauce in a sauceboat or pour it over the pudding.

Rice pudding

Creamy rice pudding

■ Yield: 4 servings
■ Time needed: 1 hour
■ Difficulty: *

Ingredients: 5 tbsp. rice, 7 tbsp. granulated sugar, 1 teaspoon vanilla extract, 3 egg yolks, ¼ teaspoon cinnamon mixed with 1 teaspoon sugar, peel of 1 lemon, 2 cups milk, ¾ cup light cream.

Pour the milk into a saucepan and add the cream and the sugar (1) with a few strips of lemon peel (only the yellow part, not the white pith underneath which is bitter). Bring this to a boil and then pour in the rice, stirring continuously with a wooden spoon. Reduce the heat to its lowest point and simmer the cream for approximately half an hour or until the rice is tender and all the milk has been absorbed. The mixture should now be very thick but at the same time soft (2). Remove the lemon peel from the rice (3), take the pan off the heat, and add the vanilla and the egg yolks one at a time (4), making sure to blend in each yolk before adding the next.

Return the pan to low heat and bring mixture to just below the simmer (5). Be sure not to let the rice boil, or the yolks will scramble. Pour the cream into individual dessert bowls and sprinkle the top of each one with the cinnamon sugar. If the pudding is not to be eaten at once, cover the bowls with tin foil and place them in the refrigerator.

This dessert is particularly good for children's snacks.

One can also serve the dessert with a fruit sauce or a hot chocolate sauce. To prepare a chocolate sauce, combine 1 cup cocoa, ½ cup sugar, and a teaspoon of potato starch or cornstarch in a pan. Add 2 cups hot milk, a little at a time, and simmer the sauce for about 10 minutes, stirring constantly. Remove the pan from the flame and add, if desired, either 1 cup of hot *espresso* coffee (or strong American coffee) or a small quantity of light cream or whipped cream (this can be sweetened with confectioners' sugar).

Bring the fruit or chocolate sauce to the table in a sauceboat so that guests can serve themselves.

1 Pour the milk into a saucepan and add the cream and sugar.

2 Stir the mixture continuously while cooking until it is very thick but still soft and slightly fluid.

3 Remove the lemon peel when the rice is ready.

4 Take the mixture off the heat and add the egg yolks one at a time.

5 Put the pan back on the stove and heat to just below the simmer, but do not boil.

Creamy rice pudding

Sweet fritters

■ Yield: 4 servings
■ Time needed: 1 hour
■ Difficulty: *

Ingredients: 7 tbsp. rice, 6 tbsp. flour, 7 tbsp. sugar, 1 tsp. baking powder, confectioners' sugar or granulated sugar, preferably flavored with vanilla, 3 "large" eggs, ⅓ cup raisins, dark rum, oil for frying, 2 cups milk, peel of 1 lemon (yellow part only), pinch salt.

Soak the raisins in a small amount of rum. Pour the rice into the boiling milk (1) and cook it until the milk has been completely absorbed. Remove the rice from the stove and let it cool slightly. Add the sugar (2), the egg yolks (one at a time) (3), the sifted flour (4), lemon peel, baking powder, pinch of salt, raisins (5), and the stiffly beaten egg whites (6).

Heat a fair amount of oil to 370°F and fry spoonfuls of the rice mixture in it (7). Fry only a few fritters at a time and turn them carefully (8). Lift them out of the pan and lay them on paper towels to drain off the excess oil (9). Place the fritters on a plate and sprinkle them with sifted confectioners' sugar or granulated sugar (10).

Ground cinnamon can also be added to the sugar. The fritters are delicious if eaten immediately and very hot: if you have to wait, keep them in a 200-degree oven.

1 Bring the milk to a boil, add the rice, and cook, stirring continuously.

2 When the milk has been absorbed, remove the rice from the stove and add the sugar...

3 ...and the egg yolks one at a time, thoroughly mixing in each yolk before adding the next.

4 Add the sifted flour a little bit at a time...

5 ...the baking powder, the grated lemon peel, a pinch of salt, and the sultana raisins.

6 Beat the egg whites until stiff, and carefully fold them into the mixture.

7 Heat the oil and fry spoonfuls of the rice mixture in this.

8 Fry only a few fritters at a time; turn them carefully.

9 Drain the fritters when crisp and golden and place them on paper towels.

10 Sprinkle the fritters with granulated or confectioners' sugar before serving.

Rice pudding with dates

■ Yield: 4 servings
■ Time needed: 1 hour
■ Difficulty: *

Ingredients: 5 tbsp. rice, 7 tbsp. sugar, 7 oz. *mascarpone* (or American cream cheese) 5 oz. lady fingers, ½ lb. dates, 3 egg yolks, 1 orange, Grand Marnier or other orange liqueur, 2 cups milk, ¾ cup light cream.

Pour the milk into a saucepan with the cream. Add the sugar and a few strips of orange peel and bring to a boil. Pour in the rice, stirring with a wooden spoon, and simmer until the rice has completely absorbed the liquid: this will take about 30 minutes. Pit the dates. Finely chop about half of them, thinly slice the rest.

Remove the orange peel from the rice, and add the egg yolks, one at a time, the *mascarpone* or cream cheese, the remaining orange peel, grated, and the finely chopped dates.

Pour the strained juice of the orange and ¾ cup Grand Marnier into a dish and dip the lady fingers into this mixture one by one. Arrange the lady fingers on the bottom of a large bowl, pour in some of the rice mixture, and continue alternating layers of lady fingers and rice, finishing with the rice mixture on top. Put the dessert in the refrigerator for a few hours. Before serving, decorate with the sliced dates. A photograph is on page 234.

Chocolate rice balls

■ Yield: 4 servings
■ Time needed: 1 hour
■ Difficulty: *

Ingredients: 1 cup minus 2 tbsp. rice, ¼ cup sugar, 3½ oz. semi-sweet chocolate, 2 oz. (about ⅓ cup) mixed candied fruit, 3 tbsp. butter, 2 cups milk, ½ cup brandy.

Put ½ cup of milk aside and bring the rest to a boil with 1 cup of water. Add the rice, the sugar, and the butter, and cook, stirring frequently, for about 25 minutes. Take the rice off the heat and let it cool. Soak the candied fruit in the brandy, drain it, and add it to the rice. Mix well. Shape the rice mixture into little balls about the size of a walnut. Melt the chocolate with the remaining ½ cup of milk in the top of a double-boiler, let it cool slightly, and, before it hardens, dip the rice balls in it. Finally, put each of the little chocolate-covered balls in a paper case, and keep in the refrigerator.

Rice Imperatrice

■ Yield: 6 servings
■ Time needed: 1½ hours
■ Difficulty: **

Rice ingredients: ½ cup rice, about ⅔ cup mixed candied fruit, ¼ cup granulated sugar, 3 tbsp. confectioners' sugar, ½ vanilla bean or ½ tsp. vanilla extract, 2 cups milk, ¾ cup heavy cream, whipped, a few candied cherries and some candied orange peel to decorate, kirsch, maraschino, 2 tbsp. butter, 2 tbsp. red currant jelly, 3 tbsp. puréed apricots, oil, salt.
Custard ingredients: 4 egg yolks, 1 cup milk, ½ cup sugar, ½ vanilla bean or ½ tsp. vanilla extract, ¼ oz. powdered gelatin.

Pour the milk into a saucepan and bring it to a boil. Add sugar, butter, and a pinch of salt and take it off the stove. Add the vanilla bean, cover, and let stand for 15 minutes. (You may omit this step and add ½ teaspoon vanilla extract along with the puréed apricots to the cooked rice.)

Soak the candied fruit in kirsch. Cook the rice for a few minutes in boiling water, pour into a strainer, rinse under lukewarm water, and drain. Pour rice into a saucepan and cover it with hot milk, removing the vanilla bean. Bring to a boil and let simmer for 25 to 30 minutes, then pour mixture into a bowl and mix in the puréed apricots. (Make the apricot purée by forcing canned apricots or jam through a sieve.) Add the drained candied fruit and let the mixture cool. In the meantime, prepare the custard. Bring 1 cup of milk to a boil, take it off the stove, add the vanilla and let sit, covered for 10-15 minutes. Alternatively, you may stir ½ teaspoon vanilla extract into the cooked custard. Beat the egg yolks with the sugar until they are thick and lemon-colored and then slowly blend in the milk (with the vanilla bean removed), stirring constantly. Pour the mixture into a heavy-bottomed saucepan or into the top of a double boiler and cook the custard, stirring constantly over very low heat, or over gently simmering water. *The custard must not simmer or it will curdle.* When the custard has thickened enough to coat a spoon, take it off the heat and add the gelatin, softened for 5 minutes in 2 tablespoons water. Let custard cool and blend into the rice mixture. As soon as the ingredients begin to gel, fold in whipped cream, sweetened with confectioners' sugar.

Film a smooth-sided mold with oil and pour in the mixture, levelling it with a spoon. Refrigerate about 4 hours. Unmold the custard onto a plate and decorate with cherries and candied orange peel. Serve with red currant jelly dissolved in a few spoonfuls of maraschino.

Rice mousse

■ **Yield: 4 servings**
■ **Time needed: 1 hour**
■ **Difficulty: ***

Ingredients: 1 cup plus 2 tbsp. rice, 1 cup minus 2 tbsp. sugar, 2 cups milk, 1 teaspoon vanilla extract, 1 cup heavy cream, whipped, Grand Marnier (or other orange liqueur), 3 navel oranges.

Wash the rice and partially cook it in boiling water. Bring the milk to a boil with the vanilla, add the rice, and cook for about 20 minutes. Remove from the stove and mix in 5 tbsp. of the sugar (1).

Cut off the ends of two oranges (2). Score parallel lines along the length of the oranges (3) and peel off the rind along these lines (4). The flesh underneath should be intact. Separate the sections and, if possible, remove the remaining white pith from them (5). Cook the remaining 9 tablespoons sugar with ⅓ cup water and the juice of the remaining orange (6) until the syrup darkens slightly—about 320°F. Dip the orange segments into this syrup (7) and let the liquid drip off. Add a jigger of liqueur, again heat the syrup to 320°F, and then dip the orange segments in it a second time. Fold the whipped cream into the rice (8). Pour the mixture into a glass bowl (9) and place the caramelized orange segments on top (10). Refrigerate the dessert for a few hours before serving.

1 Cook the rice in the vanilla-flavored milk and add the sugar.

2 Cut the ends off two oranges.

3 Score parallel lines lengthwise in the peel about an inch apart.

4 Peel the oranges following the cut lines, thus avoiding damage to the flesh.

5 After having separated the sections, carefully remove the white pith.

6 Prepare a syrup by cooking sugar, water, and the juice of one orange.

7 One at a time, dip the orange sections into the syrup, holding them with kitchen tongs.

8 Once the rice is cold, add the whipped cream, folding it in delicately with a whisk.

9 Pour the rice mixture into a glass bowl or into individual dessert bowls.

10 Finally, decorate the rice with the caramelized orange sections.

Apricots Condé

■ **Yield: 4 servings**
🕒 **Time needed: 1½ hours**
■ **Difficulty: ***

Ingredients: 8 large ripe but firm apricots, 1 cup minus 2 tbsp. rice, ½ cup sugar, about ⅔ cup mixed candied fruit, 8 candied cherries, 2 tbsp. butter, 2 "large" eggs, 1 vanilla bean or 1 tsp. vanilla extract, 2 cups milk, kirsch, pinch of salt.

Chop the mixed candied fruit into small cubes and soak them in a small amount of liqueur. Wash the apricots, divide them in half, and remove the pits. Prepare a syrup by bringing ¼ cup sugar and ½ cup water to a boil on the stove. Add the apricots to the syrup and let them simmer for 4 to 5 minutes. Drain them and put them aside until they have cooled. Bring the milk to a boil together with the salt and the vanilla bean and then take it off the stove. (If you do not wish to use a vanilla bean, stir 1 teaspoon vanilla extract into the cooked rice when you add the candied fruit.)

Wash the rice, blanch in boiling water, drain, and rinse under lukewarm water (1). When the rice is well drained, pour it into a pan in which you have melted 2 tablespoons butter (2). Brown the rice lightly and then add the milk, removing the vanilla bean (3). Continue to cook the rice, stirring constantly with a wooden spoon. After about 20 minutes the rice will have completely absorbed the milk; remove it from the stove, add the remaining sugar (4), let it cool slightly, and then mix in the egg yolks, one at a time (5).

Drain the candied fruit and add it to the rice mixture (6). Pour the rice into a buttered ring mold, packing it with a spoon (7), and put it into the refrigerator for at least a couple of hours. Unmold the ring onto a round plate (8) and put four apricot halves in the center (9).

Place the remaining apricots in a crown on top of the rice ring. As a final touch decorate with candied cherries. Add a small quantity of kirsch (or any other liqueur of your choice) to the apricot syrup and pour it over the dessert.

Refrigerate until ready to serve.

1 Blanch the rice in boiling water, drain, and rinse by plunging into lukewarm water.

2 Melt 2 tablespoons butter in a pan and pour the well-drained rice into it.

3 Brown the rice lightly, then add the boiling milk, removing the vanilla bean.

4 When the rice has absorbed all the milk, take it off the stove and add the remaining sugar.

5 Allow the mixture to cool slightly and then add the egg yolks one at a time.

6 Finally mix in the drained candied fruit and stir well.

7 Pour the mixture into a buttered ring mold and pack it down evenly.

8 After refrigerating for a few hours, unmold the rice ring onto a plate.

9 Place four apricot halves in the center of the ring and the remaining ones on top.

Apricots condé

SOUPS

Minestroni

The term soup usually embraces all those dishes that consist of a liquid such as broth, water, or milk to which are added, according to the recipe, vegetables, cereals, meat, eggs, cheeses, bread, pasta, or rice.

The first soup to make history is without a doubt the one that caused Esau to lose his primogeniture (first-born status) to his brother Jacob. As the story goes, Esau was so hungry that he surrendered all his privileges as the first-born just to have the lentil soup his brother was eating. Another famous legume soup is the one remembered in the story of the celebrations that took place on the occasion of the wedding of Catherine of Valois to Henry V of England in which the archbishop, leading the other dignitaries, brought soup and wine to the newlyweds' bedroom.

Soups date back to a time when cookbooks were virtually unknown. To make soups, one trusted recipes that were handed down orally or in more recent times, were scribbled in notebooks. In this way each family developed its own culinary tradition, giving rise to the numerous variations that are still found today in Italy in villages only a few miles apart. Even in the darkest moments in the history of humanity, we find that "a bowl of soup" has often been offered to the poor hungry soul so he could have his fill and take comfort from it. Then there was the famous ham bone that was passed from home to home, or better, from "soup to soup" in Lucchesia, from its owner to the last inhabitant of the village—another lovely story of human solidarity in the name of soup.

The way in which a soup is made, the ingredients that it contains, how it is cooked and eaten, and how and when it is served at the table offers a brief summary of the life of a town or region. For example, we find soups made with rice where the production of this cereal is highest; soups made with the ribs, pig's feet, and rind of pork where the pig reigns supreme; and slow-cooking soups where families are still gathered around a hearth and where the woman of the household is queen. People today are familiar with many of the soups of Italy as well as those of other cuisines. The meeting and blending of cuisines is perhaps one of the most interesting phenomena of our times. It allows us to enjoy the specialities of other countries and to export our own culinary traditions. Unusual foods and recipes that combine ingredients in seemingly incredible ways have now become familiar. To taste them means to enter for a moment into the traditions and customs of another people, and to learn to use even unfamiliar ingredients without prejudice, obtaining the best from them both in flavor and nutritional value.

Regional Soups

The *brodera* of Piedmont is a speciality of the Vercello area prepared on the day the family pig is butchered because the warm blood of the freshly killed pig is added to the broth made with spareribs and rice. Also in Piedmont there is a soup typically served on All Soul's Day which is made with split chick-peas, pork rind, and seasonings and left to simmer for a long time. In nearby Lombardy you will find the famous Milanese minestrone, a hearty country soup that has become such a refined dish that it is served in restaurants as an after-theater snack. It is made with beans, peas, potatoes, and other vegetables in season along with sautéed bacon or pork fat and, for a truly authentic soup, pork rind. Both rice and/or homemade pasta (usually *maltagliati*—that is, roughly cut pieces of pasta) can be added, in which case the vegetables in the minestrone are fewer and the pasta becomes the most important ingredient. Milanese minestrone is almost always served lukewarm in rough earthenware bowls. The minestrone-type soups with barley from the Trento and Alto Adige regions are typically winter dishes and are served steaming hot. The Trento minestrone calls for a ham bone along with the vegetables and pearl barley, and in the Alto Adige they put bacon in the soup. They are usually served in earthenware bowls that keep the soup hot. In the Veneto region there are a number of rice soups owing to the fact that the Doges of the city—the Serenissima Repubblica—used to import large quantities of rice from the Orient. *Risi e Bisi* is certainly the most typical dish of the region. It is made with rice flavored with a sauté of bacon, onion, and parsley and mixed with plenty of peas. Other variations exist, such as rice and spinach, rice and fennel, and even an excellent soup that combines rice and pasta. The pasta is always homemade and is added to the Veneto beans to make that marvelous soup called *pasta e fasoi* (pasta and beans). The nearby Friuli region is not to be forgotten: there meals always begin with a bowl of steaming soup, which, in fact, is the most important dish of the whole cuisine. There is the famous *jota* soup which combines beans, sauerkraut, cornmeal and pork, or the simpler soups of beans and vegetables to which neither rice nor pasta is added because the soups are already quite hearty. In Liguria the addition of *pesto* enhances the flavor of their minestrone, which is almost always made with spring vegetables and borage. A speciality of La Spezia is the *mesciua,* an ancient soup containing chick-peas, tuscan beans, wheat and flavored with Ligurian oil. The original recipe calls for *farro* (spelt, or German wheat), which was considered the key to the success of this soup. In Sardinia, as well as in the regions of Lazio and Umbria, one finds a soup of vegetables and spelt which is flavored with fresh *pecorino* cheese (Romano) and mint leaves. The *malfattini* is quite popular in Emilia-Romagna. The *malfattini* (roughly-cut pasta) are homemade, combined with aromatic herbs and spring vegetables, flavored with plenty of Parmesan. In Tuscany and Marche bean soups with vegetables, sausages, pork, and pasta are typical winter dishes made without meat during days of abstinence. Scholars of the Lazio region hold the broccoli soup in high regard. It is a typical Roman dish prepared with broccoli, pork rind, pork fat, and tomato sauce. The *virtu,* is a minestrone from Abruzzo which combines broad beans, kidney beans, chick-peas, lentils, pork rind, pigs feet, and pork ear with all the vegetables of the season. Another Abruzzo soup is made with wild spring chicory combined with eggs, broth, Romano, pork fat, and aromatic vegetables.

How to Prepare Soups

Vegetable soups are those that are made with one or more vegetables or legumes plus pasta, rice, cereals, and sometimes meats such as tripe and gizzards. Vegetable soups have solid regional origins and are not very different today from the soups that were made many years ago. The choice of available vegetables is naturally limited by the season, and it is clear that spring and summer are the ideal times of the year to make these dishes.

There are a few rules that it is wise to follow in making these vegetable soups in order to obtain the best results. The vegetables should not be cut into pieces that are too small, or they will fall apart during cooking, and they should be cleaned and washed under running water. Never soak vegetables in water for more than a few minutes because they will lose their freshness and some of their vitamins.

Many of these soups are prepared by first sautéing very finely chopped onion or garlic, to which can be added traditional flavorings such as celery, carrot, and parsley, as well as pork fat, bacon, and ham. This chopped preparation is called *il battuto* (from *battere,* to beat) because housewives used to beat the pork fat and other ingredients with rhythmic blows of a knife on a wooden chopping board in order to mince the ingredients finely and uniformly. The fat used for the sauté is usually either oil or butter. Oil is used more often because most of these soups are eaten lukewarm and butter solidifies in an unappetizing manner as it cools. When pork fat or bacon is used no other fat need be added because the melted pork fat or bacon provides more than enough fat for the sauté. Onion and garlic are the basis of any sauté while herbs are optional. When legumes are to be used in a soup the sauté is a necessity, but it is optional when making soup with other vegetables. No hard-and-fast rules exist, but let us say that a sauté will give more flavor to the soup and is especially suitable with vegetables of delicate taste such as zucchini, winter squash, and leeks.

The addition of aromatic herbs and spices, though optional, is also important because they make the soup more flavorful and inviting. Naturally one must not overseason a soup with herbs and spices or their aroma will smother the taste of the vegetables. The most suitable herbs for use in soups are bay leaf (essential when meat is added to a soup along with vegetables), thyme, rosemary, and sage, the minced leaves of which give a wonderful aroma to a soup. Parsley and basil are to be considered absolutely necessary for any soup. Other possibilities include chives, scallions, marjoram, fennel seeds, and savory.

The most frequently used spices are pepper (both white and black), red chili, pepper, paprika, and nutmeg.

These soups can also be prepared without a preliminary sauté by simply putting the diced vegetables (the pieces should not be too small) directly into a pot with cold water and a bouillon cube.

As an alternative to a bouillon cube, either soy sauce or tamari can be used. Soy may be substituted for bouillon cubes and other ingredients used to intensify the flavor of soups, and it has the advantage of being rich in vitamins and minerals. Tamari is soy sauce enriched with other vegetables and is particularly suited for use in all kinds of soups. Both soy sauce and tamari are added to soups that are already cooked, before serving.

Whether the soup has been prepared with a preliminary sauté or without, it should always be cooked over very low heat in a pan with a tightly fitting lid. The ideal soup pot would be an old earthenware crock, which should be placed on a flame-control device over low heat so that the vegetables will stew slowly. In fact, the longer the soup cooks, the better it gets. However, while it is important that the vegetables be well cooked, they should still be whole and not reduced to a purée when the soup is done.

The cooking times of soups are quite long, ranging from a minimum of two hours to a maximum of four. Long cooking times are characteristic of recipes that include pork cuts such as pork rind or pig's feet. A pressure cooker is useful for making soups as it cuts cooking times in half (35 to 40 minutes, timed after the whistle) and captures the steam in which the vegetables have cooked, thus preventing the minerals and vitamins from being lost.

What to Cook in Soups

The ingredients usually added to vegetable soups and minestrone-type soups are rice and pasta but, as we have seen, many regional dishes include other ingredients such as spelt (a type of wheat), barley, oatmeal, and soft wheat.

Pasta — The most suitable kinds of commercially prepared pasta for vegetable soups are the short ones like smooth or fluted small *maccheroni, paternostri, conchigliette* (little shells), *farfalline* (little butterflies), and *fidelini* or *capelli d'angelo* (both hair-fine noodles). Naturally the soup will be even better and more nutritious if fresh pasta (homemade or bought in special stores) is used. Both pasta made with flour and eggs and pasta made with semolina or whole-wheat flour and water are suitable. The shapes of homemade pasta usually used are *maltagliati* (roughly-cut odd shapes), wide, medium, and thin *tagliatelle* (flat noodles), *quadrucci* (little squares), *farfalline* (bowties), *galani* (ribbons), or small spaghetti.

It should be remembered, of course, that whole-wheat pasta not only adds flavor but also minerals and proteins to the soups.

Rice — Rice is used especially often in soups in northern Italy, where it is also cultivated on a vast scale. The most suitable kind of rice is the short-grained variety that has a high starch content. The nutritional properties of rice are more or less the same as those of pasta, except that rice is richer in starch, has less protein, and is almost totally without fats.

Brown rice is a worthy addition to soups because this rice has not been refined or polished and thus has all its original nutritional qualities.

Spelt or German wheat — This is a variety of wheat which originally grew wild and was used by the first inhabitants of Italy to make the *puls,* which could be considered the first soups. Today it is also called mountain wheat because it is grown in the mountains. It is polished before use and has many good properties, as is true of all foods that are not industrially refined. Before it is used it should be soaked for at least six hours, as is done with legumes, then cooked together with the vegetables of the soup.

Barley — This was the most frequently used cereal in soups of the 19th century both because of its nutritional properties (it is high in calories, vitamins, and minerals) and because it is easily digested by both children and the elderly. Today it is not used very often because the Italian pearl barley needs to be soaked before cooking.

Oats — Oats are used only in flaked form (the same form that is used to make oatmeal). Before being added to soups, oats are browned in butter in a pan or toasted in the oven (stir frequently) so that they will lose their moisture and become crisp and brown without burning. The properties of this cereal are many, and they strongly belie the definition given a famous English dictionary, according to which oats are only "food for horses." Oats, in fact, provide energy and have a good caloric value (380 calories for every 3½ ounces). They are rich in phosphorous, iron, and vitamins, especially vitamin B 1. Oats also contain an important growth hormone, auxin.

Proportions and cooking times — In preparing vegetable soups one should calculate two ladles of broth per person (about ⅔ cup), to which will be added 1½ ounces dried pasta or 3 tablespoons raw rice. If adding fresh pasta, the quantity should be increased to about 2 ounces per person. The proportions are more or less the same for the other cereals except barley and oatmeal, for which one should calculate 2 tablespoons per person.

The cooking time varies according to the type and size of the pasta. The cooking time for the small pasta generally used in soups is about 10 minutes. Homemade pasta—both egg and whole-wheat—requires shorter cooking times (3 to 5 minutes). Rice takes from 15 to 18 minutes to cook. The cereals that require soaking have longer cooking times, from 40 to 60 minutes. Oats only need to be added to the soup 5 minutes before it is removed from the stove.

Vegetable Soups

Smooth vegetable soups have as their base vegetables that are steamed or boiled and then puréed. To the puréed vegetables are added other ingredients such as oil or butter, bouillon, or vegetable broth. They may either be served plain or fortified with pasta, rice, barley, oats, or toasted bread.

If the vegetables are to be steamed, they are first trimmed, washed under running water, and cut into medium-size pieces. They are then put in a pressure cooker or steaming pot. Alternatively, the vegetables may be boiled just as for a minestrone, though these soups, unlike minestrone, hardly ever use a preliminary sauté. A well-made vegetable purée should be completely smooth and the different flavors should be thoroughly blended. To obtain such a smooth purée one has to use an electric mixer blender or food processor. Once the vegetables are puréed, oil or butter is added, and sometimes also cream or yogurt. The choice between a bouillon cube or a vegetable cube to enhance the flavor is left to personal preference. Another way of obtaining a vegetable purée is to mince the raw vegetables in an electric blender, combine them with some broth, and bring the mixture to a boil. In this way both the preparation and the cooking are much faster. The soup is then flavored with a bit of olive oil added at the last minute. This latter method of making a vegetable purée allows the vegetable to keep all their nutritional values. Interesting variations are those vegetable soups made with raw vegetables and served cold, such as the famous Spanish gazpacho. The most suitable vegetables for these summer soups are tomatoes, sweet peppers, carrots, lettuce, cucumbers, celery hearts, garlic, and onion.

Freezing Soups

While a good meat stock, strained and carefully degreased, can be kept in the refrigerator only 4 to 5 days, a vegetable broth will keep up to a week, especially if it does not contain beans or potatoes. Both types of broth will also keep very well in the freezer for up to three months if poured into covered containers.

The vegetables used to make vegetable soups and purées can also be frozen. They should be trimmed, washed, blanched in boiling water, allowed to cool, divided into small portions, and put into plastic containers or plastic bags (1). The air should be removed from the bag with the help of a straw (2), and the bag sealed airtight with a metal tie (3). The vegetables will keep for up to seven months and when needed can be put directly into boiling water or stock without defrosting.

Since minestrone takes a lot of time to make, it is a good soup to make ahead and freeze so that it will be ready to eat when you want it. It needs only to be heated. If you are going to freeze a minestrone it is a good idea to make it with little oil or fat. Just before you use the soup, you can add pork fat or bacon minced with parsley or a tablespoon of olive oil or a small handful of chopped mixed herbs.

Vegetable purées and some *veloutés* and simple cream soups can also be frozen, especially those that do not contain milk.

Cream should not be added to soups prior to freezing but should instead be added later when reheating the soup. Cream soups will keep very well in the refrigerator for 4 to 5 days if put in covered containers. In the freezer they will last 3 months or longer. They should be reheated in a double boiler and diluted with a little milk or stock (depending on the ingredients of the soup) if necessary.

1 After having diced and blanched the vegetables, put them into plastic bags.

2 Before closing the bags let out all the air with the help of a straw.

3 Then close the bags using a tie.

Necessary Utensils

High-sided, heavy pots are most suitable for cooking soups because such pots permit a uniform diffusion of heat throughout long cooking times.

The classic soup pot is earthenware used for vegetable soups, which allows for slow cooking over low heat, thus ensuring that the vegetables will remain whole and separate. Today the earthenware crock has almost wholly been replaced by stainless steel pots. A pressure-cooker is also handy for making soups as it can reduce cooking time significantly. Various kinds of pots and baskets for steaming vegetables are available. You might consider investing in one as steaming is an especially good way of cooking vegetables to preserve taste and nutritional value. Steaming is the preferred method of cooking vegetables for purées, cream soups, and *veloutés*. Small earthenware pots, heat-resistant porcelain, and pyrex, are ideal for making soups that need to go into the oven to be gratinéed. For serving soups, it is nice to have a beautiful soup tureen, either the classic kind that comes with two-handled cups for light soups or broths, or the

plainer, country type with earthenware soup plates or bowls.

The necessary utensils for preparing vegetables for soups include small pointed paring knives for peeling and slicing and either a food mill with interchangeable disks or an electric food processer to slice, chop, and purée vegetables. For chopping one can also use a spring-mechanism utensil, and to purée one can use an ordinary blender. There are many other utensils that are useful but not essential, such as a parsley-mincing device, an onion chopper, a rocker, (a half-moon-shaped knife with two handles), a chopping board, and a wooden or marble mortar and pestle.

Some Useful Hints

Vegetables should be washed repeatedly under running water, drained, and then cut into pieces that are not so small that they will disintegrate during cooking. It is a good rule to divide vegetables into two groups according to their cooking times. Put those that have long cooking times on one side of your work surface and those that cook quickly on the other. This way, you will remember in what order to put them into the pot.

Oil, butter, or other fats can be added directly to the soup or in a sauté. In the first instance the oil or butter is put into a pot along with all the diced vegetables and cold water. More often, the oil or butter is not added at the beginning but rather as part of a sauté that is added when the base of the soup has cooked. In the second instance the soup vegetables are added to the sauté when the onions have become almost transparent and the meat, if any, has rendered its fat. The vegetables are gently fried for a few minutes, and then broth (or water and bouillon cubes) is added.

Aromatic herbs are essential, because they make soups fragrant and inviting. The most suitable herbs are parsley, basil, marjoram, mint, thyme, dill, and chives.

Minestrone made without a sauté almost always requires the addition of a meat or vegetable bouillon cube of a good meat stock.

Soups or minestrone should be served directly from a soup tureen if meant to be eaten hot. If a minestrone is to be eaten lukewarm, as is done in Italy in summer, it should be put into individual bowls and left in a cool place (not the refrigerator) for at least two hours before it is brought to the table, where it should be offered with good olive oil, pepper, and grated cheese. The best way to heat minestrone just out of the refrigerator or freezer is in a double boiler. If the recipe allows, sprinkle Parmesan cheese on the surface of the minestrone and put it in the oven to gratinée.

Milanese minestrone

■ **Yield: 4 servings**
■ **Time needed: 3 hours**
■ **Difficulty: ***

Ingredients: 14 tbsp. rice, 12 oz. pinto beans shelled, or ⅔ cup dried white or pinto beans soaked overnight, 1 cup peeled, seeded, and juiced tomato, fresh or canned, ¼ lb. asparagus tips, 2½ oz. lean green bacon thickly cut, 3 tbsp. butter, 2½ oz. (about ⅔ cup) grated Parmesan cheese, 3 carrots, 2 potatoes, 2 zucchini, 1 leek, 1 celery heart, 1 onion, 1 clove garlic, 2 bay leaves, ¼ tsp. of rosemary, ground, bunch basil, bunch parsley, about 6½ cups light stock, freshly ground pepper, salt.

Put half of the butter in a pot, add the blanched bacon chopped together with the onion and leek (1), and sauté over moderate heat. When the ingredients are soft, add the asparagus tips, the carrots, the potatoes, and the zucchini, all diced, the beans, the chopped celery (2), and the remaining butter. Season with salt and pepper and cook over moderate heat for a few minutes, stirring (3). Add a *bouquet garni* of several sprigs of parsley and a bay leaf (4), the rosemary, and the tomato pulp (5). Pour in the stock (6) and continue cooking until the beans are tender. Add the rice (7) and, just before the soup is done, flavor it with a finely chopped mixture of basil, bay leaf, garlic, and parsley (8). Let the minestrone sit for a few minutes before serving. Serve the Parmesan cheese separately.

1 After having melted the butter in the pot, add the bacon chopped with the onion and leek.

2 Add all the diced vegetables and the beans to the sauté.

3 Season with salt and pepper and sauté the vegetables for a few minutes, stirring.

4 Add parsley and bay leaf to the minestrone, tied in a *bouquet garni*.

5 Add the rosemary and the tomato pulp, crushed, to the softened vegetables.

6 Cover the vegetables with the stock, put a lid on the pot, and continue cooking over very low heat.

7 When all the vegetables, especially the beans, are done, pour in the rice.

8 Just before taking the minestrone off the stove, flavor it with chopped aromatic herbs.

Milanese minestrone

Minestrone primavera

■ **Yield: 4 servings**
■ **Time needed: 2 and ½ hours**
■ **Difficulty: ***

Ingredients: ½ lb. large egg pasta *quadrucci* (squares), ½ lb. green beans, ½ lb. fresh peas, 12 oz. fresh pinto beans, ⅝ oz. dried boletus mushrooms, ½ lb. chopped plum tomatoes, 2 potatoes, one zucchini, 2 tbsp. of pesto (see p. 178), oil, salt.

Cook the beans in boiling water and drain them when two-thirds done. Soak the mushrooms in warm water, wash them well, squeeze out the excess moisture, and chop them. Bring about 2 quarts of salted water to a boil, add the beans and green beans, and let cook for half an hour. Add the diced zucchini and potatoes, the peas, tomatoes, mushrooms, a few tablespoons of oil, and salt. When the vegetables are very tender, add the pasta. Stir well and cook until the pasta is done. Before taking the soup off the stove add the basil and garlic and let sit a few minutes before serving.

Barley and bean minestrone

■ **Yield: 4 servings**
■ **Time needed: 3 hours**
■ **Difficulty: ***

Ingredients: ½ lb. pearl barley, 1 lb. fresh pinto beans shelled, or 1 cup dried white or pinto beans, soaked overnight, 3½ oz. pork rind, the fat scraped off, 3 tbsp. grated Parmesan cheese, 2 oz. pork fat, 2 bay leaves, 1 onion, 1 stalk celery, 2 potatoes, 1 sprig parsley, 1 tbsp. excellent olive oil, 1 tbsp. tomato paste, pepper, salt.

Finely chop the pork fat, onion, and parsley together, put them in a pot, add a tablespoon of oil, and sauté gently. Add the barley, stir well, and cover with 4 cups water. Add the pork rind, partially cover and let simmer for at least 2 hours, stirring now and then with a wooden spoon.

In the meantime, cook the beans separately in boiling water with bay leaves for the same amount of time as the barley. Add the beans and their cooking liquid to the barley, and then add the diced potatoes, and the tomato paste, diluted in a little hot broth. Season with salt and pepper.

Let the soup simmer for another 40 minutes. Sprinkle with grated Parmesan and serve in warmed bowls.

Ligurian minestrone

■ **Yield: 4 servings**
■ **Time needed: 2 hours**
■ **Difficulty: ***

Ingredients: 5 oz. your favorite pasta, ½ lb. fresh pinto beans, shelled, or ½ cup dried white or pinto beans, soaked overnight and then boiled until half tender, ¼ lb. spinach, ¼ lb. beets, 4 tomatoes, 2 potatoes, 1 onion, 1 clove garlic, 1 stalk celery, ½ small cabbage, small bunch parsley, 1 tbsp. pesto, salt.

Bring 6 cups lightly salted water to a boil, and add the beans, the roughly chopped cabbage, the chopped spinach and beets, the cut up potatoes, and the tomatoes, peeled, seeded, and juiced. Finely chop the garlic clove together with the onion, celery, and parsley, add them to the vegetables, and continue cooking with the lid ajar for about an hour or until the beans are tender. Drain the potatoes, mash them with a fork, and return them to the pot. Bring to a boil again, add the pasta, stir, and continue cooking for another 15 to 20 minutes. A few minutes before removing the minestrone from the stove flavor it with the chopped basil. Let it sit for a few seconds so the fragrance of the basil can be absorbed and serve in earthenware bowls. This is also excellent served cold or lukewarm.

Vegetable minestrone with marjoram

■ **Yield: 4 servings**
■ **Time needed: 2 hours**
■ **Difficulty: ***

Ingredients: ½ lb. pasta (not too small), ½ lb. green beans, 1 lb. pinto beans, shelled, or 1 cup dried white beans, soaked overnight, ½ lb. peas shelled, 2 potatoes, 2 whole cloves garlic, peeled, 1 tsp. marjoram, 3 tbsp. grated Parmesan cheese, oil, pepper, salt.

Cook the beans in boiling water and drain them when half-done. Sauté the garlic in a pot with a few tablespoons oil; when it is golden remove it and add the well-drained beans, the peas, the cut-up green beans, and the diced potatoes. Stir well for a few minutes, cover with plenty of water, season with salt and pepper, and bring to a boil. Cook over medium heat, adding the pasta and marjoram when the vegetables are cooked. Stir, cook until done.

Serve with grated Parmesan or other cheese.

Pasta and beans

- **Yield: 4 servings**
- **Time needed: 3 hours (plus soaking time for the beans)**
- **Difficulty: ***

Ingredients: About 1¼ cups dried white or pinto beans, ½ lb. egg pasta, preferably *maltagliati*, 1 cup peeled, seeded, juiced tomato, fresh or canned, 1 tbsp. butter, grated Parmesan, 1 carrot, 1 onion, 1 small stalk celery, small bunch parsley, oil, salt.

Soak the beans overnight in cold water. Finely chop the onion, carrot, celery, and parsley and put in a pot (1). Add the butter and 2 tablespoons oil, and sauté over moderate heat. Add the crushed tomato pulp (2) and the well-drained beans (3), cover with water (4), season with salt, and bring to a boil over moderate heat.

When the beans are cooked, push about half of them through a sieve (5), (or purée in a blender), return the puréed beans to the pot, and return to a boil. Add the pasta (6) and cook until done. Stir frequently because the pasta, in such a thick broth, will tend to stick to the pot.

Sprinkle with of grated Parmesan and pepper. Serve, spooning olive oil over each portion.

1 Place the chopped onion, carrot, celery, and parsley in a pot.

2 Sauté the chopped vegetables in oil and butter, and then add the tomato pulp.

3 Add the drained beans to the sautéed vegetables.

4 Cover the vegetables with plenty of cold water and slowly bring to a boil.

5 When the beans are cooked, force about half of them through a sieve and return them to the pot.

6 Finally, add the pasta to the bean broth and cook until done, stirring frequently.

Pasta and beans

Barley soup

■ **Yield: 4 servings**
■ **Time needed: 2 hours (plus soaking time)**
■ **Difficulty: ***

Ingredients: 6-8 oz. pearl barley, 3½ oz. *prosciutto* ham in one slice, 1 oz. (about ¼ cup) grated Parmesan cheese, 1½ tbsp. butter, 1 onion, 1 carrot, 1 stalk celery, 1 bay leaf, about 6 cups stock, 1 cup light cream, salt.

Soak the barley in plenty of cold water for 2 hours, or as the instructions on the package direct.

Finely chop the onion, celery, and carrot and sauté in a pot with the butter. When the vegetables have become soft add the diced *prosciutto* ham and cook gently, stirring with a wooden spoon.

Drain the barley well, add it to the sauté, let cook for 5 minutess while stirring, and then add the stock. Add the bay leaf, cover, and let simmer over low heat for about 1½ hours, stirring often. When almost done, taste the soup and correct the seasoning. Just before removing the soup from the stove, add the cream and grated Parmesan cheese.

Chicory and egg soup

■ **Yield: 4 servings**
■ **Time needed: 1 hour**
■ **Difficulty: ***

Ingredients: 1¼ lbs. chicory, 2 eggs, 1 oz. bacon, 1 stalk celery, 1 smallish onion, 2 carrots, 3 tbsp. oil, chopped garlic and parsley, about 6 cups stock, 2 tbsp. grated Romano cheese, pepper, salt.

Trim the chicory, wash it well under running water, and cook it in plenty of boiling water. Drain it when well done, and leave it under cold running water for 2½ hours so that it will lose some of its characteristic bitter taste. Chop the celery and carrots, put them in a pot, cover them with the stock, and cook them over moderate heat. In the meantime, finely chop the onion with the bacon, add the chopped garlic and parsley, and fry this mixture in the oil in a pan. Drain the chicory, squeezing out the excess moisture, chop it roughly, and add it to the sauté. When ready to serve add the chicory sauté mixture to the stock with the vegetables, stir well, and pour into a soup tureen in which two eggs have been beaten with 2 tablespoons grated Romano cheese. Add a pinch of freshly ground pepper and a pinch of salt. Stir well.

Pea soup

■ **Yield: 4 servings**
■ **Time needed: 1½ hours**
■ **Difficulty: ***

Ingredients: 1 lb. frozen peas or 2 lbs. fresh peas, shelled, ½ lb. *ditalini* (small tubular pasta), 1 small onion, 3½ oz. bacon, thickly cut, 3 tbsp. lard, 3 tbsp. good tomato sauce, 1 tbsp. chopped parsley, oil, pepper, salt.

Dice the bacon and sauté it in a pot with some oil, the lard, and the sliced onion. When the ingredients have become golden, add the peas and the tomato sauce, diluted in a little warm water. Stir the mixture, season with salt and pepper, and cook in a covered pot over moderate heat until the peas are tender.

Cook the pasta separately in plenty of salted water. Drain it when *al dente* (firm to the tooth), add it to the peas, and thin the soup with some of the cooking water from the pasta (the soup should appear quite thick). Just before removing it from the stove garnish with the parsley and serve.

Pumpkin soup

■ **Yield: 4 servings**
■ **Time needed: 1½ hours**
■ **Difficulty: ***

Ingredients: 1 pumpkin or butternut squash weighing about 2¼ lbs., 1 lb. dried pasta *maccheroni* or *ditalini* (small tubes), 2 cloves garlic, small bunch parsley, small piece hot chili pepper, grated Parmesan cheese, oil, salt.

Sauté the crushed garlic in a pot with ½ cup oil. When the garlic is golden remove it and add the peeled and sliced pumpkin or squash and the hot pepper. Season with salt, cover with cold water, bring to a boil, and cook until the pumpkin or squash as disintegrated into a pulp and the liquid has thickened.

Cook the pasta separately in boiling water, drain it when *al dente*, and add it to the pumpkin. Add enough of the pasta cooking water to obtain a fairly thick soup. Add the parsley as a finishing touch and let simmer for a few minutes longer.

Serve the soup with plenty of grated Parmesan cheese.

Turnip and rice soup

■ **Yield: 4 servings**
■ **Time needed: 1½ hours**
■ **Difficulty: ***

Ingredients: 1 lb. turnips, 14 tbsp. rice, 2½ oz. salt pork, 2 oz. (about ½ cup) grated Parmesan cheese, 2 tbsp. butter, 1 tbsp. chopped parsley, 1 small onion, pepper (optional), salt.

Peel, wash, and slice the turnips. Cook them in lightly salted boiling water and drain them when still firm. Warm them in butter in a small pan, stirring frequently. Sauté the finely chopped onion until soft in the salt pork, pour in about 2 quarts water, add salt, bring to a boil, and add the rice. Cook over moderately high heat, stirring often with a wooden spoon. A few minutes before taking the soup off the stove add the turnips and the parlsey.

Pass with plenty of grated Parmesan cheese. If you want a more savory first course, substitute a light meat stock for the water and sprinkle the soup with a good pinch of ground pepper.

Turnip and rice soup

Gazpacho

■ **Yield: 4 servings**
■ **Time needed: ½ hour**
■ **Difficulty: ***

Ingredients: 2 green peppers, 1 fresh cucumber, 1 onion, 1 lb. ripe tomatoes, 1 clove garlic, 1 fresh or dried hot chili pepper, 2 slices stale bread or 1 stale roll, pinch cumin seeds, some wine vinegar, 3-6 tbsp. olive oil, pepper, salt.

Soak the roll in a few tablespoons vinegar. Cut the ends of the cucumber, peel and slice into rounds (1). Cut the peppers in half lengthwise, remove the seeds and ribs, and dice (2). Cut the onion into rounds, then into pieces (3). Prepare the tomatoes in the same way (4). Squeeze the vinegar out of the bread, put the bread into a mortar. Add the clove of garlic and the hot pepper, and pound the mixture to a paste, incorporating olive oil, to taste (5), cumin, and a pinch of salt and pepper. Put all the vegetables into a blender (6) or food processor and blend for a few seconds to make a rough purée (7). Then add the prepared garlic mixture (8), and enough water to make a fairly fluid soup. Blend again briefly. Season with pepper (9) and add a few ice cubes (10).

Gazpacho is a vegetable soup to be eaten in warm weather. It is customary to accompany it with a plate of the same vegetables, diced.

1 Cut the ends off the cucumber, peel it, and cut it into ¼-inch rounds.

2 Cut the peppers lengthwise, remove the seeds and ribs, and cut into strips then squares.

3 Peel the onion and cut it first into rounds and then into little pieces.

4 Wash and dry the tomatoes well, and cut them first into slices and then into pieces.

5 Pound the bread, garlic, and chili pepper in the mortar, and incorporate the oil.

6 Put all the previously prepared vegetables into an electric blender...

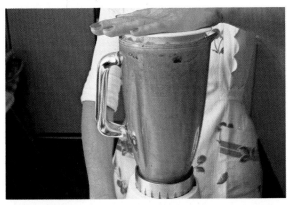

7 ...put the lid on the blender, and blend the vegetables into a rough purée.

8 Blend the bread, garlic, hot pepper, oil, and cumin mixture into the puréed vegetables.

9 After having added a sufficient quantity of water to make a fluid soup, season with plenty of pepper...

10 ...and before serving finish the preparation by adding a few ice cubes to the cold soup.

Cold puréed tomato soup

■ Yield: 4 servings
■ Time needed: 40 minutes
■ Difficulty: *

Ingredients: 4 or 5 ripe fleshy tomatoes, 1 onion, 1 tbsp. chopped basil, 1 small cucumber, ¼ lb. cooked tongue, some sugar, 4-5 tbsp. light cream, juice of ½ lemon, 1 teaspoon Worcestershire sauce, pepper, salt.

Blanch the tomatoes in boiling water, peel them, remove the seeds, and chop them. Either force them through a sieve, collecting the purée in a bowl, or purée in a blender or food processor. Add a scant teaspoon of sugar and put the purée in the refrigerator to cool. Finely chop the onion, wrap it in a cheesecloth, and squeeze out its juice. Add the onion juice to the tomato purée, season with salt, and add the Worcestershire sauce, the lemon juice, 4 or 5 tablespoons of light cream, pepper, and salt. Mix well and pour the soup into a soup tureen. At the last minute add the diced cucumber and tongue, stir, and sprinkle with basil.

Puréed mixed vegetable soup

■ Yield: 4 servings
■ Time needed: 1½ hours
■ Difficulty: *

1¼ cups drained canned white beans or shelled fresh pinto beans, 1¼ cups frozen or shelled fresh peas, 5 oz. seeded, peeled pumpkin or butternut squash, 5 tbsp. butter, 2 zucchini, 2 stalks celery, 1 carrot, 1 onion, 1 leek, bread croutons, about 8 cups stock.

Boil all the vegetables, diced, and the legumes, in 4 cups stock. Force all the vegetables through a sieve or purée in a blender or food processor, add the remaining stock, and let boil for a few minutes. Take the pot off the stove and blend in 2 tablespoons of the butter, in pieces, stirring with a whisk.
Serve with croutons fried in the remaining butter.

Puréed potato soup

■ Yield: 4 servings
■ Time needed: 2 hours
■ Difficulty: *

Ingredients: ¾ lbs. potatoes, ¼ lb. small carrots, 2½ oz. (about ⅔ cup) grated Parmesan cheese, 1 stalk celery, 1 small onion, 6 cups meat stock, 1 cup light cream, 2 tbsp. butter, freshly ground black pepper, salt.

Boil the diced potatoes and carrots in the stock. Sauté the finely chopped onion and celery in the butter, add the potatoes and carrots, both vegetables forced through a sieve, and dilute with the stock. Season with salt and pepper, bring to a boil, and take the pot off the stove.
Blend in the cream, stir, and bring to the table. Serve the grated Parmesan cheese separately.

Puréed tomato soup

■ Yield: 4 servings
■ Time needed: 1 hour
■ Difficulty: *

Ingredients: ¾ lbs. ripe tomatoes, 1 small onion, 1 potato, a few basil leaves, 1 clove garlic, 3 tbsp. butter, 6 cups stock, 1 stalk celery, 4 oz. bread croutons, toasted or fried in butter, 2 oz. grated Parmesan cheese (about ½ cup), olive oil, freshly ground pepper, salt.

Finely chop together the onion, celery, basil leaves, and the clove of garlic. Gently sauté the chopped vegetables and herbs in a few tablespoons of oil and half of the butter. After a few minutes add the seeded and chopped tomatoes, the peeled potato, salt, and pepper. Cover with stock and cook for about half an hour. Force all the ingredients through a sieve (or purée in a blender or food processor), pour soup back into the pot and bring to a boil. If the soup is too thick add more boiling stock. Just before serving add the remaining butter.
Serve the grated cheese and croutons separately.

Chick-pea soup

■ Yield: 4 servings
■ Time needed: 3 hours (plus soaking time for the chick-peas)
■ Difficulty: *

Ingredients: 14 oz. dried chick-peas, 10 oz. *lasagnette all'uovo* (small egg-pasta lasagna or egg noodles), 3 anchovy fillets, drained, 2 cloves garlic, ½ tsp. rosemary, excellent olive oil, pepper, salt.

Soak the chick-peas in warm water overnight. Drain them, put them in a pot, cover with cold, lightly salted water, add ¼ teaspoon rosemary and a peeled clove of garlic, and cook until done. Sauté the remaining rosemary and garlic, peeled and crushed with the side of a knife, in a pan in about ½ cup oil. Season with pepper. When the garlic is golden remove it and add the mashed anchovy fillets. Pour the sauté into the chick-pea soup and bring to a boil. Add the pasta and cook until done, stirring frequently so that it will not stick to the bottom of the pot.

Potato soup

■ **Yield: 4 servings**
■ **Time needed: 35 minutes**
■ **Difficulty: ***

Ingredients: 5 oz. short pasta, 2 oz. smoked bacon, 2 tbsp. butter, 2 potatoes, 1 onion, 6 cups stock, freshly ground pepper, salt.

Finely chop the onion and sauté it in a pot with the butter and chopped bacon. Add the stock, bring to a boil, and pour in the pasta and the potatoes, very thinly sliced. Season with salt and pepper. Cook over moderate heat (if the soup becomes too thick add more stock) and let the soup sit for a few minutes before serving.

Pasta and artichoke soup

■ **Yield: 4 servings**
■ **Time needed: 1½ hours**
■ **Difficulty: ***

Ingredients: ½ lb. pasta of your choice, 1 lb. artichokes, ½ cup peeled, seeded, juiced tomato, fresh or canned, 2½ oz. pork fat, 1 clove garlic, ½ onion, ½ stalk celery, small bunch parsley, grated Romano cheese, excellent olive oil, freshly ground pepper, salt.

Chop the pork fat with the onion, garlic, celery, and parsley. Put the chopped ingredients in a pot and sauté in a few tablespoons oil. Add the chopped tomato pulp, season with salt and pepper, and cook for a few minutes. Trim the artichokes, removing the thorns, the tough parts of the leaves, and the chokes. Cut them into small segments and add them to the other ingredients in the pot, stirring well. Add about 6 cups water and cook over moderate heat until the artichokes are almost tender. Correct the seasoning, add the pasta, and cook until done. Sprinkle with plenty of Romano cheese before serving.

Rice and lentil soup

■ **Yield: 4 servings**
■ **Time needed: 2 hours and 50 minutes (plus soaking time)**
■ **Difficulty: ***

Ingredients: 5 oz. small dried lentils (about ⅔ cup), ½ cup rice, 1 oz. pork fat, bunch parsley, 1 clove garlic, 4 ripe plum tomatoes, 1 beef bouillon cube, 2 tbsp. grated Parmesan cheese, 3 tbsp. excellent olive oil, freshly ground pepper, salt.

Soak the lentils overnight in a bowl with plenty of cold water. The following morning drain the lentils, pour them into a pot, cover with about 6 cups water, and cook over very low heat, adding salt only at the end of the cooking time. Chop the pork fat with the garlic and the parsley almost to a paste, and sauté the mixture in another pan with two tablespoons of oil. Then add the peeled, seeded, and crushed tomatoes (crush them with a fork), stir, and pour in 6 cups of water in which you have dissolved the bouillon cube. Season with salt and bring the liquid to a slow boil. About 15-20 minutes before the lentils are cooked, add the rice and cook it just until *al dente* so that the rice and lentils are done cooking at the same time. Add the cooked lentils to the rice soup just a second before taking it off the stove. Mix the grated Parmesan cheese into the soup, add a pinch of pepper, and pour it into a soup tureen.

Rice and pea soup

■ **Yield: 4 servings**
■ **Time needed: 45 minutes**
■ **Difficulty: ***

Ingredients: 2½ lbs. fresh peas, shelled, or 2 cups frozen peas, 1½ cups rice, 3 tbsp. butter, 2 oz. bacon, 1 small onion, two tbsp. oil, 1 tbsp. chopped parsley, 6 cups stock, 2 tbsp. grated Parmesan cheese, freshly ground pepper, salt.

Sauté the chopped bacon, the sliced onion, and the parsley with the oil and half of the butter. After a few minutes add the peas, stir well, season with salt and pepper, and add a little hot stock. Cook over moderate heat for about half an hour, add the remaining stock, bring to a boil, and add the rice. Cook the soup, stirring frequently, and when the rice is almost cooked blend in the remaining butter, in pieces, and the cheese. The soup should turn out to be very thick and should be served good and hot, with more grated Parmesan cheese passed around at the table.

Ligurian cabbage soup

- **Yield: 4 servings**
- **Time needed: 1½ hours**
- **Difficulty: ***

Ingredients: 1 Savoy cabbage weighing about 2¼ lbs., 1 cup rice, 1 onion, 2 stalks celery, 1 small carrot, about 6 cups fish stock, 3 tbsp. oil, bunch parsley, ½ clove garlic, whole freshly ground pepper, salt.

Trim, wash and shred the cabbage. Finely chop the celery, onion, parsley, and garlic and sauté gently in a pot with two tablespoons oil. Add the cabbage and cook until soft. Pour in the hot, strained fish stock (made simply with fish scraps and bones). Cook slowly for an hour, then add the rice, stir, and cook until done. Check the soup for seasoning and add pepper and the remaining oil.

Fava bean and artichoke soup

- **Yield: 4 servings**
- **Time needed: 1½ hours**
- **Difficulty: ***

Rice and pea soup

Ingredients: 3 lbs. fresh broad beans, (fava beans), shelled, or ½ lb. dried fava beans, soaked overnight, ½ lb. onions, 6 medium-size artichokes, about 1 cup excellent olive oil, 1 stalk celery, 1 lemon, salt.

Soak the beans in cold water. Clean the artichokes, removing the tough outer leaves, the thorns, and the chokes, and cut them into slivers. Put the artichokes into water acidulated with the juice of the lemon. Peel the onions and chop them roughly with the celery. Put these vegetables in a pot, add the beans and artichokes, and pour in the olive oil and about 6 cups water. Season with salt and cook until the beans are tender. Serve hot.

Rice and asparagus soup

■ Yield: 4 servings
■ Time needed: 1 hour 15 minutes
■ Difficulty: *

Ingredients: 14 oz. asparagus, 14 tbsp. rice, 2 oz. fatty *prosciutto* ham, ½ onion, 2 tbsp. butter, 6 cups stock, 2 tbsp. grated Parmesan cheese, excellent olive oil, salt.

Wash the asparagus, cut off the tops, and thinly slice the green part of the stalks, discarding the tough white ends. Sauté the asparagus slices, the chopped onion, and ham in a pot with the butter and oil, add a little stock, and cook for 10 to 15 minutes. Add the rice, mix it well with the other ingredients, and cover with the remaining stock. Bring to a boil and cook until done.
Boil the asparagus tips separately in a little salted water. Drain when firm and add them to the soup. Sprinkle with Parmesan.

Lettuce soup

■ Yield: 4 servings
■ Time needed: 1 hour
■ Difficulty: *

Ingredients: 2 heads Romaine lettuce, 6 cups meat stock (or chicken stock), 1 onion, 5 tbsp. butter, 1 tbsp. white flour, about ½ cup grated Parmesan, salt.

Trim the heads of lettuce, discarding the outer leaves. Wash, drain and cut into thin shreds. Finely chop the onion and sauté it until soft with 3 tablespoons butter. Add the flour, stir, and when the mixture starts to brown add the boiling stock a little at a time, stirring constantly. Bring to a boil, add the lettuce, and cook over low heat for 15 minutes covered. Correct the seasoning and serve with bread croutons fried in butter and grated cheese.

Ligurian soup

■ Yield: 4 servings
■ Time needed: 45 minutes
■ Difficulty: *

Ingredients: ½ lb. *trenette, linguine,* or other thin flat spaghetti, 1 cup peeled, seeded, juiced tomato, fresh or canned, about ⅔ cup grated Parmesan cheese, 2½ oz. pork fat or ham fat, 3 cloves garlic, 1 tbsp. chopped basil, 6 cups light stock, olive oil, pepper, salt.

Finely mince the fat with the garlic, put the mixture in a pot, add two tablespoons oil, and sauté. Add the sliced tomato pulp and the stock, correct the seasoning, and bring to a boil. Add the pasta, broken up, and cook until done. Remove the pot from the stove, add the basil and half of the cheese, and serve with the remaining cheese.

Puréed carrot soup

■ Yield: 4 servings
■ Time needed: 1½ hours
■ Difficulty: *

Ingredients: 1¾ lbs. small, young carrots, 5 tbsp. butter, 1 onion, bunch parsley, 1 small white celery heart, 1 tbsp. finely chopped parsley, meat or vegetable stock, milk or light cream, bread croutons fried in butter, pepper, salt.

Scrape the carrots, wash them, and slice thinly. Chop the onion and sauté it in 3 tablespoons butter until soft but not brown. Add the carrots and the celery heart tied in a *bouquet garni* with the parsley. Season with salt and pepper, and add enough stock to cover. Cover the pot and simmer until the carrots have become soft.
Removed the *bouquet garni*, force the carrots through a sieve and pour the purée into a pot. Thin it as you wish with stock milk or cream and heat over low flame. Sprinkle with chopped parsley. Serve with fried croutons.

Broths and Zuppe

There has been much discussion about the nutritional value of broth, considered by some to be very great and by others almost nonexistent. Actually broth of any kind is not a nourishing food; it only has a refreshing and tonic effect. This is not true, of course, if the broth is enriched with other ingredients such as cheeses, vegetables, eggs, meats, or cereals. The *zuppe* are closely related to broths *(brodi)*. They are soups made from broth and bread to which other natural ingredients are sometimes added. The original recipes, in fact, called for ingredients that were available to everyone. The famous *Zuppa Pavese* is a good ilustration of this. History recounts that in 1525, Francis I, defeated in Lombard territory by Charles V, was wandering around the countryside downcast and hungry. He entered a farmhouse and saw a peasant woman who was preparing a broth of beans and herbs. The king told her who he was and asked for something to eat. The poor woman broke some stale bread into a bowl and wet it with a ladle of broth. This, however, did not seem enough for a king, and the woman, not knowing what to offer him, ran out to the henhouse and found two fresh eggs which she broke into the soup, creating a small masterpiece.

The common element and principal characteristic of all *zuppe* is bread. But be careful, because not all kinds of bread are suitable for such soups. One should not use soft or sweetened commercial breads or seasoned breads, but plain French or Italian loaves or homemade bread. Black bread, rye bread or pumpernickel are also suitable. The bread is usually thickly sliced and toasted before being put in the bowls into which the steaming soup is then poured. Sometimes the toasted bread is rubbed with a clove of garlic, giving fragrance and aroma to the soup, and sometimes the bread is covered with plenty of cheese before the broth is added.

How to Prepare Broth

To obtain a good meat broth one must follow certain rules.

—Choose a flavorful cut of stewing beef or veal such as chuck, the plate, or rump. Beef cuts are best when taken from an adult animal and well aged. For a chicken broth use a whole hen or just the bones of a chicken, plus the neck and giblets.

—If possible, add a leg bone with its marrow. Wrap the bone in cheesecloth so that the marrow, which is delicious eaten plain or spread on toast, will not fall out. You might also use pieces of beef shin or a calf's foot. If using veal or other white meats enrich the broth with a piece of beef or with bouillon cubes.

—Keep in mind that to produce 4 cups of broth you need at least 1 pound of meat and about 8 cups of water to start. Some people believe that broths are more nutritious if the meat and other ingredients are covered with cold water—rather than warm or hot water—and then slowly brought to the simmer.

—Bring the broth to a boil in a covered pot. If necessary, remove any scum that rises to the surface as the broth reaches a boil. The scum is the albumin of the blood.

—Lower the heat as soon as the broth begins to boil and let it simmer gently for two and a half or three hours. You can reduce the cooking time by using a pressure cooker. The broth must simmer rather than boil or the meat will disintegrate, the water will evaporate too quickly, and the broth will become cloudy.

—At this point add the aromatic herbs (parsley, basil, celery leaves, bay leaf) tied in a bunch or in a cheesecloth bag *(bouquet garni),* and the vegetables (a clove of garlic—which, alternatively, can also be inserted into the meat—a big stalk of celery, a carrot, a medium-size onion stuck with one or two cloves, and, if you wish, a chopped tomato). Lastly, season with salt, but do not add too much because the broth becomes more concentrated as it simmers and hence all the flavors become stronger.

—When the broth is done, degrease it by skimming the fat from the surface using a spoon. This can be done more easily if the broth is put in the refrigerator and the fat allowed to coagulate.

—Finally, remove the larger pieces of meat, the vegetables, and the herbs and strain the broth through a sieve with a very fine wire mesh or, even better, through a triple layer of rinsed cheesecloth.

From meat broth you can make a consommé or concentrated broth by simmering the broth a second time for about an hour after having added half again the quantity of water or some minced meat. Before it is served, the broth needs to be clarified. To do this whisk in 2 or 3 beaten egg whites 10 minutes before the cooking time is over and let the broth stand over very low heat without simmering. The egg whites can also be added with the minced meat if you keep the broth just below the simmer throughout cooking. The consommé is then strained through fine cheesecloth. It is served in the spcial two-handled cups, plain or with a granish or flavored with fortified wines.

If one wants to make a meat stock quickly an equal amount of minced meat can be substituted for whole meat and the soup prepared in the same way. The minced meat can be later used to make meatballs. For all meat broths, from chicken broth to rabbit broth, the process is the same. When using a variety of meats in the same broth, one must keep in mind that each meat will have a different cooking time.

Vegetable broths are made with a choice of mixed vegetables—usually carrots, potatoes, onions, celery, and tomato—and may be flavored with a clove. The ingredients are covered with cold salted water, brought rapidly to a boil, and left to simmer for about 2 hours. A pressure cooker will cut the cooking time in half. The vegetables can be used for purées and cream soups.

And finally a brief mention of instant broths, that is, broth made with water and bouillon cubes or granules. These are the easiest and quickest broths to make though they are not necessarily the most economical. To make them, all one has to do is dissolve the bouillon cube or granules in boiling water (usually one bouillon cube or one teaspoon of granules for every cup of water). The broth may be seasoned with salt and flavored with a knob of butter or a tablespoon of oil and some grated cheese, as one wishes. To make these instant broths more flavorful or to vary their taste a little, one need only add some minced fresh vegetables or herbs or even a little Port or other fortified wine.

Garnishes for Broths

First, there are garnishes that are usually passed separately with the soup so that each person at the table can help himself to a spoonful. These simple garnishes can enrich a consommé sipped from a cup without making it into a complicated soup and without masking the delicacy of the flavors. The most common such garnishes are bread croutons, which may be plain or stuffed. Croutons are sautéed in oil or butter or toasted in the oven before being served with the broth. There are also various vegetable garnishes for which Italians have different names. Small herbs are a mixture of the leaves of parsley, chervil, fennel, celery. *Verdure frastagliate* (jagged vegetables) are the leaves of lettuce, sorrel, or celery cut with special molds. *Giuliane* (julienned) are vegetables are cut into very thin, regular slices. *Pastorella* denotes a garnish of asparagus tips or very thin slices of mushrooms. Usually the vegetables used to garnish a broth are boiled first, both to remove any bitter taste that

could spoil the broth and to prevent them from making the broth cloudy.

Other garnishes that are quite easy to prepare are small slices of cooked tongue, shredded chicken, turkey breast, or slices of omelet. These three ingredients can also be used in combination to create an especially tasty and refined decoration. If one has time and is willing to work a little bit, there are some elaborate but very delicate garnishes that can be prepared. Among the most elegant garnishes are small turnovers of puff pastry and tiny puffs made with choux paste. Either garnish may contain delicate fillings of cheese or ham. Then there are the various soup custards that are made from a basic mixture of broth and eggs and cooked in the oven in a double boiler. Once the custard has solidified it is cut into dice, lozenges, or squares. The basic recipe can be varied by the addition of other ingredients such as chicken, game, fish, tomatoes, or carrots. Another garnish for broths and consommés are those refined dumplings that in French are called *quenelles* and in Italian *morbidelle*. *Quenelles* can be of various kinds, depending on their basic ingredient. Usually they are made with ground meat, poultry, game, fish, or shellfish, which is mixed with eggs and a binder such as softened bread, a white sauce, puréed boiled potatoes or rice, or even thick cream. *Quenelles* are formed using two spoons or a pastry bag fitted with a round tip, and they are poached, either on the stove or in the oven, in very gently simmering salted water broth. Before using the *quenelle* paste it is best to test its consistency by cooking one dumpling with a bit of cream. If the *quenelle* is too soft, the yolk or white of an egg should be added to the pasta. After they are cooked, the *quenelles* should be removed with a slotted spoon to soup bowls or a soup tureen and covered with boiling broth. There are also dumpling garnishes, a smaller version of the German spaetzle, based on flour and bread crumbs, which are mixed with chopped poultry, liver, or ham, and egg. These dumplings are cooked in boiling water for a few minutes, after which they are drained and added to the hot broth before serving.

Regional Zuppe

Starting with Lombardy the original tripe *zuppa,* calls only for tripe, bacon, celery, carrot, onion, and rye bread. Piedmont offers a variety of *zuppe,* two of which are of particular interest. The soup is made with turnips or Savoy cabbage, flavored with garlic and bacon, and cooked in a good broth. The second is from the Vercello area and contains frog meat flavored with basil, sage, and parsley. In the Alto Adige region the *zuppe* have a base of browned flour to which is added, ingredients such as sauerkraut, onions, or tripe. Flour is a principal ingredient of the *paparot,* a typical *zuppa* from Friuli, which is made with spinach, cornmeal and a little white flour. These ingredients are diluted with boiling broth. The Veneto region boasts the unforgettable *sopa coada,* a soup that is cooked slowly for many hours in the oven. This *zuppa* is comprised of alternating slices of bread soaked in broth and layers of meat covered with gravy. The original recipe calls for pigeon meat, but the soup can also be made with any fowl. The *panada* is also made in the Veneto region. This tasty bread soup is one of the many versions of the recipe appearing in regions, from Lombardy, where it is made with butter and Parmesan, to Calabria, where tomatoes are added and the basic condiments are oil and Romano. In Tuscany the classic *zuppe* are made with unsalted bread, vegetables (including tomatoes and garlic) and broth or water, flavored with "extra virgin" olive oil. The *acqua cotta* (cooked water), a famous *zuppa* of Grosseto, is an example, as is the *pappa al pomodoro* (tomato and bread soup), a simple *zuppa* found everywhere in the region for which local *casareccio* bread is essential. This soup is good reheated, as is the *ribollita* (boiled-again soup). The nearby Lazio region offers some *zuppe* that are savory and light, made with capon or hen broth. In the Molise region and Calabria there are the famous *zuppe* made with nettles and thistles, and the *licurdia,* an onion soup from Calabria flavored with Romano, hard ricotta cheese and the ubiquitous hot red pepper.

Onion soup

- **Yield: 4 servings**
- **Time needed: 1½ hours**
- **Difficulty: ***

Ingredients: 1¼ lb. yellow onions, 1 loaf French bread, 3 tbsp. butter, 3 tbsp. flour, ½ lb. Swiss cheese, 4 cups broth, 1 cup dry white wine, 2 or 3 tbsp. brandy, pinch nutmeg, freshly ground pepper, salt.

Slice the onions and sauté them in a pot with half of the butter (1) for about 10 minutes over low heat. They should become transparent. Season with salt, pepper, and nutmeg, sprinkle with flour, stir well, and pour in the wine (2) and the brandy. Let the liquids evaporate, pour in the broth (3), and bring to a boil. Cover with a lid and let simmer over low heat for about 45 minutes.

Slice the bread, butter both sides of the slices, and put them on a piece of aluminum foil. Put the bread in the oven until it is lightly toasted. Arrange the slices of toast in a single layer on the bottom of a casserole (4), cover them with half of the shredded cheese, and pour in the onion soup (5). Cover with the remaining cheese, cut in this slices (6). Put the casserole in a 450-degree oven for ten minutes, or until the cheese turns golden.

1 Slice the onions quite thinly and sauté them in half of the butter.

2 After adding the flour to the sautéed onions, stir well and add the wine.

3 When the onions have become soft, cover with the broth and bring to a boil.

4 Arrange a layer of sliced bread (toasted in the oven until golden) on the bottom of a casserole.

5 Pour the boiling onion soup over the bread, making sure to cover it completely.

6 Cover the soup with the remaining cheese, cut into very thin slices.

Onion Soup

Pavese soup

■ **Yield: 4 servings**
■ **Time needed: 20 minutes**
■ **Difficulty: ***

Ingredients: 8 very fresh eggs, 1 loaf French bread (or 8 slices ordinary bread), 4 tbsp. butter, 4 cups excellent meat broth, plenty of grated Parmesan cheese, salt.

Pour the broth into a pot and bring it to a boil. Taste it and correct the seasoning if necessary. Slice the French bread or cut the slices of regular bread in half diagonally, and fry them on both sides in hot butter. Remove the bread slices from the skillet with a slotted spatula (1) and arrange them on paper toweling to drain off the excess butter. Arrange a few slices of bread in soup bowls or in special earthenware bowls (2), break two eggs into each bowl (3), and sprinkle with plenty of grated Parmesan cheese. Slowly pour boiling broth into the bowls (4), being careful not to let it fall directly on the eggs (the yolks must not break). This very delicate soup of ancient origin is especially good if served for supper.

1 Fry the bread slices in hot butter and remove them from the skillet when nice and golden.

2 Arrange a few slices of sautéed bread in individual soup plates or in special earthenware bowls.

3 Break two eggs gently into each bowl so they rest on the slices of bread.

4 Pour the boiling broth into the bowls, being careful not to let it fall directly on the eggs.

Pavese soup

Ribollita

- Yield: 4 servings
- Time needed: 2 hours (plus soaking time)
- Difficulty: *

Ingredients: 12 oz. dried pinto or white beans, 1 small onion, 1 leek, 2 cloves garlic, 1 small, firm red cabbage, 1 stalk celery, 3 tbsp. tomato sauce, ½ tsp. each thyme and rosemary, bread croutons, olive oil, pepper, salt.

Soak the beans overnight in cold water. The following day drain them, put them in a pot, cover with salted cold water, and boil until tender. Blanch the cabbage leaves in boiling water, drain and cut into thin slices.

Chop the onion, leek, celery and garlic and sauté until golden with a little oil. Add the cabbage and the herbs, tied in a cheesecloth bag, stir for a few minutes, and then add the tomato sauce diluted with a little of the water from the beans. Season with salt and pepper and continue cooking over moderate heat. Then add the beans with part of their cooking water, and let cook for a few minutes. Remove the herb bag and serve the *ribollita* with the toasted croutons.

Cipollata

- Yield: 4 servings
- Time needed: 1½ hours (plus soaking time)
- Difficulty: *

Ingredients: 1¾ lbs. yellow onions, 1¼ cups tomato pulp, 1 oz. pork fat, 1 bunch basil leaves, 3 eggs, Parmesan, olive oil, pepper, sliced bread, salt.

Thinly slice the onions, cover with cold water, and let them soak for 2 hours Chop the pork fat to a paste and sauté it in two or three tablespoons of oil. When the pork fat is brown, add the well-drained onions, season with salt and pepper, add the basil leaves, and let stew over low heat.

When the moisture in the pan has almost evaporated, add the sieved or chopped tomato pulp, cover the pan, lower the heat to its lowest setting and cook for an hour. Correct the seasoning, add the eggs beaten with Parmesan, and remove from the stove, stirring vigorously. Serve with slices of toasted bread, or arrange the slices in bowls and pour the soup over them.

Potato soup

- Yield: 4 servings
- Time needed: 1 hour
- Difficulty: *

Ingredients: 4 medium-size potatoes, 4 medium-size onions, 1 egg, ½ cups heavy cream, 6 cups chicken broth, 1 sprig parsley, about ¾ cup Parmesan, salt.

Peel the potatoes and onions, cut them into big pieces, and cook in the broth for half an hour. Put the vegetables through a food mill (or purée with some of the broth), recombine the vegetables and the broth, return the soup to the stove. Correct the seasoning and bring to a boil. In the meantime, in a separate bowl beat together the egg, the grated cheese, and cream, and turn this mixture into a soup tureen. Slowly pour in the boiling soup, stirring vigorously. Sprinkle with chopped parsley and serve.

Fava and artichoke soup

- Yield: 4 servings
- Time needed: 1½ hours
- Difficulty: *

Ingredients: 5 artichokes, 1¼ lbs. fresh pinto or fava beans or ¾ cup dried fava beans or white beans, soaked overnight and boiled until half tender, 10 oz. fresh peas or 1 cup frozen peas, 4 medium-size potatoes, 2 onions, ½ lb. canned tomatoes, 6 cups broth, 1 lemon, 1½ tbsp. butter, olive oil, large pinch oregano.

Remove the outer leaves and the chokes of the artichokes, then cut them into small pieces and put them into water acidulated with lemon juice. Shell the beans if you are using fresh fava beans. (If using dried beans, simply drain them.) Shell the peas, peel and dice the potatoes and onions.

In a large saucepan sauté the onions in the butter and oil. When they turn golden add all the vegetables except the peas and let them brown lightly. Pour in the broth and add the tomatoes. Halfway through the cooking time add the peas, and when the beans are almost tender add a pinch of oregano. Serve with Parmesan.

Tuscan chick-pea soup

- Yield: 4 servings
- Time needed: 4½ hours (plus soaking time)
- Difficulty: *

Ingredients: About 1¼ cups dried chick-peas, ½ lb. small young beets, 1 onion, 2 anchovy fillets, drained, 1 clove garlic, 1 tbsp. tomato paste, 3 tbsp. grated Romano cheese, 1 meat bouillon cube, 3 tbsp. oil, 8 slices Italian bread brushed with olive oil and toasted in the oven, pepper, salt.

Soak the chick-peas overnight in salted cold water. The following morning clean the beets, wash them under running water and boil until tender.

Thinly slice the onion and sauté until golden in a pot with the oil, adding the crushed clove of garlic, and the anchovy fillets, in pieces. Add the drained chick-peas, stir well, and then add the well-drained and chopped beets. Stir again and cover all the ingredients with about 8 cups of warm water in which you have dissolved the bouillon cube and the tomato paste. Simmer gently for about 4 hours, keeping the pot tightly covered. Halfway through the cooking time taste the broth and add salt.

Arrange two toasted bread slices in individual soup bowls, cover with the chick-peas and their thick broth, and sprinkle with grated Romano and freshly ground pepper.

Tuscan chick-pea soup

Tomato and bread soup

■ **Yield: 4 servings**
■ **Time needed: 1 hour**
■ **Difficulty: ***

Ingredients: 1¾ lbs. ripe tomatoes, ½ lb. stale bread, 1 onion, a few leaves fresh basil, 6 cups broth (or water), "extra virgin" olive oil, freshly ground black pepper, salt.

Chop the onion very finely, put it into a pot with two tablespoons of oil and sauté over low heat without letting it color. Add the diced bread (1), and let it absorb the oil, stirring continuously. When the bread is lightly browned, add the peeled and chopped tomatoes (2), mix well (3), and let cook gently for a few minutes. Then add the broth, a little at a time, until you obtain a soup that is not too thick (4). Season with salt and pepper and let the soup cook for about 30 minutes, stirring occasionally. Just before taking the soup off the stove add the chopped basil leaves and a few tablespoons olive oil.

Serve the soup hot or cold, as you prefer. It is also very good reheated.

1 Stir in the diced bread and let it absorb the oil.

2 When the bread is brown, add the peeled and chopped tomatoes...

3 ...mix well and cook gently for a few minutes, then...

4 ....add the broth, a little at a time until you obtain a soup.

Tomato and bread soup

Farmer's soup

■ Yield: 4 servings
■ Time needed: 3 hours (plus soaking time)
■ Difficulty: *

Ingredients: ½ lb. (1 cup) dried white beans, 4 oz. a ham or pork rind, 1 small onion, 2 cloves garlic, 1 stalk celery, 1 carrot, 1 sprig parsley, ¼ Savoy cabbage, ¼ medium-size red cabbage, 1 bunch beets, 1 potato, 2 tbsp. tomato paste, 8 thin slices stale wholewheat bread, 2 tbsp. grated Parmesan cheese, 3 tbsp. oil, plenty of black pepper, salt.

Soak the beans overnight in plenty of cold water. The following morning drain them and boil them with pieces of ham or pork rind over low heat. Season with salt only when the beans are tender.

Meanwhile, finely chop the onion, garlic, celery, carrot, and the parsley, and sauté them in a pot with the oil. Then add the beets, the diced potato, and the two kinds of cabbages, cored, and cut into thin strips. Season with salt and pepper and cook slowly for 15 minutes. Stir in the tomato paste, diluted with some of the cooking water from the beans.

Purée half of the cooked beans in a food mill, blender, or food processor and stir into the sautéed vegetables. Then add the remaining beans and their water and let the soup boil softly for 15 minutes, stirring occasionally with a long wooden spoon. To serve, pour the soup over slices of bread arranged in individual bowls, sprinkle with grated Parmesan and ground pepper, and bring to the table.

Emilian fava soup

■ Yield: 4 servings
■ Time needed: 2 hours (plus soaking time)
■ Difficulty: *

Ingredients: ½ lb. dried fava beans, pinto beans, 2 oz. chopped bacon, ½ lb. diced beef, 1 large onion, 6 ripe plum tomatoes, ½ clove garlic, small bunch parsley, a few leaves fresh basil, 2 tbsp. grated Parmesan cheese, 1½ bouillon cubes, 3 tbsp. oil, freshly ground pepper, salt. An accompaniment: 5 oz. bread croutons fried in butter or lightly toasted.

Soak the beans overnight in plenty of cold water. The following morning sauté the chopped onion with the bacon and a tablespoon of oil in a pot. As soon as the onion starts to color add the seeded and chopped tomatoes, and mix well, stew slowly for 10 minutes. Add the diced meat and a few minutes later the drained beans. Prepare a broth by dissolving the bouillon cubes in about 5 cups water, and pour enough broth over the other ingredients to barely cover them. Simmer slowly for about two hours, or until the beans are soft, adding more broth or boiling water if necessary. Season with salt and freshly ground pepper. Drain 1 cup of the beans force them through a sieve, and return them to the broth, to make the soup thicker. Finish the soup by adding the grated Parmesan cheese, the remaining oil, a little more freshly ground pepper, and a mixture of finely chopped parsley, basil, and garlic.

Serve the soup in individual bowls with croutons browned in butter or toasted.

Zuppa rustica

■ 4 servings
■ Time needed: 1½ hours
■ Difficulty: *

Ingredients: 4 tbsp. butter, ½ lb. celery hearts (1 large or 2 small), ½ lb. carrots, ½ lb. potatoes (2-3 small), plenty of meat broth, ½ small Savoy cabbage, 1 onion, ½ meat bouillon cube, 8 stale slices French or Italian bread, grated Parmesan cheese, pepper, salt.

Cut the carrots, celery, and potato in rounds of the same size. Separately prepare the cabbage by slicing it into julienne strips. Sauté the finely chopped onion in half of the butter. Add the cabbage and cook slowly for a few minutes. Season with salt and pepper and add the other vegetables. Pour in about 6 cups of broth, cover the pot, and simmer slowly for 1 hour, adding half of a meat bouillon cube dissolved in some broth near the end of the cooking time. Fry the bread crusts in the remaining butter until golden, arrange in soup plates, and pour in the soup. Serve with Parmesan.

Florentine bean soup

■ Yield: 4 servings
■ Time needed: 3 hours
■ Difficulty: *

Ingredients: ½ lb. (1 cup), small dried white beans, soaked overnight, ¼ small red cabbage, 1 large onion, 1 ham bone, 1 carrot, 1 stalk celery, 1 leek, 2 ripe tomatoes, peeled, seeded, and juiced, 1 bouillon cube, 4 cloves garlic, ¼ tsp. rosemary, crushed, 4 slices Italian bread, 2 oz. (about ½ cup) grated Parmesan cheese, olive oil, salt.

Farmer's soup

Chop the onion with a clove of garlic and sauté in a few tablespoons oil until soft. Roughly chop the carrot, celery, leek, and tomato pulp and add them to the sauté along with the beans, the ham bone, and about 8 cups water in which you have dissolved the bouillon cube. (If you have used dried beans, add their soaking liquid as part of the 8 cups water.) Season with salt, cover the pot, and let simmer over low heat until the beans are very tender. Drain and set aside one cup of beans and push the rest through a sieve or purée in a blender or food processor together with the broth they were cooked in. Put the purée back on the stove and add the well-washed cabbage leaves, sliced in thin strips.

While the cabbage cooks, sauté the rosemary and two crushed cloves of garlic in a few tablespoons of oil. When the garlic turns golden (it must not burn) remove it. Add the sauté and the reserved whole beans to the soup and pour the soup into a tureen lined with slices of bread that have been toasted and rubbed with a clove of garlic. Serve the soup with the Parmesan cheese.

Potato and pepper soup

■ **Yield: 4 servings**
■ **Time needed: 1½ hours**
■ **Difficulty: ***

Ingredients: 2 medium-size potatoes, 2 sweet yellow or green peppers, 2 cucumbers, 2 ripe tomatoes, 1 small onion, 3 tbsp. butter, 3 tbsp. grated Parmesan cheese, 6 cups broth (it can be made with a bouillon cube), 2 tbsp. oil, pepper, salt, bread croutons toasted in the oven or fried in butter.

Cut the peppers in half lengthwise, remove the seeds and whitish ribs, and cut into thin strips. Peel the cucumbers and dice them. Blanch the tomatoes in boiling water, peel them, remove the seeds, and cut them into pieces. In a pot sauté the thinly sliced onion in the butter and the oil. First add the peppers and potatoes, letting them cook briefly, and then add the cucumbers and tomato pulp. Stir well and cook uncovered for a few minutes, stirring occasionally. Season with salt and pepper, cover with the broth, bring to a boil, and let the soup simmer gently for about an hour. Serve the soup in a tureen, passing the cheese and croutons around separately, or else distribute the croutons in individual bowls, sprinkle with Parmesan cheese, and pour in the soup.

Cabbage soup

■ **Yield: 4 servings**
■ **Time needed: 1 hour and 15 minutes**
■ **Difficulty: ***

Ingredients: Sliced stale bread, 1 medium Savoy cabbage, 2-3 cloves garlic, olive oil, 4 peppercorns, 5 juniper berries or 1 clove, 1 bay leaf, Parmesan, salt.

Choose a good firm cabbage. Remove the outer leaves and the tougher ribs of the leaves and chop the cabbage roughly. Cover the cabbage with salted water and set it on the stove to boil. Add the peppercorns, the juniper berries or clove, and the bay leaf, all wrapped in a piece of cheesecloth. Drain the cabbage when done, saving the little cooking water that remains. Remove the bag of herbs. Brown the slices of bread in oil and rub them with the garlic. In a casserole (preferably of earthenware) arrange a layer of cabbage and cover with a layer of bread slices. Add a little of the cabbage-cooking water, drizzle with olive oil, and season with salt, if necessary. Continue to alternate layers of cabbage and bread, ending with cabbage. Sprinkle with Parmesan and put the casserole in a 450-degree oven for 10 minutes. Serve the cabbage soup immediately after taking it out of the oven.

Mushroom soup

■ **Yield: 4 servings**
■ **Time needed: 1½ hours**
■ **Difficulty: ***

Ingredients: 1¼ lbs. mushrooms, 3 tbsp. butter, small bunch parsley, 1 clove garlic, 1 medium-size onion, 6 cups broth, 1 stalk celery, 1 carrot, about ½ cup grated Parmesan, sliced bread fried in butter, oil, pepper, salt.

Sauté the chopped garlic, onion, and parsley in 2 tablespoons butter and a few tablespoons oil in a pan. Clean the mushrooms, cut into slices or pieces, and sauté with the other ingredients. Add the whole celery stalk and the carrot and cover with broth. Correct the seasoning, add pepper, and let cook, covered, for one hour. Before taking it off the stove add the remaining butter. Arrange the slices of bread in individual bowls, pour in some of the mushroom soup, sprinkle with Parmesan, and season with plenty of freshly ground pepper.

To make the soup even more nutritious and flavorful, beat two egg yolks with ¼ cup light cream and a tablespoon of grated Parmesan, and, off heat, slowly pour this mixture into the soup.

Light, Cream and Velouté Soups

These soups are all those soups that are less substantial and hearty than a minestrone or a *zuppa* but nevertheless richer than a garnished broth. They can be divided into light soups, cream soups and *velouté* soups. Puréed soups also belong to this group, but because they are usually made with vegetables we included them in the section on vegetable soups. The light soups usually have a base of meat broth to which is added pasta, rice, semolina, barley, tapioca, rolled oats or eggs or meat. The broth must always be very clear and at the same time subtle but tasty. In some recipes milk is substituted for broth, making the soups more nutritious and especially suited to children and people who need light but nourishing foods. Cream soups and *velouté* soups, on the other hand, are "bound" soups. They have a dense liquid such as white sauce or velouté sauce as a base, to which is added the ingredient or ingredients that give an individual recipe its name. The result is always very delicate and especially suited for very refined meals.

Some Useful Hints

Light Soups — Either dry or fresh pasta can be added to the broth. The former should be a small-size pasta and 1 to 1½ ounces per person is sufficient. Dry pasta should be poured into the boiling broth and stirred immediately. As soon as the broth comes to a boil again the heat should be lowered and the soup cooked until the pasta is *al dente*. Fresh pasta can be either plain or filled. Appropriate plain pasta shapes include green or white egg *tagliatelline* (small flat noodles), *farfalline* (bowties), *quadrucci* (little squares), *maltagliati* (roughly cut pasta), and *passatelli* (little pasta cylinders). The famous grated pasta, *pasta rasa* might also be used. Filled pastas that are sometimes cooked in soups include *tortellini*, *cappelletti* (little hats), and *anolini*, which are usually cooked in capon or chicken broth.

The most suitable rice for soups is short-grain. The correct quantities and cooking procedures for rice are the same as for pasta. Generally other ingredients are included in rice-and-broth soups to give them more flavor, such as aromatic herbs (*ris e erborin*, a Milanese dish, is an example) or chicken giblets. Rice is also good when cooked in milk, and therefore we have the famous cream of rice soup as well as its excellent wintertime variation made with chestnuts.

There are also various kinds of delicate soup based on cereals such as wheat semolina (to make the traditional cream of wheat soup), rice flour, rolled oats and tapioca. Like rice, cereals can be cooked in both broth and milk. Some nutritious mushes can be made with almost all cereals. The cereal is first heated in the oven to remove all traces of humidity and is then cooked in broth or milk.

Soups made with bread crumbs and crushed bread sticks are also easy to digest. They can be made with either milk or broth. Often bread crumbs are combined with grated cheese, as in several of the versions of the *minestra in paradiso* (soup in paradise). Grated cheese is also often mixed with beaten eggs, such as in the famous *stracciatella* soup. Eggs are also used to make thin omelets, similar to crepes, which are then cut into thin strips to be put into boiling broth, usually one made from chicken. These soups include the *celestina* and the *scrippelle* soups from the Abruzzo region. Of course these little omelets can be enriched with aromatic herbs, pieces of ham, tongue, chicken, turkey, et cetera.

Cream Soups and Velouté Soups — These are soups that are bound by a fairly thick sauce, usually a white sauce in the case of cream soups, and a broth-based velouté sauce in the case of *velouté* soups. Other ingredients are often included in these soups to make them even smoother and thicker such as cream, cream of rice, potato starch, cornstarch, or egg yolks.

In *velouté* soups the predominant ingredient is the velouté sauce itself, which is always present in a greater quantity than any of the other ingredients, whereas in cream soups the most important ingredient is the one that also gives its name to the soup: spinach in cream of spinach soup, asparagus in cream of asparagus, et cetera. For *velouté* soups, on the other hand, the recipe name is determined by the ingredient that is the second most abundant after the velouté sauce. Thus we have poultry *velouté* soups, *velouté* soups of game, barley, tapioca, rice, et cetera. With few exceptions, both these cream soups and *velouté* soups call for the last-minute addition of a second binding ingredient: cream for cream soups and egg yolks for the *velouté*. These ingredients should be added at the last minute because after the second binding the preparation must not boil again. These soups are somewhat complicated to make and are therefore most suitable for important dinners. They must be served hot and accompanied by garnishes served separately. The garnishes usually consist of the ingredient that gives its name to the soup: precooked rice for rice *velouté* soups, slices of chicken for chicken *velouté* soups, pheasant or partridge breast cut into thin strips for game *velouté* soups, or bread croutons of different shapes or sizes that have been lightly toasted or fried.

If a cream or *velouté* soup turns out to be too thick, add a bit of hot milk to a cream soup or hot broth to a *velouté*. If the soups are too thin you can add a cornstarch mixed to a smooth paste with cold milk or water. You may also add a potato that has been boiled and puréed with milk or broth.

Egg-drop soup

- **Yield: 4 servings**
- **Time needed: 20 minutes**
- **Difficulty: ***

Ingredients: 3 eggs, plenty of grated Parmesan cheese, 1 tbsp. chopped parsley, 6 cups broth, nutmeg, salt.

Beat the eggs in a bowl and add 4 to 5 tablespoons grated Parmesan cheese (1), the parsley (2), a pinch of salt, and a pinch of nutmeg. Dilute with ½ cup cold broth and stir well (3). Bring the remaining broth to a boil. Slowly pour in the egg mixture and cook over moderate heat, stirring continuously, for 3 to 4 minutes (4). The egg will cook and form little clots, giving the soup an interesting texture. Serve immediately, accompanied by grated Parmesan.

In the Marche region bread crumbs are added with the grated cheese and the egg mixture is bound with a teaspoon of white flour and flavored with grated lemon peel. In Rome the soup is usually made according to the recipe given above (sometimes without parsley), though sometimes three tablespoons of fine semolina is added.

1 Break the eggs into a bowl and beat them with a whisk while adding the Parmesan cheese.

2 When the mixture has become smooth blend in a tablespoon of chopped parsley.

3 Gradually add ½ cup cold broth to the mixture and mix well.

4 Bring the broth to a boil and pour in the egg mixture very slowly, stirring continuously.

Passatelli soup

■ **Yield: 4 servings**
■ **Time needed: 45 minutes**
■ **Difficulty: ***

Ingredients: ¾ cup dry bread crumbs, 4 oz. (about 1 cup) grated Parmesan cheese, 3-4 tbsp. flour, 1½ oz. beef bone marrow, 3 eggs, grated peel of ½ lemon, 6 cups broth, nutmeg, salt.

Combine the flour, Parmesan cheese, bread crumbs, eggs, lemon peel, chopped bone marrow, a pinch of salt, and a pinch of nutmeg (1). Mix the ingredients with your fingers (2), and knead the dough until it is smooth and quite firm. Add more bread crumbs if needed.

Place the special utensil for making *passatelli* on top of the dough and bear down so as to obtain little cylinders (3). With a knife scrape the cylinders onto a floured plate (4). Bring the broth to a boil, add the *passatelli* (5), and take the soup off the stove as soon as the *passatelli* come to the surface. If you do not have the special utensil, put the dough into a potato ricer and press the *passatelli* directly into the boiling broth (6).

1 After having combined the flour with all the other ingredients, flavor with a little nutmeg.

2 Starting from the center blend the eggs into all the other ingredients using your fingertips.

3 Bear down on the dough with the special utensil for *passatelli* forming little cylinders of dough...

4 ...that you can scrape with a knife onto a floured plate.

5 Bring the broth to a boil and, using a wooden spoon, add the *passatelli*.

6 If you do not have the special utensil for *passatelli* you can make them with a potato ricer.

Passatelli Soup

Cream of asparagus

- Yield: 4 servings
- Time needed: 1 hour
- Difficulty: *

Ingredients: 1 lb. asparagus, 5 tbsp. butter, 1 tbsp. flour, 1 small onion, ½ cup heavy cream, 2 heaping tbsp. grated Parmesan cheese, a few leaves of fresh chervil (or 1 tsp. dried chervil), 4 cups or more broth, pepper, salt.

Wash the asparagus, remove the white part of the stalks, and cut the green part into small pieces (1). Boil the asparagus, warm it in a little butter, and then force it through a sieve (2) or purée in a blender or food processor. Chop the onion and sauté it in a pot with half of the remaining butter. Add the flour, mix until completely smooth, and then add the broth a little at a time. Bring to a boil, stir in the puréed asparagus (3), correct the seasoning, add pepper, and simmer very slowly for 15 minutes. Strain the soup through a sieve, pour it back into the pot, and bring it to a boil again. Take it off the stove and enrich it with the remaining butter, cut in pieces and the light cream (4). Garnish with chervil leaves.

1 Remove the white part of the stalks from the asparagus and cut the rest into little pieces.

2 After boiling the asparagus warm it in butter, force it through a sieve or purée in a blender.

3 Add the asparagus to the sauce prepared with the broth, stirring constantly.

4 Take the soup off the stove and enrich it with the remaining butter and the cream.

Cream of asparagus

Cream of chicken soup

- **Yield:** 4 servings
- **Time needed:** 2½ hours
- **Difficulty:** *

Ingredients: 1 2½ lb. chicken, 11 tbsp. butter, 7 tbsp. flour, 2 leeks, 1 celery stalk, 1 carrot, 4 cups light broth, 1 cup heavy cream, salt.

Rinse the chicken and poach it in the broth with the white part of the leeks, the celery, and the carrot. Add salt if necessary. Drain the chicken when well done, remove all the bones and skin, cut the meat from the breast into strips, and mince or finely chop the rest. Pound the minced meat with a pestle in a mortar (1) or grind in a blender or food processor. Mix in, a little at a time, 3 tablespoons butter (2) and ½ cup cream (3). Melt 4 tablespoons of the remaining butter in a pot, blend in the flour (4), stir until smooth and add the lukewarm broth a little at a time (5). Bring to a boil, skimming any surface scum (6), pour the soup through a sieve (7), and put it back on the stove. When heated, take it off the stove, add the chicken pieces and the chicken purée (8), and mix well with a whisk (9). Finish the soup by adding the remaining butter and cream, mixing well. If the soup is too thick, add broth.

Cream of chicken and ham with vodka

- **Yield:** 4 servings
- **Time needed:** 2½ hours
- **Difficulty:** *

Ingredients: 1 2½ lb. chicken, 11 tbsp. butter, 7 tbsp. flour, 2 leeks, 1 celery stalk, 1 carrot, 4 cups or more light broth, 1 cup light cream, ¼ lb. fatty ham (preferably country ham or *prosciutto*), 2 tbsp. vodka, salt.

Prepare the soup as indicated in the recipe for Cream of chicken soup. When adding the puréed and sliced chicken add the finely chopped ham and flavor with a few tablespoons of vodka.

1 Poach the chicken in a light broth, drain it, bone it, and pound part of it in a mortar (or processor).

2 Thoroughly mix the chicken with some soft butter.

3 Gradually add part of the cream to the butter and chicken mixture.

4 Melt a little butter in a pot and blend in the flour, stirring until smooth.

5 Slowly add the warm broth, stirring continuously.

6 Bring the soup slowly to a simmer and remove any surface scum with a spoon.

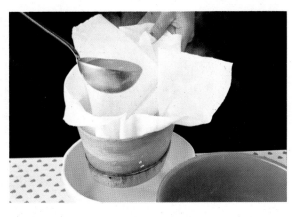

7 Pour the cream soup through a sieve lined with cheesecloth.

8 After heating the soup over low flame, finish by adding the puréed and sliced chicken...

9 ...and the remaining butter and cream, stirring well with a whisk.

Cream of mushroom soup with cheese

- ■ Yield: 4 servings
- ■ Time needed: 45 minutes (plus soaking time for the cheese)
- ■ Difficulty: *

Ingredients: 1 lb. fresh mushrooms, 7 tbsp. butter, 1 tbsp. potato starch or cornstarch, 10 oz. *fontina* cheese, 2 cups milk, 2 egg yolks, 1 clove garlic, 1 cup heavy cream, pepper, salt.
As an accompaniment: Bread croutons fried in butter or lightly toasted.

Cut the *fontina* cheese into thin slices, put it in a bowl, cover it with the milk, and let stand for about 6 hours. Clean the mushrooms well by rubbing them with a damp cloth, cut them into pieces, and sauté them in a pan with 3 tablespoons of the butter, the garlic clove, and a pinch of salt. Melt the remaining butter in a pot, blend in the potato starch or cornstarch, stir well to dissolve any lumps, and then add the cheese with the milk. Stir continuously with a wooden spoon and cook over low heat until the cheese melts and the mixture is smooth and thick like a custard sauce. Blend in the cream, take the soup off the stove, and mix in the egg yolks, one at a time. Season with salt and pepper and add the mushrooms and their juices, removing the garlic. Serve the cream of mushroom soup with the fried or toasted croutons.

Cream of endive soup

- ■ Yield: 4 servings
- ■ Time needed: 1 hour
- ■ Difficulty: *

Ingredients: 1½ lbs. Belgian endive, 2 tbsp. flour, 3 tbsp. grated Parmesan cheese, 5 cups broth (made with beef bouillon cubes), 2 egg yolks, 2 tbsp. Port, salt.

Wash the endive and cook for about 20 minutes in boiling salted water. Drain the endive, squeeze out the excess moisture, and blend in an electric blender or food processor with 2 cups broth until smooth. Correct the seasoning. Now melt the butter in a pot, blend in the flour, stir, and add the vegetable purée. Stirring constantly, add the remaining broth, boiling hot, a little at a time. Simmer the soup gently for about 20 minutes, stirring frequently with a wooden spoon, and then add the Port. In a soup tureen beat the egg yolks with the cheese and pour in the soup very slowly. Serve good and hot with more cheese.

Cream of bean soup

- ■ Yield: 4 servings
- ■ Time needed: 2½ hours
- ■ Difficulty: *

Ingredients: ½ lb. (1 cup) dried white beans, soaked overnight, 1 potato, 1 carrot, 1 onion, 1 stalk celery, 3 tbsp. butter, 1¼ cups milk, 1 cup heavy cream, salt.

Place the beans in their soaking water on the stove, add the carrot, onion, celery and potato, and simmer until tender about 2 hours. Drain the beans and vegetables reserving a good 2 cups of the cooking water and force through a sieve or purée in a blender or food processor. Dilute the purée with the milk and the reserved cooking water. Put the soup back on the stove and simmer for about twenty minutes, removing any scum that comes to the surface of the soup. Blend in the butter, in pieces, and the cream.

Cream of carrot soup

- ■ Yield: 4 servings
- ■ Time required: 1 hour and 10 minutes
- ■ Difficulty: *

Ingredients: 1 lb. carrots, 1 small onion, 4 cups broth, 7 tbsp. butter, 1 tbsp. tomato paste, 3 tbsp. white flour, ½ cup light cream, 2 tbsp. grated Parmesan cheese, nutmeg, freshly ground pepper, salt.

Scrape the carrots, wash them, cut them into thin slices, and put them in a pot with the finely chopped ground pepper, salt, and a pinch of nutmeg and cook covered over low heat, occasionally adding a little hot broth. When the carrots are soft, purée them in an electric blender or food processor with 2 tablespoons butter, the tomato paste, and the remaining broth. In a separate pot melt the remaining butter, blend in the flour, and stir in the carrot mixture a little at a time. Continue stirring with a wooden spoon over low heat as the soup slowly thickens. Let the soup simmer for about ten minutes, then add the light cream and the grated cheese. Stir again and serve. The soup can be accompanied by croutons fried in butter or toasted in the oven. It is best served as the main course of a light supper.

Shrimp bisque

■ **Yield: 4 servings**
■ **Time needed: 2 hours**
■ **Difficulty: ****

Ingredients: 1 lb. shelled raw shrimp, 12 tbsp. butter, 5 tbsp. flour, 6 egg yolks, ¼ cup chopped carrot, ¼ cup chopped onion, ¼ cup chopped celery, bunch parsley, 6 cups chicken or fish broth, 1 cup heavy cream, a few pinches nutmeg, freshly ground pepper.

Slowly cook the carrot, onion, and the celery in a pot with 3 tablespoons butter. Add three-quarters of the shrimp (1), and cook until the shrimp are done. Force all the ingredients through a sieve with the help of a wooden spoon (2) or puree in a blender or food processor. Melt 4 tablespoons butter in a pot, add the flour and mix until smooth. Dilute, gradually add 4 cups broth and bring to a boil, stirring constantly. Remove any surface scum and add the bunch of parsley, a pinch of pepper, and a pinch of nutmeg. Let the sauce simmer for about 15 minutes over moderate heat, stirring frequently with a wooden spoon, then strain through a cheesecloth-lined sieve. Mix the puréed shrimp and vegetables into the prepared sauce (3) and dilute with the remaining broth, boiling hot. Put the soup back into a pot, and as soon as it is on the verge of simmering pour in the egg yolks beaten with the cream (4). Once again bring just below the simmer, stirring continuously, then remove from the stove.

Meanwhile, in a mortar pound half of the remaining shrimp with the remaining 5 tablespoons butter and push the mixture through a sieve. (Alternatively, you may blend the shrimp with the butter in a blender or food processor, in which case you needn't push the mixture through a sieve.) Finish the preparation by adding the shrimp butter a little at a time while beating with a whisk (5) and garnish with the remaining boiled and chopped shrimp.

This delicate *velouté* soup is especially suitable as a main-course supper dish. It can also be made with crayfish tails and served in individual porcelain cups garnished with additional whole crayfish tails cooked in butter and a little cream.

1 Cook the chopped vegetables in butter until soft and then add some of the shrimp.

2 When the shrimp are cooked force them through a sieve with a spoon or grind in a blender.

3 Mix the cooked, puréed shrimp and vegetables into the previously prepared soup base.

4 Just before taking the soup off the stove add egg yolks beaten with cream.

5 Add the shrimp butter a little at a time, beating with a wire whisk.

Shrimp bisque

Cream of artichoke soup

■ Yield: 4 servings
■ Time needed: 2 hours
■ Difficulty: **

Ingredients: 1¼ lb. artichoke bottoms (6 to 8 large), 7 tbsp. butter, 5 tbsp. flour, 6 egg yolks, 1 tsp. snipped chives, 6 cups broth, 1 cup heavy cream, a few pinches nutmeg, pepper, salt.

Melt 3 tablespoons butter in a pot, add the flour, and let it brown lightly while stirring with a wooden spoon. Gradually add 4 cups broth, stirring continuously. Season with a few pinches of pepper and nutmeg, and let cook over low heat for about 15 minutes. Pour the sauce through a sieve and set it aside.

Boil the artichoke bottoms in a little broth, save a whole one, and force the rest through a sieve or purée in a blender or food proceesor. Mix the puréed artichokes into the prepared soup base, add 1¼ cups broth, and force the soup through cheesecloth-lined sieve with a spoon. Bring to a boil, pour in the egg yolks beaten with the cream, and remove from the stove. Season with salt, add the remaining butter, in pieces, and garnish the soup with the remaining artichoke bottom, cut into small pieces, and the chives. Serve immediately.

Cream of chicory soup

■ Yield: 4 servings
■ Time needed: 50 minutes
■ Difficulty: *

Ingredients: 1½ lbs. chicory, 1 tbsp. lemon juice, 3 tbsp. butter, 3 tbsp. flour, 2½ oz. bacon, 3 cups broth, 1 cup milk, ½ cup heavy cream, 3 tbsp. grated Parmesan cheese, pepper, salt.
As an accompaniment: Thin fingers of wholewheat bread fried in butter.

Wash and drain the chicory and blanch it for 5 minutes in boiling salted water acidulated with lemon juice. Drain the chicory, let it cool, chop it, and put it into a pot in which you have already sautéed the bacon, diced, in 3 tablespoons of butter.

Stir the chicory with the butter and bacon and let cook slowly for a few minutes. Sprinkle with a little salt and pepper, stir in the flour, add the boiling broth a little at a time, and then add the milk. Finally, add the cream as well. Let the soup simmer for a quarter of an hour and then add the grated Parmesan cheese. Pour the soup into individual bowls and serve. Serve the wholewheat bread fingers on four individual plates, one plate for each person.

Cream of celery soup

■ Yield: 4 servings
■ Time needed: 1 hour
■ Difficulty: *

Ingredients: 2 whole bunches celery, ½ onion, 1 cup heavy cream, 2 egg yolks, 1 tbsp. butter, 1 tbsp. flour, 4 cups broth, pepper, salt.

After having removed a few of the tougher outer stalks, boil the celery in a pot of water until nearly tender and drain it. In another pot cook the chopped onion in the butter until the onion is soft but not brown. Add the flour and stir until smooth. Add the boiling stock a little at a time.

Cut a couple of celery stalks into strips and set aside. Add the rest of the celery to the broth and let it cook for about 20 minutes. Put the celery and broth through a sieve. Return the soup base to the stove and season with salt and pepper. Beat the egg yolks with the cream in a soup tureen, pour in the celery soup base, mix well, and garnish with the reserved strips of celery.

The soup can be accompanied by bread croutons, either fried in butter or toasted.

Cream of oat soup

■ Yield: 4 servings
■ Time needed: 1½ hours
■ Difficulty: *

Ingredients: 3 heads Boston or Bibb lettuce, 3 tbsp. butter, ⅓ cup rolled oats (not the quick-cooking kind), pulverized in a blender, 1 egg yolk, 1 tbsp. chopped parsley, 2 cups milk, 4 cups broth, ½ cup heavy cream, salt.
As an accompaniment: Thin slices of oat bread buttered and lightly toasted in the oven.

Wash the lettuce leaves well, and cook them for ten minutes in salted boiling water. Drain them, chop them and let them stew gently in a pot with 2 tablespoons butter. When they are soft, melt the remaining butter in the pot and add the oats. Stir with a wooden spoon and add the hot milk a little at a time, stirring continuously. Let the soup cook slowly for half an hour, stirring frequently, and then put it through a food mill or purée in a blender or food processor.

Put the purée back into the pot and add the broth. Heat it slowly and then pour the soup in a thin stream into a soup tureen in which you have beaten the egg yolk with the cream. Garnish the soup with the finely chopped parsley and serve accompanied by the oat bread, buttered and toasted in the oven just before serving. This nutritious soup is especially suited to the elderly and convalescent but is also good for someone who wants to try something a bit unusual.

Cream of oat soup

HOT AND COLD SAUCES

Hot Sauces

Sauces are creamy preparations of various thicknesses that are used to flavor and garnish certain foods. Normally they are divided into cold sauces and hot sauces. The first sauces were doubtless cold, but soon man learned to use the juices of sautéed meats or roasts to obtain something more appealing. The first known hot sauces are of ancient Jewish origin, including a gravy made by adding various herbs to the broth of boiled meats and the famous *arroset*, a sweet sauce with which the Jews garnished lamb, and probably the sauce in which Jesus Christ soaked the bread given to Judas during the Last Supper. The Romans also used herbs and spices for their hot sauces, among which was the *sapa* made with boiled grape. Perhaps the *sapa* is an ancestor of the sauce that is made today with the juice of white grapes. The great moment for sauces,

however, was the Renaissance, when they were not only served to enrich dishes, but were also used to help disguise "off" tastes and to preserve foods. *Peverada* sauce dates to the Renaissance and is still used today to season game. In 1500, when Catherine de Medici was wed to the king of France, many recipes for sauces and other dishes served at the Medici court were taken to France by Italian chefs, who at that time were the most famous in the world. In France these recipes were elaborated and perfected to the point that now, especially in the realm of sauces, French cuisine is the most refined. It was the French who invented the "mother sauces" from which, with the addition of other flavorings, many other sauces are derived. Some of these sauce variations have become classics, while others remain relatively unknown.

Basic Sauces and Variations

Sauces are composed of fats (butter, oil), liquids (milk, broth, meat juices, tomato juice, wine, vinegar, lemon juice), aromatic herbs, spices, and, binding ingredients (eggs, flour, potato starch, cornstarch). In traditional practice the base of a hot sauce is always the juice in the bottom of a pan left by a piece of sautéed, poached, or roasted meat, poultry, or fish. A brown sauce can be made from the juices of red meat, white sauce can be derived from white meats (chicken, veal), and sauces of various kinds can be made from the juices of game or fish. In homemade sauces these juices can be replaced by concentrated meat stock or even bouillon cubes or the gravy from a roast.

Precisely because hot sauces are made with a variety of ingredients, they require special care. The sauces must be cooked over very low heat or in a double boiler to prevent the sauce from boiling and breaking down. Finally, one must handle the delicate binding process carefully, particularly when raw eggs are the binding agent.

Among the hot sauces there are four great basic sauces called "mother sauces," from which are derived infinite variations.

Brown sauce — The classic recipe for brown sauce, which is called *sauce Espagnole,* is quite complicated. A simpler brown sauce can be prepared by following the recipe or by binding the juice of stewed or braised meat with flour or potato starch and flavoring the resulting sauce with a piece of fresh butter. Among the most important variations of brown sauce is *demi-glace sauce,* which is made by reducing brown sauce and adding other flavorings. Then there are *Madeira sauce, Marsala sauce,* and *cacciatora sauce,* all made by combining brown sauce with the wine in which game has been marinated, *salsa alla diavola,* made by flavoring brown sauce with vinegar, pepper, and French mustard, and *sauce Robert,* a brown sauce containing onions and mustard. Brown sauce and its variations are particularly recommended for grilled meats.

Velouté Sauce — This light sauce is made with butter, flour, boiling stock, and aromatic herbs. Veal, chicken, or fish stock may all be used as the base. If water is substituted for stock you have a mock velouté sauce. The addition of various other ingredients gives rise to many other light sauces such as mushroom or truffle sauce, and spicy sauces flavored with paprika and curry as well as the so-called sauce of the Pope, which is made with onions, capers, olives, and vinegar. Velouté sauce and its variations are good with eggs, poultry, fish, and vegetables.

White Sauce — Also called bechamel sauce, is perhaps the best known and most commonly used sauce. Invented by a great chamberlain of the Sun King, the original version called for a *blond roux* (a binding mixture of flour and butter that is allowed to color) blended with cream and flavored with chopped parsley, onion, and scallions. Today the cream is replaced by milk and the aromatic herbs have disappeared, though a pinch of nutmeg is always recommended. By varying the proportions of milk to flour you will get a thicker or thinner sauce. Among the most famous of the many variations of white sauce are Mornay sauce, made by adding egg yolks and grated cheese, the *sauce Aurore,* whose rosy color is imparted by a dab of tomato sauce; *sauce soubise,* flavored with onions, and *Villeroi* sauce, a white sauce enriched with puréed mushrooms or truffles. White sauce and its variations are good binding sauces for casseroles, gratinéed dishes and stuffed meats, fish, and vegetables.

Hollandaise sauce — We consider hollandaise one of the "mother sauces" because it is the base of many other well-known sauces. Hollandaise is made by emulsifying eggs with butter and lemon juice. If the sauce should separate, it must be put into another container, allowed to cool, and reconstituted by the addition of another egg. Béarnaise sauce, the most famous hollandaise variation, is flavored with tarragon. There is orange flavored hollandaise, or Maltaise sauce, made by mixing in finely chopped orange peel and orange juice. A creamy hollandaise, mousseline sauce, is made by folding in whipped cream. Choron sauce is made by adding thick tomato purée to hollandaise. Foyot sauce is made by stirring in meat juices. Hollandaise sauce and its variations go well with white meats and vegetables.

Necessary Utensils

How to Serve Hot Sauces

Let us begin with a few recommendations concerning the best pots and pans in which to prepare sauces. For the best results use a pan heavy enough to heat foods slowly and evenly or a double boiler. The old earthenware pots, which must always be used with a flame-control device are classics, but there are also modern pots with unusually heavy bottoms that can be used. The traditional *ponzonetto* made of unlined copper is ideal for some sauces because of its concave bottom, that allows for perfectly even cooking. It is also very practical because of its long handle. The equipment used for *bagna cauda* (a sauce typical of the cuisine of Piedmont, made with oil, garlic, anchovies, and parsley) is worth a special mention. It consists of a small pot set over a small candle. The candle provides low, uniform heat while also giving a nice intimate glow to the room.

Food processors are very useful for making sauces; they chop, blend, mix, and knead. A blender with a glass container is also very helpful.

We must not forget all those small utensils that can facilitate the preliminary preparations, such as a juicer (an electric model is very practical if one has to squeeze many citrus fruits), a lemon slicer, a garlic press, and a parsley chopper. Sieves of varyious sizes, all with a fairly fine mesh, are essential as are long-handled wooden spoons (used ones, by the way, will not absorb odors as readily as new spoons), a whisk with which to blend sauces without deflating them, a hand or electric beater for beating egg whites or whipping cream, and a spatula with which to collect the last traces of a sauce from a mixing bowl.

Finally there are sauce boats and gravy boats of various types, including the traditional porcelain gravy boat that rests on a special plate and has its own spoon, metal gravy boats of contemporary design and heat-resistant sauce boats for holding sauces that must be kept hot until the very last minute.

Roasted or sautéd meats are served with hot sauces, boiled meats are served with cold sauces (the *peara,* a hot sauce from the Veneto region made with bone marrow and pepper is an exception), and stewed meats are served with their own juices. Sauces containing vegetables and herbs, such as ketchup and *sauce Robert* go well with steaks and grilled meats, as do all the sweet-and-sour sauces and fruit sauces, which are especially suitable for pork. For roasts choose between a simple deglazing sauce made with pan juices and some other more elaborate sauce, such as a chicken-liver sauce or *peverada* sauce, which goes well with roast chicken. For thin slices of beef and veal scallops, cream-based sauces are suitable, especially those flavored with herbs, spices, mushrooms, or truffles.

One must make a distinction between strongly flavored sauces that determine the character of a dish made with boiled or raw vegetables, and less assertive sauces that are used as fillings or toppings. Included in the first group are *salsa bastarda* (mock velouté sauce), various velouté sauces, and béarnaise sauce, all of which are used with boiled vegetables, and savory and spicy sauces such as *bagna cauda,* anchovy sauce, and hot mayonnaise, all of which are good with raw vegetables. On the other hand, mild sauces with a milk or cream base, with or without eggs or cheese, are ideal for filling or napping boiled vegetables. White sauces are especially good with vegetables that are to be gratinéed in the oven.

There are also some marvelous sauces for fish, especially boiled fish. There are those made with wine and butter, such as Bercy sauce, and those made with eggs, such as hollandaise or mousseline.

These sauces are to be served hot in warmed sauce boats. If a sauce is not to be used immediately, the pan of sauce should be put into a pot of hot water. In other to prevent skin forming pour a little melted butter over the sauce.

White sauce

■ Yield: 4 servings
■ Time needed: 20 minutes
■ Difficulty: *

Ingredients: 3 tbsp. butter, 4 tbsp. flour, 2 cups milk, nutmeg (optional), freshly ground white pepper, a few pinches of salt.

Heat the milk almost to a boil. Put the butter in a saucepan and melt it over low heat. Blend in the flour (1) and stir with a wooden spoon to dissolve any lumps. Let the mixture bubble for a few seconds and then very slowly add the boiling milk (2) (it can be lukewarm or even cold if you stir the sauce constantly) and continue cooking over moderate heat until the sauce boils. Simmer the sauce 5 minutes, stirring constantly (3), season with salt and pepper and nutmeg, and take the sauce off the stove. It should appear soft and velvety. If you don't use the sauce immediately, drizzle the surface with melted butter or dot with cold butter, which will spread over the surface of the sauce as it melts.

You can enrich the white sauce with ½ cup grated Parmesan cheese (4) and egg yolk (5), making it into a Mornay sauce, which is especially good with boiled fish or vegetables and for gratinéed dishes.

If you want a more aromatic and more strongly flavored sauce, sauté some very finely minced onion and a pinch of thyme and ground bay leaf in the butter before adding the flour.

White sauce can be used in many ways—as a poured sauce, as a sauce medium for gratinéed dishes, as a basic ingredient for croquettes and mousses, and as a filling. The thickness of the sauce should vary according to its use. If the sauce is to be poured on eggs, vegetables, fish, etc., it must be very fluid, and thus prepared with 1½ tablespoons flour per cup of milk. For gratinéed dishes the proportions given above are fine. If you want to use the sauce to make croquettes, soufflés, or fillings, increase the flour to 5 tablespoons per cup of milk.

1 Melt the butter in a saucepan over low heat and slowly blend in the flour.

2 After having let the mixture cook briefly slowly add the milk, stirring continuously.

3 Let the sauce boil for five minutes, stirring constantly with a wooden spoon.

4 To enrich the white sauce, remove the sauce from heat and add grated Parmesan cheese...

5 ...and, after the sauce has cooled a little, add an egg yolk.

White sauce

Velouté Sauce

- **Yield: 4 servings**
- **Time needed: 20 minutes**
- **Difficulty: ***

Ingredients: 2 tbsp. butter, 3 tbsp. flour, 2 cups chicken or veal stock, ¼ cup mushroom stems, parsley, freshly ground white pepper, nutmeg.

Melt the butter in a saucepan, add the flour (1), mix well and cook slowly until the mixture barely starts to color. Pour in the boiling stock a little at a time (2) and continue cooking, stirring constantly with a wire whisk (3). As soon as the sauce begins to simmer remove any surface scum and add the mushroom stems (4), a bunch of fresh parsley (5), a bit of white pepper and nutmeg. Let the sauce simmer very slowly for 15 minutes, and then strain it through a sieve (6). If you want a particularly smooth and velvety sauce, line the sieve with cheesecloth (7). If the sauce is not to be used immediately, drizzle it with a thin layer of melted butter or dot the surface with cold butter (8). To keep the sauce warm, place it in a pan set in or over hot water (9); when ready to serve, stir the sauce well so that it becomes perfectly smooth and creamy (10). The amount of flour can be increased or diminished, depending on the thickness desired. This sauce is served with boiled fish and meats.

1 Melt the butter in a saucepan, blend in the flour, and stir well with a whisk.

2 Slowly add boiling veal or chicken stock, stirring constantly.

3 Continue to cook over low heat, stirring with a whisk, until the sauce boils.

4 After having removed any surface scum, add the mushroom stems, well washed and dried...

5 ...then flavor the sauce by adding also a bunch of fresh parsley.

6 When the cooking time is up, strain the sauce through a fine-mesh sieve.

7 If you want an especially velvety sauce, line the sieve with cheesecloth.

8 If you do not use the sauce immediately, dot the surface with butter.

9 If you have to keep the sauce hot while waiting to bring it to the table, set it in or over hot water...

10 ...and when ready to serve, stir the sauce well to make it perfectly smooth and creamy.

Brown sauce

■ **Yield: 4 servings**
■ **Time needed: 1½ hours**
■ **Difficulty: ***

Ingredients: 1 medium-size onion, 2 tbsp. butter, 1 oz. bacon, 3 tbsp. white flour, 1 beef bouillon cube or 1 tablespoon meat extract, a few mushrooms, *bouquet garni* containing a sprig of thyme, 6 sprigs parsley, and bay leaf (or, if using dried thyme, tie all herbs in a cheesecloth bag), ½ cup dry white wine, a few peppercorns, 2½ cups cold water, salt.

The original recipe for brown sauce is quite long and complicated because it calls for a basic stock made with veal meat and bones, ham bones, and fresh pork rind. Here we give a simplified version that is also very good. Serve in a warmed sauce boat with sautéed or grilled meat, or use as a base for other sauces, or as an enrichment for the pan juices of roasted or braised meats. It can also be used to garnish poached eggs, braised sweetbreads, and similar foods.

To make the sauce proceed as follows: Cut the onion into very thin slices and put it in a fairly narrow saucepan with a heavy bottom (1). Add the sliced bacon and the butter (2), and cook over moderate heat, stirring often with a wooden spoon, for about 12 minutes. When the onion is golden brown and the fat has become foamy, add the flour (3) and stir for a few minutes to brown the flour slightly. Add the wine (4) and stir until it has almost all evaporated. Add the cold water, the bouillon cube or meat extract (5), some salt and pepper, the washed, drained, and chopped mushrooms, and the *bouquet garni* (6). Bring to a boil, then lower the heat and let the sauce simmer, stirring occasionally and periodically skimming the grease that forms on the surface (7). Let the sauce cook for 40 minutes, and then strain it through a sieve lined with cheesecloth (8), lightly pressing the various ingredients to extract their flavors before discarding them (9). Taste the sauce and correct the seasoning if necessary. The sauce can be used right away, or it can be cooled and kept in a sealed container in the refrigerator.

1 Cut the onion into very thin slices and put it into a heavy-bottom saucepan.

2 Add the sliced bacon and butter to the onion.

3 Let the onion sauté until it is golden brown, and then mix in the flour.

4 Stir until the mixture has browned lightly; add the white wine...

5 ...and when the wine has evaporated, add the water and the bouillon cube or meat extract.

6 After adding the mushrooms, add a *bouquet garni* of thyme, parsley, and bay leaf.

7 As the sauce cooks, periodically skim grease that forms on the surface.

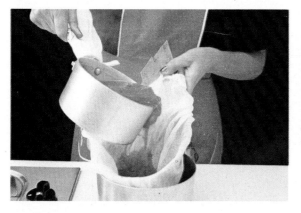

8 When the sauce has finished cooking strain it through a sieve lined with cheesecloth...

9 ...pressing the ingredients lightly with a wooden spoon before discarding them.

Brown sauce

Hollandaise

■ **Yield: 4 servings**
■ **Time needed: 45 minutes**
■ **Difficulty: ***

Ingredients: 1½ sticks butter, 2 egg yolks, 2 tablespoons good-quality white wine vinegar, lemon juice, freshly ground white pepper, salt.

This sauce should be prepared just before serving. If the sauce must wait, keep it warm in a double boiler over tepid water. Excess heat will make the sauce separate. In a narrow pot with fairly high sides, combine the vinegar, a pinch of freshly ground white pepper (1), and a few pinches of salt, and simmer until the vinegar is reduced to a teaspooon.

Take the pan off the stove and add a tablespoon of cold water, the egg yolks (2), and 2 tablespoons of butter cut in little pieces (3). The pan may be placed directly over low heat, but it is safer to cook the sauce in a pan of hot water (you can also use a double boiler, so that the temperature remains constant). Maintain the water in the bottom pan just below the simmer. Stir the sauce with a wire whisk (4) or with a wooden spoon. As soon as the sauce begins to thicken, beat in the remaining butter, cut in pieces (5), alternately adding drops of cold water (6). The water (a tablespoon) is added to keep the sauce from separating. Continue to cook being careful not to let it come near the simmer, until it appears thick (7). Strain the sauce through a sieve lined with cheesecloth (8), blend in a few drops of lemon juice (9), and taste the sauce, correcting the seasoning if necessary. Serve the hollandaise in a warmed sauce boat. Hollandaise is good with poached fish and poultry, hot boiled or steamed vegetables and poached eggs.

This sauce separates easily. There are some things that can be done should the sauce begin to thin or curdle. At the first sign of trouble take the sauce off the heat, add a tablespoon of cold water, and beat the sauce rapidly, with the bottom of the pan immersed in cold water. A second way is to put a teaspoon of lemon juice in a bowl and to beat in the sauce a teaspoon at a time until it re-emulsifies. A third method is to let the sauce cool and blend it by teaspoons into another egg yolk, until a mayonnaise-like cream results.

1 Pour the vinegar into a sacuepan and add a pinch of freshly ground white pepper.

2 After the vinegar is reduced, take the pan off the stove and add the egg yolks.

3 Add 2 tablespoons butter, cut into small pieces.

4 Set the pan in a larger pan filled with hot water and cook the sauce over low heat, stirring with a whisk.

5 As soon as the sauce begins to thicken, beat in the remaining butter, again cut in pieces...

6 ...alternately adding drops of cold water (about 1 tablespoon in all).

7 Cook the sauce, without letting it come near the simmer, until it reaches the correct thickness.

8 At this point strain it through a sieve lined with cheesecloth...

9 ...add a few drops of lemon juice, and serve immediately.

Béarnaise

- **Yield: 4 servings**
- **Time needed: ½ hour**
- **Difficulty: ***

Ingredients: 1½ sticks butter, 1 tbsp. finely chopped scallions, 3 egg yolks, 2 sprigs of chervil and 1 small sprig of fresh tarragon, or 1 dried chervil and tarragon, 5 tbsp. dry white wine, 5 tbsp. excellent wine vinegar, peppercorns, salt.

In a saucepan combine the chopped scallions, a few peppercorns, crushed in a mortar, the white wine, the vinegar, and the tarragon (1). Reduce the liquid by two-thirds over moderate heat, and then let the mixture cool. In the meantime, beat the egg yolks in a bowl and add a tablespoon of hot water (2). Return the herb reduction to the stove and slowly pour in the egg yolks, beating with a whisk (3). Then add the butter a few pieces at a time, stirring constantly (4), and finally add the salt. Cook the sauce over low heat, continuing to stir with the whisk (5). Remove the béarnaise from the heat when it appears as thick as a mayonnaise (6).

Stretch a double thickness of cheesecloth over a bowl, pour in the sauce (7), and twist the cloth in order to extract the most flavor possible from the herbs in the sauce (8). Finally, garnish the sauce with the finely chopped fresh tarragon (9) or dried tarragon.

Serve the sauce lukewarm with grilled meats, roast beef, boiled or roast fish, or boiled or poached eggs.

Choron sauce

- **Yield: 4 servings**
- **Time needed: ½ hour**
- **Difficulty: ***

Ingredients: a good béarnaise sauce (see above), 2 tbsp. concentrated tomato sauce or tomato paste.

Prepare a béarnaise sauce according to the recipe. Before removing the sauce from the stove, add lukewarm tomato sauce or tomato paste, stirring for a few minutes. Remove the herb sprigs from the sauce (dried herbs need not be strained out) and pour the sauce into a sauce boat. Choron sauce is good with grilled meats and hard-boiled eggs.

1 In a saucepan combine the scallions, pepper, wine, vinegar, and sprigs of herbs.

2 In a separate bowl, beat the egg yolks with a whisk, and add a tablespoon of water.

3 Put the saucepan with the herb reduction back on the stove and slowly mix in the egg yolks.

4 Finish the sauce by adding the cut-up butter a little at a time and seasoning with a pinch of salt.

5 Cook over moderate heat (the sauce should never simmer), continuing to stir with the whisk.

6 When the sauce is about the same thickness as mayonnaise take it off the stove...

7 ...pour it into a bowl over which you have stretched a double thickness of cheesecloth...

8 ...and strain the sauce by twisting the cloth to extract the most flavor from the herbs.

9 Sprinkle the sauce with finely chopped fresh tarragon and mix well.

Béarnaise sauce and Choron sauce

Mousseline sauce

■ **Yield: 4 servings**
■ **Time needed: ½ hour**
■ **Difficulty: ***

Ingredients: a hollandaise sauce (see page 332), 1 cup heavy cream, whipped.

Prepare a hollandaise sauce. Take it off the stove and fold in the whipped cream a little at a time. Pour the sauce into a warm sauce boat and serve immediately. Mousseline sauce can be served with poached fish or hot vegetables, especially asparagus and artichokes.

Maltais sauce

■ **Yield: 4 servings**
■ **Time needed: ½ hour**
■ **Difficulty: ***

Ingredients: a hollandaise sauce (see page 332), 1 juice orange.

Prepare the hollandaise sauce. Wash and dry the orange, grate a little of the peel (about 1 teaspoon), and squeeze and strain the juice. Take the hollandaise sauce off the stove and mix in first the orange juice, then the peel. Pour the Maltaise sauce into a warm sauce boat and serve with boiled asparagus or artichokes.

The hollandaise sauce can be replaced by a hot or cold mayonnaise.

Foyot sauce

■ **Yield: 4 servings**
■ **Time needed: ½ hour**
■ **Difficulty: ***

Ingredients: a béarnaise sauce (see page 335), 1 beef bouillon cube, 2-3 tbsp. stock or hot water.

Prepare a béarnaise sauce. When it is almost ready, add the bouillon cubes dissolved in a few tablespoons of hot stock or water. Continue stirring until the sauce has reached the right thickness, keeping the heat very low. Pour the sauce into a warm sauce boat. This sauce is especially good with tournedos, beef medallions, or grilled lamb chops.

Parsley sauce

■ **Yield: 4 servings**
■ **Time needed: ½ hour**
■ **Difficulty: ***

Ingredients: 1 large bunch fresh parsley, 1 clove garlic, ½ cup oil, 4-5 tbsp. white wine vinegar, pepper, salt.

Wash and dry the parsley, remove the large stems, and chop finely with the peeled garlic. Put the chopped mixture in a saucepan, season with salt and pepper, and pour in ½ cup oil and 4 to 5 tablespoons of vinegar (a greater amount of vinegar can be used if desired). Put the pan on the stove and let the sauce simmer for 6 or 7 minutes. Pour the parsley sauce into a sauce boat and let it cool before serving.

Parsley sauce is good with boiled beef, tongue, poached or baked sausages, and baked or boiled potatoes. Leftover cold meats are much more appetizing when served with sauce.

Sweet-and-sour pepper sauce

■ **Yield: 4 servings**
■ **Time required: 2½ hours**
■ **Difficulty: ***

Ingredients: 1 lb. sweet red peppers, 1 lb. rice tomatoes, 4 onions, 1 clove garlic, 7 tbsp. sugar, ⅓ cup raisins, 1 tsp. cayenne pepper, pinch pepper, 1 tsp. ground ginger, 1 cup wine vinegar, oil, salt.

Soak the raisins in cold water. Chop the onions with the garlic. Cut the red peppers into strips and chop the tomatoes. Put ½ cup oil in a pot (preferably of earthenware) and add the onions, peppers, and ground hot pepper. Stir and cook until the vegetables soften. Then add the tomatoes.

Let the mixture cook for 10 minutes and then force it through a sieve or purée in a blender or food processor. Return the purée back to the pot and add the drained and chopped raisins, vinegar, sugar, salt, pepper, and ginger. Let the sauce simmer over low heat for about 2 hours, stirring occasionally with a wooden spoon.

Let the finished sauce cool, then pour it into glass jars. Cover the jam with aluminum foil and seal with a piece of string or a rubber band. Keep in a cool, dry place. Serve the sauce with boiled beef, chicken, and capon.

Orange Sauce

■ **Yield: 4 servings**
■ **Time needed: 1 hour**
■ **Difficulty: ***

Ingredients: 3 very juicy oranges, 2 lemons, 1⅛ cups sugar, 1 cup concentrated meat stock, dry white wine, 1 jigger Curaçao or other orange liqueur, pepper, salt.

Remove only the colored part of the peel of the oranges and lemons, leaving behind the underlying white pith (1). Cut the peel into very thin strips (2), blanch for 3 minutes in lightly salted water, drain and spread out on a dish towel to dry. Squeeze the juice of the oranges and lemons, strain it, and put it aside (3). Put the sugar in a non-aluminum pan with about ½ cup white wine (4), and let boil until the sugar begins to color, stirring occasionally with a wooden spoon. As soon as the sugar has turned golden pour in the orange and lemon juice (5). Continue boiling the sauce over low heat for 4 or 5 minutes.

Add the stock (6) and the orange and lemon peel (7) and simmer the sauce gently, skimming periodically (8), for 5 minutes, or until the sauce has thickened a little. Season with salt and a pinch of pepper. If the sauce turns out to be too thin, thicken it with a teaspoon of cornstarch dissolved in a few tablespoons of white wine, or sift the starch directly into the sauce (9). When the sauce is almost as thick as honey, take it off the stove and add the liqueur. Mix well and serve hot.

This sauce is good with duck, roast turkey, and other poultry, and with pork and ham. It can also be added to the pan juices of roasts, poultry or pork. You can garnish roasts and other dishes that are to be served with this sauce with the peels in the sauce and pass the rest of the sauce separately.

This sauce takes very well to canning and is a good way to have it always on hand.

1 Peel the oranges and lemons, removing only the colored part of the peel without the white part.

2 With a small knife, cut the peel first into pieces and then into very thin strips.

3 Squeeze the oranges and lemons and strain the juices into a bowl.

4 Put the sugar in a non-aluminum pan and add the white wine.

5 As soon as the sugar turns golden add the orange and lemon juice.

6 After letting the sauce boil for a few minutes, mix in the meat stock...

7 ...sitr well, and add the orange and lemon peels.

8 Simmer the sauce gently, skimming occasionally.

9 If the sauce is too thin, sift in a little cornstarch.

Orange sauce

Apple sauce

■ **Yield: 4 servings**
■ **Time needed: 1½ hours**
■ **Difficulty: ***

Ingredients: 2¼ lbs. firm, tart baking apples ½ cup sugar, 1 lemon, 4-5 white cloves, dry mustard, ground cinnamon, a little white wine, pepper, salt.

Peel and core the apples, cut them into pieces, and put them in a stainless steel, cast iron, or enameled pan. Do not use a pan of unlined cast iron or aluminum (1). Sprinkle the apples with the juice of a lemon (2), add a few pieces of lemon peel, 4 or 5 cloves, cinnamon to taste (3), and about ½ cup white wine (4).

Put the pan on the stove and cook until the apples have disintegrated and all the liquid has been absorbed (5). At this point add the sugar (6), a pinch of salt, and a pinch or two of pepper and dry mustard. Remove the lemon peel and the cloves and force the apples through a sieve (7). Put the sauce back on the stove and let it thicken, stirring continuously, until it resembles a thick jam (8).

If you like, you can prepare a greater quantity of applesauce and put it up in glass jars. In this case increase the sugar to 1 cup for every 2 pounds apples. Put the sauce into jars while it is still hot (9), and seal the jars hermetically (10).

1 Peel and core the apples, cut them into pieces, and put them in a pan.

2 Add the lemon juice to prevent the apples from turning brown, a few pieces of lemon peel...

3 ...the cloves (use only 1 or 2 if you want a mild clove flavor) and the cinnamon.

4 Add about ½ cup dry white wine.

5 Put the pan on the stove and cook the apples, stirring, until they have completely disintegrated.

6 Add the sugar by spoonfuls and stir well to mix the ingredients.

7 After having removed the lemon peel and the cloves, force the apples through a sieve.

8 Put the purée back on the stove and let it thicken until it resembles a thick jam.

9 If you wish to preserve the sauce, put it into glass jars while still hot...

10 ...seal the jars hermetically, and store the jars in the refrigerator.

—343—

Tangy grape

■ **Yield: About 2 cups of sauce**
■ **Time needed: 1½ hours**
■ **Difficulty: ***

Ingredients: 6 lbs. sour white grapes.

In order to make this sauce successfully, one must use large white grapes that are still immature and sour.

Wash the grapes carefully to eliminate any traces of pesticides and dry them well with a clean dish rag. Detach the individual grapes from the bunch, put them all in a large bowl, and crush them with your hands (1). Force the grapes through a sieve with the help of a spoon, extracting as much of the grape juice and pulp as possible (2). Discard the seeds and skins and pour the juice and pulp into a stainless steel pan or into an unlined copper *ponzonetto*. Put the pan on the stove, and let the grape mash simmer gently, occasionally skimming the surface of the sauce (3). Simmer the sauce until reduced by two-thirds. Take the pan off the stove and let the sauce cool. When it is cold pour it into one or more bottles and seal (4). For prolonged storage, seal the bottles hermetically and store them in a cool, dry place. This sauce goes well with poultry (especially duck) and with boiled and roasted meats.

1 Detach the individual grapes from the bunch, put them in a bowl, and crush them with your hands.

2 Extract the juice and pulp by forcing the grapes through a sieve with a spoon.

3 During cooking, skim the sauce occasionally with a slotted spoon.

4 When the sauce is cold ladle it into one or more bottles.

Bagnetto rosso

- **Yield: 6-8 servings**
- **Time needed: 2½ hours**
- **Difficulty: ***

Ingredients: 2¼ lbs. ripe tomatoes, 1 carrot, 1 large onion, 2 cloves garlic, 1 stalk celery, 1 hot red chili pepper, 1 tbsp. sugar, 1 tbsp. good wine vinegar, 10 tbsp. good olive oil, a few pinches salt, fresh ground pepper (optional).

Chop the celery, onion, carrot, and garlic. Wash, seed, and chop the tomatoes. Put the chopped vegetables and tomatoes in a saucepan, preferably earthenware, season with a few pinches of salt and hot pepper (1), and add the sugar (2), the vinegar, and 2 or 3 tablespoons oil (3). Put the pan on the stove and let cook over very low heat for about 2 hours, stirring occasionally (4). Put the sauce through a sieve or food mill or purée in a blender or food processor (5) and mix in another ½ cup olive oil (6). Taste the sauce, correct the seasoning, and serve.

This sauce, typical of Piedmont region, is usually served with mixed boiled meats including beef, capon, *cotechino* sausage, tongue, calf's head, and veal. Piedmont cooks also prepare a *bagnetto rosso* for use during winter that includes 4 or 5 red and yellow peppers and spices.

1 Put the chopped vegetables and tomatoes in a pan and add a little hot pepper.

2 Mix in a tablespoon sugar...

3 ...and then add a tablespoon white wine vinegar and two or three tablespoons olive oil.

4 Put the pan on the stove and cook the sauce over very low heat, stirring occasionally.

5 When the sauce is cooked put it through a sieve or a food mill into a bowl...

6 ...and finally, before serving, blend in another ½ cup olive oil.

Bagnetto rosso

Ketchup

■ **Yield: 2 cups sauce**
■ **Time needed: 1½ hours**
■ **Difficulty: ***

Ingredients: 2¼ lbs. ripe tomatoes, 3 red peppers, ¼ cup sugar, 2 onions, 1 carrot, 1 stalk celery, 1 clove garlic, 1 bay leaf, 2 whole cloves, thyme, cinammon, 1 teaspoon dry mustard, 1 teaspoon cornstarch, 1¼ cups white wine vinegar, ½ cup oil, freshly ground pepper, salt.

Chop the onion, carrot, celery, and garlic and sauté them in a pan with the oil (1). Add the tomatoes, cut in pieces (2), and bring the mixture to a boil, skimming the surface (3). Add the peppers, cut in pieces (4), the sugar (5), vinegar (6), dry mustard, the cornstarch, mixed to a smooth paste with a little tomato juice or water, the bay leaf, cloves, and a pinch each of thyme and cinnamon. Season with salt, add a good pinch of freshly ground pepper, and let cook slowly for several hours, or until the sauce becomes quite thick. Force the sauce through a sieve (7), pour it back into the pan, and let it boil for a few more minutes. It should be thick and velvety.

Let the ketchup cool. If you wish to store it, pour into jars or bottles and seal them hermetically (8). Keep in the refrigerator or freezer. Ketchup is served with boiled or grilled meats and fish.

1 Chop the aromatic vegetables and sauté them in oil.

2 When the vegetables are soft add the cut-up tomatoes...

3 ...bring the mixture to a boil, and skim the surface of the sauce with a slotted spoon.

4 Add the peppers, seeded, deribbed, and chopped.

5 Stir in ¼ cup sugar...

6 ...then add 1¼ cups white wine vinegar.

7 When the cooking time is over, force the sauce through a sieve with the help of a wooden spoon.

8 If you wish to store the sauce for a long period of time, put it into jars and seal.

Deviled sauce

- ■ Yield- 1¼ cups sauce
- ■ Time needed: 45 minutes
- ■ Difficulty: *

Ingredients: 1 tin anchovy fillets, drained, ½ cup sugar, 1 cup red wine vinegar, ½ cup white wine, 3-4 scallions, 3 cloves garlic, 4-5 hot red peppers, ¼ tsp. sage, ½ tsp. tarragon, 2 bay leaves, pinch thyme, ¾ oz. dried boletus mushrooms (optional), 1 teaspoon dry mustard, 1 tbsp. whole peppercorns, salt.

Put the sugar in a stainless steel pan and melt it over low heat. When it turns a light nut brown take it off the heat and slowly add the white wine, standing back in case the mixture splatters. Put the caramelized sugar aside and keep it warm so that it will not harden. Soak the mushrooms in warm water. Finely chop the scallions and put them in another stainless steel pan, and add a tablespoon whole peppercorns, crushed in a mortar, the crushed garlic cloves, the tarragon, bay leaves, thyme, and sage. Add the vinegar, put the pan on the stove, and simmer until the liquid is reduced by one fourth. Add the flavored vinegar to the caramelized sugar (if the mixture has hardened, warm it gently to melt again), add the drained and chopped mushrooms, the mustard, the anchovies, the hot peppers, and a pinch of salt. Boil for about 5 minutes, stirring and skimming. Take the sauce off the stove and strain it while still hot through a cheesecloth-lined sieve, squeezing the ingredients well to extract all their flavor. Taste the sauce and add more salt if necessary. Put the sauce into bottles, seal them, and store in a cool, dry place.

Deviled sauce

Bagna cauda

■ Yield: 4 servings
■ Time needed: ½ hour
■ Difficulty: *

Ingredients: 1 cup olive oil, 4 tbsp. butter, 5 or 6 cloves garlic, 1 tin anchovy fillets, drained.

If you do not have the special pot used for making the *bagna cauda* use an ordinary small saucepan with a long handle. The saucepan can be made of earthenware, copper, or heat-proof porcelain. Slice or crush the garlic and put it into a pan (1). Add the oil and the butter (2) and heat over very low flame, stirring with a wooden spoon (3). When the fat is hot, add the drained anchovies, chopped and pounded in a mortar (4) or mashed with a fork. Stir until the anchovies have dissolved. Be careful never to let the sauce boil. Serve the sauce immediately, keeping it warm at the table over an alcohol burner. The sauce is used chiefly as a dip for raw vegetables such as peppers, Jerusalem artichokes, celery hearts, cabbage leaves, and cauliflower. The vegetables should all be washed and soaked in ice water acidulated with lemon juice so that they will stay firm.

1 Crush or slice the garlic cloves and put them in a pan.

2 Add 1 cup olive oil and the butter, in pieces...

3 ...and heat the mixture over very low heat, stirring with a wooden spoon.

4 Finally add the drained anchovies which have been pounded in a mortar.

Bagna cauda

Caper and olive sauce

■ **Yield: 4 servings**
■ **Time needed: ½ hour**
■ **Difficulty: ***

Ingredients: 1½ tbsp. pickled capers, ¼ cup pitted green olives, 9 flat anchovy fillets, drained, 1 clove garlic, small bunch parsley, oil, vinegar, salt.

Wash and dry the parsley and remove the large stems. Squeeze the liquid out of the capers and chop them together with the olives and anchovies. Chop the parsley separately. In a pan, preferably of earthenware, heat ½ cup oil until hot, then add the crushed garlic and sauté briefly. Add the chopped capers, anchovies, and olives and sauté gently for a few minutes. Stir in the chopped parsley and two tablespoons vinegar. Leave the sauce on the heat for a few more minutes, correct the seasoning, and remove from the heat. Remove the clove of garlic and pour the sauce into a sauce boat. Serve the sauce lukewarm or cold with boiled meat.

Smitane sauce

■ **Yield: 4 servings**
■ **Time needed: 20 minutes**
■ **Difficulty: ***

Ingredients: 1 rather large onion, 1 cup sour cream, ½ cup dry white wine, 2 tbsp. butter, salt.

Finely chop the onion, put it into a little saucepan, add the butter, and sauté over low heat until the onion is soft but not at all colored. Add the wine and let it boil until it reduces substantially. Add the sour cream and heat thoroughly, stirring continuously but do not let it boil. Finally season with salt and a little lemon juice if desired. The sauce is good with poultry and game.

Mint sauce

■ **Yield: 4 servings**
■ **Time needed: ½ hour**
■ **Difficulty: ****

Ingredients: 12 tbsp. butter, 2 scallions, 2 egg yolks, 1 large bunch fresh mint, ½ cup white wine vinegar, ½ lemon, pepper, salt.

After removing and discarding the stems, finely chop the mint leaves along with the scallions and put the chopped mixture in a pan. Add the vinegar and simmer over lively heat, stirring with a whisk, until the liquid has almost completely evaporated. In a pan set over simmering water. Beat the egg yolks with the juice of half a lemon and a tablespoon of cold water. Strain in the vinegar reduction and season with salt and pepper. Beat with a whisk until the egg yolks thicken, then add the butter a small piece at a time, whisking constantly. Let the sauce cool and serve it in a sauce boat with roast lamb.

English caper sauce

■ **Yield: About 3 cups**
■ **Time needed: ½ hour**
■ **Difficulty: ***

Ingredients: 1¾ sticks butter, 6 tbsp. flour, 3 cups milk, 1 tsp. Worcestershire sauce, 4 tbsp. small pickled capers, pepper, salt.

Add a pinch of salt to the milk and bring it to a boil. Melt 4 tablespoons butter in a saucepan, blend in the flour, and stir. Add the boiling milk a little at a time, and simmer the sauce over low heat, stirring continuously, for about 5 minutes. With the pan off heat, add the remaining butter ½ tablespoon at a time, beating constantly with a whisk. Finally add the Worcestershire sauce, the capers, rinsed and patted dry, and a good pinch of pepper. Stir gently. Pour the sauce into a warmed sauce boat and serve with lamb or game.

Romano sauce

■ **Yield: 4 servings**
■ **Time needed: ½ hour**
■ **Difficulty: ***

Ingredients: ¼ lb. bacon, 1 cup peeled, seeded, juiced tomato, fresh or canned, 1 small onion, 2 tbsp. oil, 2 tbsp. grated Romano cheese, 2 tbsp. Worcestershire sauce, freshly ground black pepper, salt.

Finely chop the onion, put it into a small pan with the oil and the diced bacon, and sauté over moderate heat. Add the tomato pulp, crushed with a fork, and cook the sauce until it has thickened. Finish the preparation by adding the Worcestershire sauce, a pinch of salt, the cheese, and plenty of freshly ground pepper. Serve the sauce hot with beef steaks and roast beef.

Cold Sauces

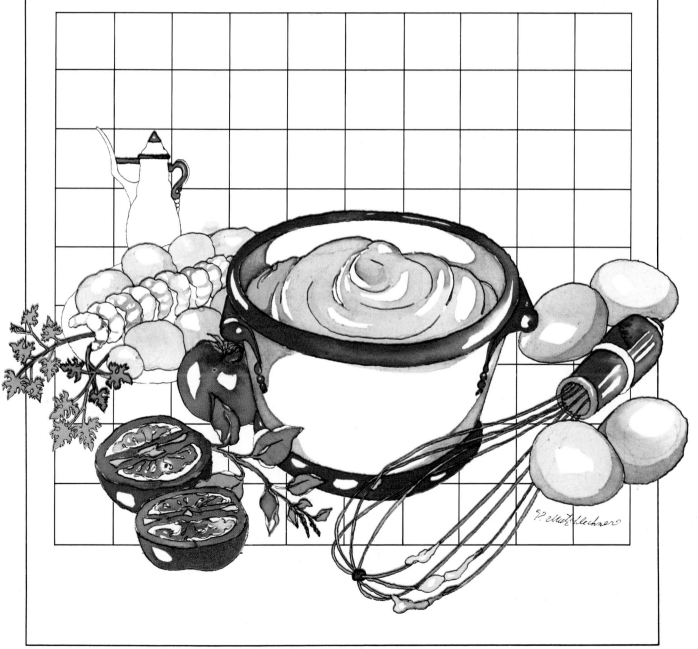

It is very difficult to establish the origins of cold sauces because of the infinite modifications that they have undergone over the centuries. Experts and scholars see the origin of the first cold sauce in the famous *liguamen* of Roman times. *Liguamen* was a liquid that was made by fermenting fish, salt, and other ingredients for days and days in the sun and then mixing in aromatic herbs. The condiment had a mildly cheesy smell and was used to flavor virtually any food, much as we use salt. Even before Roman times peoples of the Mediterranean had invented various simple sauces made by mixing oil and aromatic herbs. The great nutritional qualities of oil had already been discovered; indeed, oil was considered of divine origin and the olive tree was dedicated to the cult of the goddess Minerva. The same aromatic herbs we use today grew wild all along the coasts : garlic, onion, thyme, parsley, chives, and mint. Basil was still unknown, however, and was not imported from India until much later on. With the passage of time lemon juice and vinegar were added to these first simple sauces, partly because the sharp taste of these ingredients could disguise the taste of meat or fish that were no longer fresh. Later on we find examples of sauces similar to the *salsa verde* (green sauce) that we use today, as well as sauces calling for raw or hard-boiled eggs, almonds, saffron, and spices that were the forerunners of mayonnaise. The 18th century was the golden century for all sauces, both cold and hot. They become the very triumph of the cuisine. The most important sauces are often associated with famous names and interesting anecdotes. For example, there is the legend of a soldier in the ranks of Marshal Richelieu. Unhappy with the usual unappetizing rations, he would disguise them by beating an egg vigorously with a few drops of oil and lemon juice, until he obtained a soft creamy golden sauce—mayonnaise!

Cold Sauces with Oil

Herb Sauces

The better-known cold sauces are doubtless the ones based on oil and flavored with a host of other ingredients (such as eggs, aromatic herbs, anchovies, nuts, radishes, etc.) Such sauces may accompany many hot and cold foods. The best-known cold sauce made with oil is certainly mayonnaise from which are derived an infinite number of variations. Mayonnaise is made with eggs, oil, and lemon juice beaten together until they turn into a thick cream with a nice gold color. One variation of mayonnaise is gelatin mayonnaise, a mayonnaise that is stiffened with dissolved gelatin and used to bind molded salads and to decorate cold dishes. Among the many easily prepared mayonnaise variations are the delicious chantilly sauce, made by folding in unsweetened whipped cream, the very famous äioli, a mayonnaise that is flavored with plenty of garlic, and curried mayonnaise which calls for the addition of onion and curry powder. Mayonnaise can also be given a spicy flavor by adding anchovies, mustard, capers, and cayenne pepper. Often the sauce is made more appetizing and decorative by being colored with different ingredients. Thus we have green mayonnaise, which is made by adding finely chopped herbs such as basil or parsley, or spinach leaves. A pinkish mayonnaise is made by adding tomato sauce or ketchup as in the case of the well-known Russian dressing. Then there are the richer variations that call for the addition of a substantial ingredient that completely alters the flavor of the sauce, which, for such recipes, needs to be a little more runny than usual. For example, there is tuna sauce, which is made by adding puréed tuna to mayonnaise, and seafood mayonnaise, an excellent accompaniment for cold shellfish, which is made by blending mayonnaise with minced crab, lobster, or shrimp.

Tartar sauce, another common mayonnaise-type sauce, is made with hard-boiled egg yolks and flavored with mustard and chopped spring onion.

Among the oldest cold sauces are certainly those with aromatic herbs in a liquid emulsion such as oil, vinegar, or lemon juice. Many of these sauces also have a binding agent such as bread soaked in vinegar, mashed hard-boiled egg yolks, or mustard. Herb sauces give flavor to blend foods and cut the greasy taste of fatty meat or fish. The herb sauces that we find in Italy are typically regional, using the same principal ingredients as other sauces but always including the typical local products, such as pine nuts and basil in Liguria, or black and green olives in central and southern Italy. The most famous Italian *salsa verde* (green sauce) is certainly the one from Piedmont, the *bagnet,* which is made with bread soaked in vinegar, garlic, chopped anchovies, parsley, and olive oil and seasoned with pepper. Many things can be added to the *bagnet,* including gherkins, capers, peppers, tuna, and aromatic herbs such as tarragon, chervil, fresh marjoram, basil, and mint. Then there are herb sauces that have no binding agent and are simply made by emulsifying olive oil and lemon juice and adding garlic, chopped herbs, salt, and pepper. The most famous of these simple herb sauces is parsley sauce, but there are many others such as the famous Sicilian *salmoriglio,* a sauce made with basil or oregano, that is always served with swordfish, and others that include capers, olives, and hot red pepper. Though common in all Oriental cuisines and in British cooking mint sauce is still little known in Italy, although we do find a few sauces that use mint in the Trentino-Alto Adige region and in Sicily.

Beyond the Alps we find that herbs are no longer the principal ingredient in cold sauces but are replaced by various kinds of fruit and strong spices. Many English and German sauces, for example are made with currants, blueberries, apples, and pears and served with especially fatty meats such as pork and lamb.

Flavored Butters

When speaking of sauces we could not omit the flavored butters, which, although they are not true sauces, serve the same purpose as sauces. Flavored butters are made by blending butter with other ingredients, and they function as precious complements to sauces or as elegant garnishes for simple dishes. They can also be used as fillings, decorations, and spreads for bread slices and canapés.

Flavored butters are of two kinds: those prepared with cold butter and those made with melted butter. The butter for either kind should always be very fresh and of top quality.

To make a cold flavored butter remove the butter from the refrigerator at least two hours ahead of time so that it will be soft and easy to work with. Put the amount of butter called for by the recipe in a bowl, and cream it with a wooden spoon or small whisk until light and fluffy. The other minced or puréed ingredients can now be added. It can be made into decorative slices by shaping it into a cylinder, wrapping it in tin foil and putting it in the refrigerator to cool to be cut into rounds when ready to serve. Butter prepared in this way can be served with many kinds of food depending on the way the butter is flavored. You can have very simple butters, such as garlic butter, or spicy butters made with anchovies, mustard, paprika, or grated horseradish. Aromatic herbs in general lend themselves quite well to these preparations, from parsley, principal component of the very famous maître d'hôtel butter, to tarragon, which is used as an ingredient for the famous snails *Bourguignonne*. There are even more refined variations made by blending butter with lobster meat, crab, shrimp, caviar, or salmon.

Finally, let's not forget hot flavored butters, which are made by melting butter, either directly on the stove or in a double boiler, and adding an infinity of other ingredients, such as shellfish, anchovies, herbs, lemon juice, or cayenne pepper. Such preparations are usually served with boiled or grilled fish or grilled or fried meats.

How to Serve Cold Sauces

Cold sauces are easier and take less time to prepare than hot sauces and therefore they can be made more often to perk up leftovers, to vary the flavor of a familiar dish, and finally . . . to disguise a culinary mistake. It is important to match these sauces with the right foods. When choosing a cold sauce for meats, for example, it is important to distinguish between red meats, which have a strong flavor, and white meats, which have a more delicate taste. The sauce should also be chosen according to the way the meat is cooked. For grilled meats, sauces flavored with herbs and strongly flavored ingredients such as mustard, anchovies, and chili pepper are very suitable. For boiled meats, the so-called green sauces, which are almost always based on parsley, garlic, and vinegar and blended with ingredients such as capers or anchovies, are ideal. Mayonnaise and its variations are used chiefly with cold meats, both red and white.

The question of which sauce to use is important also with fish because both poached and baked fish acquire a special touch if accompanied by the right sauce. On baked, grilled, and poached fish one can use any of the cold sauces made with oil, lemon, and garlic, and these sauces, in turn can be flavored with almost any aromatic herb and wide range of other ingredients including pine nuts, anchovies, or anchovy paste. However, the queen of cold sauces for all kinds of fish, especially for poached fish, is certainly mayonnaise and all of its variations.

The only cold sauces that are frequently used with vegetables are mayonnaise-type sauces, such as *pinzimonio,* which is especially suitable for dressing all salads and raw vegetables. Mayonnaise is also often used to bind mixed salads, which can include ingredients other than vegetables.

As far as serving cold sauces, with the exception of dishes that are meant to be combined with or masked by the sauces, cold sauces, like hot sauces, are brought to the table either in porcelain, metal sauce boats or fanciful earthenware or ceramic bowls.

Mayonnaise

■ **Yield: 4 servings**
■ **Time needed: 20 minutes**
■ **Difficullty: ****

Ingredients: 1 cup olive oil, 2 egg yolks, 1 tablespoon strained fresh lemon juice or white wine vinegar, pepper, salt.

Hand-made mayonnaise — Put the egg yolks in a bowl and add a pinch of salt and pepper (freshly ground if possible) and a few drops of lemon juice or vinegar. Beat the egg yolks with a whisk (1), then add the oil in a very thin stream while continuing to beat until you obtain a very thick mixture (2). At this point dilute the mayonnaise a little with a few drops of lemon juice or vinegar (3), then beat in more oil, then add a little lemon juice, and continue in this manner until you have used up all the ingredients. Halfway through the preparation, when the sauce has bound into a creamy emulsion, you can add the oil a little more at a time. The mayonnaise is ready when it is thick enough to cling to the whisk (4). Mayonnaise is especially recommended for boiled or grilled fish and meat, hard-boiled eggs, and cold dishes.

The success of this sauce depends on the care and

1 With a thick whisk beat the egg yolks in a bowl with a few drops of lemon juice or vinegar.

2 Add the oil in a very thin stream and continue beating until you obtain a very thick mixture.

3 Dilute the mixture with a few more drops of lemon juice or vinegar.

4 When the mayonnaise is ready it should be quite thick enough to cling to the whisk.

attention that goes into its preparation. The most common cause of failure, especially in winter, is the use of cold oil or eggs just out of the refrigerator. Thus if the day is cold, the oil should be warmed in a double boiler; the eggs should always be taken out of the refrigerator a few hours beforehand and kept at room temperature. Furthermore, the proportions of the ingredients must be respected, as much the procedure. If there is too much oil for the number of egg yolks or if the oil is added too quickly, the sauce can be saved by beating another egg yolk in a separate bowl and adding the failed sauce to it a little at a time, beating vigorously. In this way you will obtain a slightly greater amount of mayonnaise, which will be perfectly emulsified.

Mayonnaise made in a blender — Mayonnaise can be made quickly and successfully in an electric blender. With this system the egg white is used as well and therefore you get a greater quantity of sauce. Proceed as follows: Break a whole egg and one egg yolk into the blender (1), and add a pinch of salt and pepper (freshly ground) and a tablespoon of vinegar or fresh strained lemon juice. Add also about two tablespoons of oil (2) and blend at maximum speed for 5 seconds, or until the ingredients form a smooth mixture. At this point pour in the remaining oil in a thin stream (3). The mayonnaise is ready when it can absorb no more oil and a little pool of oil sits in the center. Stop the blender and stir the mayonnaise to incorporate the oil on the surface (4).

1 Break a whole egg and an egg yolk into an electric blender...

2 ...add a pinch of salt and pepper, a tablespoon of vinegar or lemon juice, and two tablespoons oil.

3 Pour the remaining oil in a thin stream into the whirlpool created by the blender blades.

4 When the sauce is ready, stir it a final time to mix in the oil left on the surface.

Aioli sauce

■ **Yield: 4 servings**
■ **Time needed: ½ hour**
■ **Difficulty: ****

Ingredients: 4 cloves garlic, 2 egg yolks, juice of 1 lemon, 1 cup olive oil, salt.

Pound the peeled garlic to a pulp in a mortar, add the egg yolks and a pinch of salt, and mix thoroughly with the pestle. Then pour in the oil in a very thin stream, alternately adding drops of lemon juice and a few drops of water as the sauce thickens. Continue with sauce as if it were mayonnaise. This sauce can also be prepared in a blender or food processor using a whole egg and an egg yolk.

Also called "butter of Provence," *äioli* is usually served with fish or raw vegetables.

Tuna sauce

■ **Yield: 4 servings**
■ **Time needed: 45 minutes**
■ **Difficulty: ***

Ingredients: 1 recipe mayonnaise (see page 360), 7 oz. tuna in oil, 6 flat anchovy fillets, drained, a little stock.

Pound the tuna in a mortar with the anchovy fillets, dilute with a few tablespoons of stock, and put the mixture through a fine sieve. You may also grind the mixture in a blender or food processor. Gently stir the tuna-and-anchovy purée into the mayonnaise, adding drops of stock should the sauces be too thick.

Serve this sauce with boiled meats.

Mustard sauce

■ **Yield: 4 servings**
■ **Time needed: ½ hour (plus resting time for sauce)**
■ **Difficulty: ***

Ingredients: 1 recipe mayonnaise (see page 360), 1 celery heart, 2 carrots, 2 tbsp. peas, juice of 1 lemon, 1 teaspoon mustard, olive oil, freshly ground pepper, salt.

Wash and thinly slice the celery. Scrape and wash the carrots and cut them into small strips or shred them coarsely. Put the celery, carrot, and mustard in a bowl and add a little oil, salt, freshly ground pepper, and lemon juice. Let stand for about an hour. Just before serving, mix in the boiled peas, cold, and the mayonnaise.

Pour the sauce into a sauce boat and serve with cold boiled or roasted meats.

Avocado sauce

■ **Yield: 4 servings**
■ **Time needed: ½ hour**
■ **Difficulty: ***

Ingredients: 3 medium-size ripe avocados, 1 onion, 2 hot red peppers, white vinegar, ½ cup oil, whole pepper, salt.

Finely chop the onion with the hot peppers. Wash the avocados and cut them in half lengthwise. Remove the pit and scoop out the pulp with a spoon. Put the avocado pulp into a bowl, mash it with a spoon, add the chopped onion and pepper, and season with salt and a little freshly ground pepper. Beat the mixture with a wooden spoon until it is creamy. Pour in ½ cup oil in a very thin stream, then stir in two tablespoons vinegar. When the sauce appears well emulsified, taste it, correct the seasoning if necessary, and bring it to the table in a sauce boat as an accompaniment for boiled meat.

Mint sauce

■ **Yield: 4 servings**
■ **Time needed: 20 minutes**
■ **Difficulty: ***

Ingredients: 2 bunches fresh mint, ¼ cup sugar, good white wine vinegar.

Wash the mint in running water (do not allow to soak in the water) and gently pat dry with paper toweling. Remove and discard the stems. Chop the mint leaves very finely with the sugar and scrape the ingredients into a bowl. In the meantime in a saucepan bring enough vinegar to cover the mint to a boil and let it boil 2 minutes to reduce it. Let it cool, and pour it into the bowl containing the mint. Mix well and pour the sauce into a sauce boat and serve with roast kid, lamb, or mutton.

If you wish, you can prepare a greater quantity of mint sauce and keep it in sealed jars or bottles. Before using it, shake the bottle because the mint settles on the bottom.

Tartar sauce

■ **Yield: about 2 cups**
■ **Time needed: ½ hour**
■ **Difficulty: ****

Ingredients: 4 hard-boiled egg yolks, 2 cups oil, some vinegar, 6 scallions with some of their green stalks, 1 teaspoon prepared mustard, pepper, salt.

Finely chop the scallions with the tender part of their green stalks. Put the hard-boiled egg yolks in a bowl and mash them with a fork until smooth, or put them through a sieve (1). Mix in the mustard (2) and the chopped scallions (you can set aside a tablespoon with which to garnish the finished sauce), and finally add the oil in a very thin stream, beating constantly (3). When the sauce has thickened, add a few drops of vinegar and a pinch of salt and pepper. The sauce should have a consistency similar to that of mayonnaise (4). If you wish to make it creamier mix in a few tablespoons of mayonnaise. Serve the sauce with boiled or grilled meat and fish.

Prepare the tartar sauce at the last minute because it separates easily. Should this happen, it can be saved in the same way as mayonnaise—by beating the sauce by teaspoons into a raw egg yolk.

1 Put the egg yolks in a bowl and mash with a fork or push through a sieve...

2 ...mix in a teaspoon of mustard, add the finely chopped scallions...

3 ...and pour the oil in a thin stream, beating continuously.

4 When ready, the sauce should have a consistency simiilar to that of mayonnaise.

Tartar sauce

Horseradish sauce

■ **Yield: 4 servings**
■ **Time needed: 20 minutes**
■ **Difficulty: ***

Ingredients: 2 oz. fresh horseradish, pinch sugar, 2 tablespoons white vinegar, 1 cup "extra virgin" olive oil, salt.

Scrape off the skin of the horseradish with a knife (1), wash and dry the horseradish, and grate it into a bowl (2). Pour the vinegar into another small bowl, add the sugar and a few pinches of salt and stir to dissolve the ingredients. Add the vinegar mixture to the grated horseradish (3), stir, and add the oil a little at a time, stirring constantly with a wooden spoon (4). The sauce should be of medium thickness. If necessary, beat in a little more oil. Taste the sauce, and add more salt if necessary. If you wish, you can add a pinch of pepper, but keep in mind that the horseradish is quite hot. This sauce is especially recommended for grilled pork chops or mixed boiled meats.

You can also make a hot horseradish sauce by adding grated horseradish to a thin white sauce enriched with a cup of cream; heat for a few seconds to blend the flavors.

1 Scrape off the skin of the horseradish with a small knife...

2 ...wash and dry the horseradish, and grate it into a bowl.

3 Dissolve the sugar and a pinch of salt in the vinegar and add it to the horseradish...

4 ...and then add the oil a little at a time, stirring constantly with a wooden spoon.

Horseradish sauce

Horseradish sauce with apples

■ **Yield: 4 servings**
■ **Time needed: 20 minutes**
■ **Difficulty: ***

Ingredients: 2 oz. fresh horseradish, 1 large, tart baking apple, 1 tbsp. sugar, 2-3 tbsp. dry bread crumbs, 3-4 tbsp. good wine vinegar, some lemon juice, pinch salt.

Scrape off the skin of the horseradish with a small knife, wash and dry the horseradish and grate it into a bowl.

Peel and core the apple and cut it in half. Cut one of the halves into small pieces and combine in a saucepan with a tablespoon water and half the sugar. Cook the apple until it falls apart, then mash it well with a fork or, even better, put it through a food mill. Shred the other half of the apple and sprinkle it with a little lemon juice so that it will not turn brown.

Mix the remaining sugar, the horseradish, the cooked apple, and the raw grated apple. Add a few tablespoons vinegar, a pinch of salt, and enough bread crumbs to make a sauce neither too thick or too thin.

If you prefer a more liquid sauce replace the apple (both raw and cooked) with ½ cup heavy cream, blending it in well with the other ingredients.

This sauce is used frequently in the Alto Adige and Trentino regions, where it is called *ravanda* and is served with all kinds of boiled meats.

Horseradish and nut sauce

- ■ Yield: 4 servings
- ■ Time needed: 20 minutes
- ■ Difficulty: *

Ingredients: 15 walnuts, shelled (or 30 canned walnut halves), 1 roll or 2 slices bread, 2 oz. fresh horseradish, some milk, 1 oz. (about ¼ cup) pine nuts, 1 cup heavy cream, 1 tbsp. white vinegar, pinch sugar, salt.

Put the white part of the roll or bread in a bowl, cover with a little warm milk and let soak. Rub the skin off the walnut kernels using a thin cloth towel. To facilitate this operation blanch the walnuts for 15 seconds in boiling water.

Put the walnuts in a mortar, add the bread (squeeze out all the milk) and the pine nuts, and pound the mixture into a pulp with the pestle (1). Peel the horseradish by scraping it with a small knife wash and dry and grate it. Add the bread and nut mixture to the horseradish (2), along with the sugar, a few pinches salt, the cream (3), and the vinegar (4). Stir to blend. The sauce is recommended for boiled meats.

1 In a mortar pound the walnuts with the bread and the pine nuts.

2 Grate the horseradish and add the bread-and-nut mixture to it, mixing well.

3 Add the sugar and a few pinches of salt and dilute with the cream.

4 Finally mix in a tablespoon of white vinegar to complete the sauce.

Horseradish and nut sauce

Black olive sauce

■ **Yield: 4 servings**
■ **Time needed: ½ hour**
■ **Difficulty: ***

Ingredients: 7 oz. pitted imported Greek or Italian black olives, 1 tin flat anchovy fillets, drained, 2 oz. pickled capers, juice of 1 lemon, 1 tbsp. brandy, 1 cup olive oil, freshly ground pepper, salt.

Pound the olives, anchovies, and capers (washed well first) in the mortar (1). If you do not have a mortar you can chop the ingredients very finely. Force the pounded ingredients through a sieve (2) into a bowl and pour in the oil in a thin stream while beating constantly, just as if you were making a mayonnaise (3). Finally add the lemon juice, the brandy, a pinch of freshly ground pepper, and salt.

If you wish to store the sauce prepare a greater quantity and pour it into small jars (4) covered with wax paper before closing.

Black olive sauce is a good stuffing for hard-boiled eggs and tomatoes, and it is also delicious with boiled beef or spread on bread or toast.

1 Pound the black olives, anchovies, and washed capers in a mortar.

2 Push the mixture through a fine sieve with the back of a spoon.

3 Pour in the oil in a thin stream while beating the mixture, as if making mayonnaise.

4 You can make a sizeable amount of sauce and store it in small jars.

Black olive sauce

Vegetable Relish

■ **Yield: 4 servings**
■ **Time needed: 1 hour**
■ **Difficulty: ***

Ingredients: The core and small inner leaves of a medium-size cabbage, 2 carrots, 1 celery heart, 1 onion, 1 green pepper, 1 red pepper, 1 yellow pepper or additional red or green pepper, a few bay leaves, vinegar, cloves, whole peppercorns, salt.

Wash all the vegetables and chop them finely in separate batches. Mix the vegetables in a colander (1). In a pot, make a broth of half water and half white wine vinegar, adding a few cloves, 12 peppercorns, a few pinches salt, and 3 or 4 bay leaves. Bring the broth to a boil, then pour in the chopped vegetables and simmer them for 3 minutes. Drain the vegetables with a slotted spoon (2), turn them out on a dish towel, and pat them dry (3). Let the vegetables rest on the towel for at least 30 minutes. Put the vegetables into a bowl and mix in olive oil (4). You can use the sauce immediately or store it in the refrigerator in small sealed jars (5). Before closing the jars cover the vegetables with oil to protect them (6).

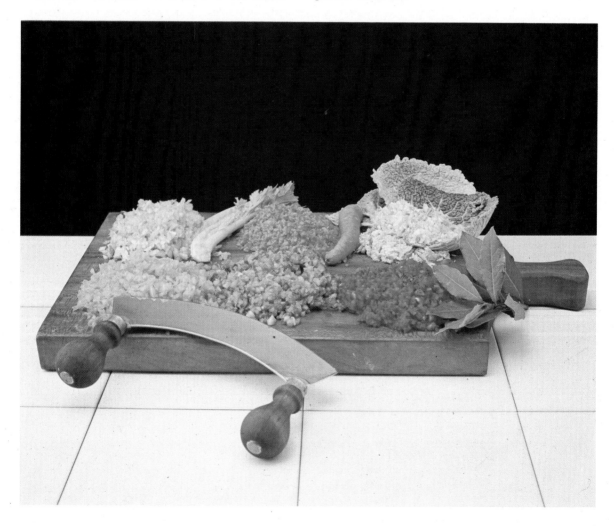

1 After having chopped all the vegetables mix them together in a colander and stir them.

2 Blanch the vegetables in a broth of water, vinegar, and spices, drain them with a slotted spoon...

3 ...spread them out on a clean dish towel, and dry them very well.

4 Put the vegetables in a big bowl, dress them with plenty of olive oil and mix well.

5 If you want to store the sauce, turn it into little jars...

6 ...and before sealing the jars cover the vegetables with a layer of oil to protect them from the air.

Bagnetto verde

- **Yield: 4 servings**
- **Time needed: ½ hour**
- **Difficulty: ***

Ingredients: 1 bunch parsley, 2 cloves garlic, 4 flat anchovy fillets, drained, 1 tbsp. pickled capers, 2 eggs, 1 roll or 2 slices bread, vinegar, oil, pepper, salt.

Put the white part of the roll or bread in a bowl, add a few tablespoons vinegar, and let it soak. Hard-boil the eggs, and mash the yolks with a fork. After removing the large stems, wash and finely chop the parsley with the garlic cloves (1) and put the chopped mixture in a bowl.

Put the anchovy fillets in a mortar, add the soaked bread (squeeze out the vinegar) and pound the ingredients to a pulp (2). Add the anchovy-and-bread mixture to the parsley, along with the drained and chopped capers and the mashed egg yolks (3). Stir until the mixture is smooth. Blend in plenty of oil, beating constantly, until you have a medium-thick sauce (4). Season with salt and pepper.

This sauce, typical of the Piedmont region, is good with boiled meats. The sauce can be varied by adding chopped gherkins or peppers and onion.

1 After having cleaned, washed, and dried the parsley, chop it finely with the garlic cloves.

2 Pound the anchovy fillets and the bread soaked in vinegar together in a mortar.

3 Add the bread-and-anchovy mixture and the mashed egg yolks to the chopped parsley...

4 ...and blend in plenty of oil,. beating constantly, until you have a medium-thick sauce.

Colbert butter

■ Yield: 4 servings
■ Time needed: ½ hour
■ Difficulty: *

Ingredients: 8 tbsp. (1 stick) very fresh butter, a beef bouillon cube dissolved in 1 tablespoon water, 1 tbsp. chopped parsley, 1 tsp. tarragon, juice of ½ lemon, freshly ground pepper, salt.

Cream the butter and beat in the dissolved bouillon cube, parsley, and tarragon. Add the lemon juice and season with salt and freshly ground pepper.
Garnish fried fish or grilled fish and meat with Colbert butter.

Anchovy butter

■ Yield: 4 servings
■ Time needed: ½ hour
■ Difficulty: *

Ingredients: 8 tbsp. (1 stick) very fresh butter, 8 anchovy fillets, drained, freshly ground pepper.

Mash the anchovies with a fork or push them through a sieve. Cream the butter and beat in the anchovies; season with freshly ground pepper.
Anchovy butter is used as a spread for canapés, as a flavoring for certain sauces, and as an accompaniment for grilled fish meat.

Shrimp butter

■ Yield: 4 servings
■ Time needed: 20 minutes
■ Difficulty: *

Ingredients: 8 tbsp. (1 stick) butter, 10 oz. shrimp, a few drops brandy, whole white or black peppercorns, 1 bunch parsley, 1 bay leaf, ¼ tsp. thyme, a few pinches salt.

Combine 2 cups salted water, the parsley, thyme, bay leaf, and a few peppercorns in a pan and let simmer for 5 minutes. Add the washed shrimp and simmer a minute or two, or until firm. Drain and peel the shrimp and pound their meat in a mortar. Cream the butter, add the shrimp paste, and stir well. Flavor with a few drops of brandy and season with salt and freshly ground pepper.

You can use the shrimp butter to make cold appetizers or as a spread for breads or crackers.

Maître d'Hôtel butter

■ Yield: 4 servings
■ Time needed: ½ hour
■ Difficulty: *

Ingredients: 8 tbsp. (1 stick) very fresh butter, juice of ½ lemon, 1 bunch parsey, freshly ground white pepper, salt.

Finely chop the parsley. Cream the butter and add the chopped parsley, a pinch salt, a bit of freshly gound pepper, and a few drops of lemon juice.
Maîte d'Hôtel butter is served with grilled fish and meats.

Garlic butter

■ Yield: 4 servings
■ Time needed: ½ hour
■ Difficulty: *

Ingredients: 8 tbsp. (1 stick) very fresh butter, 1½ oz. (1 medium head) garlic.

Peel the cloves of garlic, blanch them for a few minutes in boiling water, dry them, and pound them in a mortar (or chop very finely). Cream the butter, beat in the garlic, and force the mixture through a fine sieve.
This butter is used to make cold appetizers and to flavor sauces.

Salmon butter

■ Yield: 4 servings
■ Time needed: 15 minutes
■ Difficulty: *

Ingredients: 8 tbsp. (1 stick) butter, 2 oz. smoked salmon.

Cream the butter and add the salmon, chopped to a paste. Put the salmon butter through a sieve.
Salmon butter may be used as a filling for pastry shells or as a spread for toast or crackers.

Subject Index

Recipe Index

HOT AND COLD SAUCES